ORAL HIS
an annota

ORAL HISTORY

AN ANNOTATED BIBLIOGRAPHY

Compiled and introduced by
ROBERT PERKS

Foreword by ASA BRIGGS

THE BRITISH LIBRARY

© 1990   Robert Perks and The British Library Board

Published by
The British Library National Sound Archive
29 Exhibition Road, London, SW7 2AS

British Library Cataloguing in Publication Data

Perks, Robert
    Oral history : an annotated bibliography.
    1. Oral history - Bibliographies
    I. Title
    016.9072

    ISBN 0 7123 0505 X

Designed by The Public
Cover illustration by Matilda Harrison
Typeset by Saxon Printing Ltd, Derby
Printed in Great Britain by St Edmundsbury Press Ltd.,
Bury St Edmunds, Suffolk

CONTENTS

ACKNOWLEDGEMENTS

I would like to extend special thanks to Asa Briggs for the Foreword, and to Joanna Bornat and Paul Thompson for their helpful comments. SCONUL students Merle Read and Joy Parker assisted at various stages of the project: without their enthusiasm it would have taken twice as long. National Sound Archive staff were extremely supportive, especially Alistair Bamford who guided the whole project into print, John Killingbeck who provided helpful suggestions and guidance on *BLAISE*, Alan Ward for allowing me so much time to work on what had at first seemed a short term project, and Crispin Jewitt for rescuing me from computer madness on more than one occasion. Thanks also to the University of London Library; BLISS staff; Doc Rowe and Rosemary Dixon at London History Workshop Centre Sound and Video Archive for London references; and Anna Davin for sharing her extensive personal library.

I would also like to acknowledge the assistance of those libraries, archives, museums, oral history groups, local history groups, publishers and individuals who responded to some 500 letters sent out in the course of compilation. The following exceeded the call of duty and merit especial thanks: Jill Dilkes of Portsmouth City Records Office; Randolph Ellis; Margot Farnham of the Hall-Carpenter Oral History Archive; Elaine Finnie of Huntly House Museum, Edinburgh; Carol Greenwood of Bradford Central Reference Library; Joyce Hammond of Walsall Local History Centre; Clifford Harkness of Ulster Folk and Transport Museum; Eve Hostettler of the Island History Trust; Helga Hughes of Kirklees Sound Archive; Donny Hyslop of Southampton Museums Oral History Section; Judy Kingscott of Nottinghamshire County Library; Sav Kyriacou of the Ethnic Minorities Oral History Project; Jane Mace of Lee Community Education Centre; Rory O'Connell of the Imperial War Museum; Tom Parkinson of North Tyneside Council Community Services Unit; Sue Quinn of the Living Archive Project, Milton Keynes; Elizabeth Roberts; David Stockdale of Dundee Art Galleries and Museums; Beth Thomas of the Welsh Folk Museum; Al Thomson of the Federation of Worker Writers and Community Publishers; and Mel Wright of Lewisham Social Services.

Outside Britain I would like to thank in particular Helen Frizzell of Presbyterian Support Services (Otago) Community History Project in Dunedin, New Zealand; Mark Cranfield, Chief Oral History Officer at the National Library of Australia; and Grace Koch of the Australian Institute of Aboriginal Studies.

Finally I have once more to thank Jane Tyrtania for putting up with my frequent absences to work on this project over the eighteen months it took to complete.

FOREWORD

There has long been a need for an annotated bibliography of oral history. As Robert Perks shows in his brief but illuminating introduction, the number of historians who are interested in the use of oral evidence has greatly increased in recent years. They are not the only people, however, for whom this bibliography will be useful. Many of the articles and books cited in it have been written by psychologists and by doctors. They approach the subject in a different way. So, too, do writers of fiction and drama, who also figure in these pages. There has often been a popular dimension too. Collecting memories is an activity of a collective as well as of an individual kind.

The value of the bibliography is greatly increased by reason of the fact that it covers not only Britain and the United States, but different countries in the Commonwealth, notably Australia and Canada which have contributed substantially – and often innovatively – to the literature. And there is an important place in it also for the work of historians and anthropologists in Africa and other parts of the world where oral traditions provide the master keys to understanding.

There is scope for a detailed study of the various strands in recent intellectual and social history which together have made this bibliography not only interesting and useful but necessary, and Robert picks out a few of the relevant themes in his introduction. Nonetheless, for many users of the bibliography it will be the references to the significantly large number of works concerned with techniques and methods that will be most helpful. Guidance on how to proceed is often called for, and a practical concern runs through many of the entries.

Inevitably this bibliography is bound to be incomplete. I have noted some omissions myself. Its value, however, lies in the fact that it provides a foundation and that it is capable not only of updating but of revision. Historians used oral evidence long before the term came into fashion, and there are some history books that might have appeared in this bibliography for that reason. Yet such an exhaustive list would have been impractical. The same is true also of studies with a psychological or medical content. Obviously an immense amount of work has gone into the compilation of this work of reference, just as an immense amount of work has gone into the making of many of the books and articles cited.

The British Library National Sound Archive is a major centre of interest and activity in this country, and it is fitting that this bibliography is published by it. I have always treasured my own association with it, and it is a continuing association.

I first discussed oral history with Allan Nevins, who introduced me to the term which I have subsequently learnt was used long before him. His own enthusiasm, however, was infectious, as has been the enthusiasm of my friend and colleague Paul Thompson. Enthusiasm, indeed, as well as curiosity and concern seem to be hallmarks of oral historians. Whatever the context or the circumstances, I do not think that it will ever be lost.

ASA BRIGGS
Worcester College, Oxford,
August 1990.

INTRODUCTION

Oral history in Britain

Twenty years ago few people in Britain had heard of 'oral history'. Fewer still would have predicted the rapidity with which it would come to have such a pervasive role in local and school history, that it would fuel a re-evaluation of older people's reminiscences, or that it would create a host of new sound archives all over Britain. The Oral History Society and *Journal*, which celebrated its twentieth birthday in 1989, has changed beyond recognition from its first meeeting on 13 December 1969. Held at the British Institute of Recorded Sound, which is now the British Library National Sound Archive, the founders that day were almost exclusively historians: T.C.Barker, Brian Harrison, Raphael Samuel, Stanley Ellis, John Saville, Paul Thompson. One of the few non-academics present was Britain's 'father' of oral history, George Ewart Evans, who was only then beginning to realise that the fieldwork he had been doing for years could be termed 'oral history'.

For if the phrase itself was new, Evans was in fact part of a long tradition of historians' recognition of the value of eye witness accounts stretching back to the Venerable Bede in the eighth century and earlier. Until the wide availability of printed sources in the nineteenth century, when political history was ascendant, it would have been surprising if historians had not consulted oral sources when, as was often the case, no written sources existed. As Samuel Johnson noted in 1773 in the first documented plea for an oral history project, in this case about the 1745 Rebellion: 'You are to consider, all history was at first oral'. More recently it was the emergence of field work techniques in the second half of the nineteenth century that forged the way for social history and a rediscovery of oral sources. Engels' *Condition of the Working Class in England in 1844*, Mayhew and Charles Booth's studies of London, Rowntree's study of York, and the Webbs' histories of the co-operative movement and trade unionism are all, to some extent, what we would now term 'oral history'.

Although the tag 'oral history' had been coined reputedly by Allan Nevins in 1948 in the United States, from the outset post-war British oral history was different in emphasis from its US counterpart. Whilst the initiative was academic, the links to new approaches to studying history in Britain were clear. Key amongst these were the History Workshop movement, the emerging interest in Labour history, feminist and ethnic history, and the growth of working class autobiographical writing. All stressed the need to redress the balance of historical enquiry to embrace the experiences of 'ordinary' working class people and minority groups. Indeed the US interest in elites was to be largely anathema to British oral historians until Paul Thompson launched his National Life Story Collection in 1987, with its interest in the business world and leaders of national life.

Added to these new influences were moves towards a more source-based school history curriculum, the rising popularity of local and family history (and local studies libraries), and changing attitudes to social history in museums. Technological change, particularly the advent of affordable open-reel tape recorders and high quality cassette recorders, promoted tape recording as an efficient means of note-taking for all. As historians developed confidence in recording technology so oral history began to emerge not just as a method of gathering historical data but as a new discipline altogether in which individual life stories were paramount. Community historians and those working with older people simultaneously began to see that recording an individual's reminiscences was a two way process and that interviewees often gained personally from the whole process. This awareness received due recognition in Help the Aged's innovative slide-tape reminiscence pack *Recall*, building as it did on American psychologist Robert Butler's earlier work on the value of reminiscence and 'life review'.

Whilst Paul Thompson's pioneering work on family and work at Essex University, and important projects at Kent University in the 1970s, provided a framework, oral history's main thrust during the 1980s came from community history. It was the advent of unprecedented levels of government funding through various job creation schemes, but especially Community Programme (CP), which accounted for an explosion of activity. At the peak there were perhaps as many as one hundred CP-funded oral history schemes, many of them local history projects operated by local authority museums and libraries. Though they were inevitably varied in approach and quality, and some were grossly under-resourced and poorly-managed, taken together these projects significantly advanced oral history into new areas and new communities. They succeeded in collecting some innovative recordings and produced some outstanding publications. Most importantly they acted as a testbed for new techniques and ideas, and a training base for a whole new breed of young oral historians deeply committed to community history. However, by 1988 government priorities had changed and the vast majority of local schemes were forced to close. This tragedy was underlined by an astonishing unpreparedness of traditional archives to offer archival support. The Society of Archivists came to realise the value of oral archives very late indeed and it is still the case that relatively little attention has been given by sound archivists to oral history recording, despite the fact that it represents the majority of amateur recording activity.

After two decades of growth the development of oral history in Britain has reached something of a cross-roads. Cuts in government funding have not been confined to temporary work schemes. Higher and further education has suffered, so too have local authorities and all that means for diminishing library, museum and social services budgets. Arts funding for reminiscence theatre remains miniscule. The result is a peak of popular interest and initiatives in oral history on the one hand, but pathetically few facilities for training and archiving on the other. Many of the collections created in the 1980s still await funding to provide proper documentation and public access. The importance of this material is not in doubt: in some cases interviews chart a lost trade or a forgotten community for which no documents exist; in others the recordings give fresh insights into established areas of enquiry. Nor is the demand from teachers for oral history source material in doubt following the place awarded to oral history in the new core curriculum for history teaching in British schools.

The decline in public funding and a growing emphasis on short-term revenue earning has forced oral history into a defensive position in which it must constantly justify its existence. Some of the battles for academic respectability may have been won but the battle for funding continues. With only a handful of regional sound archives, themselves in constant difficulties, it is likely that the future of oral history recording lies to some extent with voluntary local history groups. Nevertheless there are hopeful signs, particularly the growing internationalism of oral history: not only the regular international conferences, but also the blossoming of oral history in Eastern Europe. The British Library has also belatedly recognised the need for a national initiative through the creation of a curatorship in oral history at the National Sound Archive, and there are a number of short-term funded projects, sometimes linked to local festivals or exhibitions in museums, where oral history is taking an increasing part, especially in social history displays. Ultimately it is oral history's breathtaking relevance to many debates and many disciplines outside history that will be its strength.

The bibliography: what's included

This bibliography identifies the published results of work in oral and life history, the first time it has been attempted in Britain. The aim has been to include books, pamphlets, periodicals, articles, catalogues and published recordings about, based on or using oral history, together with relevant coverage of related topics like sound archives and reminiscence therapy. Included are works published or available from 1945 up to the end of 1989. I have attempted to be comprehensive for the United Kingdom and selective for the rest of the world. North American, Australasian, and European works in translation have been included on the basis of their intrinsic interest, their relevance to oral history in Britain, or their contribution to debates about oral testimony or reminiscence.

It was not as straightforward a task as I had anticipated. Arriving at a qualifying definition of oral history for the purposes of inclusion raised a number of questions which forced decisions at an early stage. For example autobiographies, whilst being personal testimony, have generally been included only if they are written using some element of spoken history or tape recordings. Biographies are included where they are based predominantly on oral sources. Works about the technical aspects of tape recording and archival storage are included if they have direct relevance to oral history.

Sources used

Apart from a major literature search through the main oral history periodicals, an enormous array of sources have been consulted during compilation, including such bibliographies as exist, notably Paul Thompson's in *The Voice of the Past* (second edition). *BLAISE* (*British Library Automated Information Service*) proved to be invaluable by enabling a rapid on-line search of nearly 30 million records, notably *BNB* (*British National Bibliography*) since 1950, the US Library of Congress catalogues since 1968, the University of London catalogue, the British Library Humanities and Social Sciences catalogue since 1976, and Whitakers. Another on-line facility, *LISA* (*Library and Information Service Abstracts*) at *BLISS* (*British Library Information Sciences Service*) gave access to 550 library-related periodicals since 1950. Nevertheless many entries in this bibliography, having no ISBN number or being of limited circulation, do not appear in any catalogue. To unearth these I relied on personal contacts and the assistance of hundreds of libraries, archives, local and oral history groups and individuals to provide me with information.

The form of entry

The entries are arranged alphabetically by author and numbered sequentially. These identifying numbers are referred to in the subject index.

– Each entry begins with the author's (or editor's) surname followed by forenames or initials. If it is an edited work this is specified as '(ed.)' or '(eds.)'. In cases of joint or multiple authorship the form is taken from the work itself, unless this is not clear in which case they are listed alphabetically. Multiple works by a single author are listed chronologically. Where that author is also a joint or part author these works are listed in chronological order after his or her sole entry. There are cross-references for part authors whose entries appear under another name. If no individual or originating organisation is apparent the work is entered under its title.

– Below the author name(s) is the full title as it appears on the work's title page, including any sub-title. A note is made if this differs from the cover title, and if it has been translated into English from another language.

– Next is the place of publication if it is not London: all entries are assumed to have been published in London unless otherwise stated. American publications which have also been published in Britain generally show the British imprint details.

– On the same line is the name of the publisher (in shortest recognisable form) and the date of publication (*nd* appears where no date is given). This is the original date of publication except where this is otherwise specified, in which case details of new editions or reprints are given. In the case of articles it is the full title of the periodical, with volume, part and page details, which appears beneath the author details and article title.

– If the entry is a book which is part of a series this information appears next, followed on the line below by the number of pages and a note of the presence, if any, of a bibliography.

– Finally, many entries are completed by a brief annotation. Annotations are intended to give some idea of content where this is not evident from the title, to provide additional information, and to draw users' attention to works of particular merit. For these reasons there are more annotations for books than for articles.

– Entries are sometimes followed by cross-references to other related works of interest, and to other works by the same author appearing elsewhere in the bibliography.

The subject index
A detailed subject index follows the main bibliographic entries. Included are names, places, topics and concepts in alphabetical order and cross-referenced to the identifying numbers of the main entries. Larger sections are sub-divided by country. It is thus possible to identify rapidly all references to, say, oral history in museums or oral histories of coal mining, interview techniques or archival procedures, oral history school resources or oral history in libraries.

This bibliography is part of the British Library National Sound Archive's ongoing oral history programme and will be updated. For suggested entries or for information about oral history at the National Sound Archive contact:

The Curator, Oral History
British Library National Sound Archive
29 Exhibition Road
London SW7 2AS.

ALPHABETICAL LIST OF PERIODICALS CITED

Aboriginal History (Aus)
Advances in Librarianship (GB)
African Notes (Nig)
Ageing and Society (GB)
Agricultural History (GB)
American Archivist (US)
American Historical Association Newsletter (US)
American Historical Review (US)
American Journal of Occupational Therapy (US)
American Journal of Psychiatry (US)
American Studies International (US)
American University Law Review (US)
An Leabharlann: The Irish Library (Eire)
Annals of the American Academy of Political and Social
    Science (US)
Anthropological Quarterly (US)
Archivaria (Can)
Archives and Manuscripts (Aus)
Archives of General Psychiatry (US)
Assistant Librarian (GB)
Audiovisual Librarian (GB)
Australian Historical Association Bulletin (Aus)
Australian Library Journal (Aus)

BASC (British Association of Sound Collections)
    News (GB)
Behavioral and Social Sciences Librarian (US)
Biography (US)
Blackwood's Magazine (GB)
BMA (British Medical Association) News (GB)
Boston (US)
Bradford Antiquary (GB)
British Journal for the History of Science (GB)
British Journal of Clinical Psychology (GB)
British Journal of Psychiatry (GB)
British Journal of Sociology (GB)
Bulletin of the Medical Library Association (US)
Bulletin of the Society for the Study of Labour History
    (GB)
Business History (GB)
By Word of Mouth: Scottish Oral History Group
    Newsletter (GB)

California Librarian (US)
Canadian Archivist (Can)
(The) Canadian Forum (Can)
Canadian Oral History Association Journal (Can)
Canberra Historical Journal (Aus)
Cantium (GB)
Cardiff Working Papers in Welsh Linguistics (GB)
Case Conference (GB)
Catholic Library World (US)
Change (US)

Chronicle of Higher Education (US)
Clinical Gerontologist (US)
Collection Building (US)
Community Care (GB)
Comparative Studies in Society and History (GB)
Conditions Six (US)
Country Music (US)

Dimensions: A Journal of Holocaust Studies (US)
Donegal Annual (GB)
Drexel Library Quarterly (US)

East European Quarterly (US)
Educational Gerontology (GB)
Encounter (GB)
Encyclopedia of Library and Information Science (US)
English Journal (US)
Experimental Aging Research (US)
Exploring Local History (GB)

Family Heritage (US)
Feminist Studies (US)
Forest History (US)
Frontiers: A Journal of Women's Studies (US)

Garden History: The Journal of the Garden History
    Society (GB)
Generations: Bulletin of the British Society of Geriatric
    Nursing (US)
Geriatrics (US)
Gerontologist (US)
Gerontology (GB)
Gwent Local History (GB)

Health and Social Services Journal (US)
Higher Education and Research in the Netherlands
    (Holland)
(The) Historic Record (GB)
Historical Methods Newsletter (US)
Historical Social Research (W.Germany)
Historical Studies (US)
Historical Studies Australia and New Zealand (Aus)
History and Theory (US)
History in Africa (US)
History News (US)
History of Education Quarterly (GB)
History Teacher (US)
History Today (GB)
History Workshop (GB)

IFLA Journal (W.Germany)
Immigrants and Minorities (GB)
Information Development (US)
Innes Review (GB)
International Journal of Nursing Studies (GB)

International Journal of Oral History (US)
International Journal on Aging and Human
    Development (US)
International Library Review (GB)
International Review of Social History (Holland)
Irish Studies in Britain (GB)

Journal of Adolescence (GB)
Journal of Advanced Nursing (GB)
Journal of African History (GB)
Journal of American Folklore (US)
Journal of the American Medical Association (US)
Journal of Contemporary History (GB)
Journal of the East Anglian History Workshop (GB)
Journal of Experimental Psychology (US)
Journal of Genetic Psychology (US)
Journal of Geriatric Psychiatry (US)
Journal of Gerontological Nursing (US)
Journal of Gerontological Social Work (US)
Journal of Gerontology (US)
Journal of Library and Information Science (US)
Journal of Library History (US)
Journal of Nursing Care (US)
Journal of Peasant Studies (GB)
Journal of the Police History Society (GB)
Journal of Presbyterian History (US)
Journal of Psychohistory (US)
Journal of Psychosocial Nursing and Mental Health
    Services (US)
Journal of Social History (GB)
Journal of the Society of Archivists (GB)

Kalulu (Zomba)

Labor History (US)
Library Association Record (GB)
Library Journal (US)
Library Trends (US)
Life Stories (GB)
Llafur: The Journal of the Society for the Study of
    Welsh Labour History (GB)
(The) Local Historian (GB)
Local History (GB)
Local Studies Librarian (GB)
LOCSCOT (GB)
Lore and Language: The Journal of the Centre for
    English Cultural Tradition and Language (GB)

Man (GB)
Marxism Today (GB)
Melbourne History Journal (Aus)
Mental Health Nursing (US)
Morgannwg: The Journal of Glamorgan History (GB)
Morriston Other Times (GB)
Museums Journal (GB)

New Age (GB)

New Library World (GB)
New Socialist (GB)
New Society (GB)
New York Times Book Review (US)
New Zealand Journal of History (NZ)
New Zealand Libraries (NZ)
Newsletter of the History Workshop Centre for Social
    History (GB)
Nigerian Libraries (Nig)
North East Group for the Study of Labour History
    Bulletin (GB)
Nursing Forum (US)
Nursing Times (GB)

Ontario Library Review (Can)
Oral History (GB)
Oral History Association of Australia Journal (Aus)
Oral History Newsletter (Aus)
Oral History Review (US)

Pacific North West Quarterly (US)
Parliamentary Affairs (GB)
Phonographic Bulletin (GB)
Physical Educator (US)
Political Quarterly (GB)
Proceedings of the Plymouth Atheneum (GB)
Psychiatry (US)
Public Historian (US)
Public Library Quarterly (US)

Quadrant (Aus)

Radical History Review (US)
Recorded Sound (GB)
Rhode Island History (US)
Rhodesian Librarian (Rho)

Scholarly Publishing (US)
Scottish Library Association News (GB)
Signs (US)
Sing out! (GB)
Sky and Telescope (US)
Social Analysis (Aus)
Social Casework: The Journal of Contemporary Social
    Work (US)
Social Education (US)
Social History (GB)
Social History Curators' Group Journal (GB)
Social Science Information (GB)
Social Services Insight (GB)
Social Studies (US)
Social Work Education (GB)
Social Work Today (GB)
Sociological Review (GB)
Sociology (GB)
Sociology and Social Research (US)
Sound Heritage (Can)

Southern Exposure (US)
Southern History (GB)
Soviet Literature (US)
SSRC Newsletter (GB)
Studies in Western Australian History (Aus)
Studio Sound (GB)

Talk: The Journal of the National Oracy Project (GB)
Teaching History (GB)
Theatre Papers (GB)
(The) Times (GB)
(The) Times Educational Supplement (GB)
(The) Times Higher Education Supplement (GB)
(The) Times Literary Supplement (GB)

Victorian Studies (US)
Voices of Southern Struggle (US)

West Sussex Archives Society Newsletter (GB)
West Sussex History (GB)
Wilson Library Bulletin (US)

Zambia Library Association Journal (Zam)

Key to country of publication

Aus   Australia
Can   Canada
GB   Great Britain and Northern Ireland
Nig   Nigeria
NZ   New Zealand
Rho   Rhodesia
US   United States of America
Zam   Zambia

1   ABELLA, Irving and MILLAR, David (eds.)
The Canadian worker in the twentieth century
Toronto: Oxford University Press, 1978
310pp; bibliography
A survey of life in Canada between 1900 and 1940 using oral history and contemporary sources.

ABENDSTERN, Michele *see* THOMPSON, Paul

2   ABRAHAM, D.P.
"Maramuca: an exercise in the combined use of Portuguese records and oral tradition"
Journal of African History, vol.2, no.2 (1961)

3   ABRAHAMS, Roger
"Story and history: a folklorist's view"
Oral History Review, vol.9 (1981)
For related developments in folklore.

4   ABRAHAMS, Roger
Deep down in the jungle: Negro narrative folklore from the streets of Philadelphia
Hatboro, Pennsylvania : Folklore Associates, 1964
288pp; bibliography
Black urban folklore collected in a neighbourhood in South Philadelphia.

5   ABRAMS, Philip
Historical sociology
Shepton Mallet, Somerset: Open Books, 1982
353pp
For oral history, history and sociology.

6   ACKER, Alison
Children of the volcano
Westport, Connecticut: Between the Lines/ Laurence Hill, 1986
168pp
An account of the poverty, violence, toil and resilience of young people's lives in central America, based on five months of interviews in Guatemala, El Salvador, Honduras and Nicaragua.

ACKERMAN, Adele M *see* HYLAND, Diane T.

7   ADAIR, Nancy and Casey
Word is out: stories of some of our lives
San Francisco: New Glide Publications, 1978
337pp; bibliography
Lesbian oral history from a film of the same name.

8   ADAM, Rachel (ed.)
So this was Ollerton: local voices from Ollerton
Pontefract: Yorkshire Art Circus, 1986
40pp
Described as a proto-book written by the community between 28 April and 9 May 1986. Extracts from interviews about a Nottinghamshire mining village.

9   ADAM, Rachel (ed.)
When poverty knocks on the door love goes out the window: voices from Pontefract, Normanton, Castleford, Knottingley and Featherstone 1930-1945
Castleford, West Yorkshire: Yorkshire Art Circus, 1987
98pp
Life in the 'five towns' of Wakefield remembered by liquorice workers, railwaymen, miners, teachers, pub owners, munitions workers, glassworkers and others.

10   ADAM, Rachel (ed.)
Looking up
Castleford, West Yorkshire: Yorkshire Art Circus, 1989
72pp
Six people talk about their experiences of spinal injury, and the positive and negative changes that have occurred since their accidents.

11   ADAM, Rachel and VAN RIEL, Rachel
In sickness and in health
Castleford, West Yorkshire: Yorkshire Art Circus, 1987
54pp
Tales from nurses, midwives, GPs, dentists and the woman-next-door.

12   ADAM SMITH, Patsy
The Anzacs
Hamish Hamilton, 1978
372pp; bibliography
An account of the First World War as Australian soldiers and their families experienced it, based on interviews and letters.

13   ADAM SMITH, Patsy
Folklore of the Australian railwaymen
Melbourne: Macmillan of Australia, 1969; Adelaide: Rigby, 1979
308pp

14 **ADAM SMITH, Patsy**
Outback heroes
Sydney: Lansdowne, 1981
255pp
Testimony from the intrepid pioneers who
grappled with the unhospitable terrain of
Central Australia.

15 **ADAM SMITH, Patsy**
The shearers
Melbourne: Nelson, 1982
416pp
An oral history based study of sheep shearers
in Australia.

16 **ADAMOVICH, Ales**
"With the people as a co-author"
Soviet Literature, vol.5 (1979), pp.109-114
Stories of the Leningrad blockade of the
Second World War.

17 **ADAMS, Carol**
Ordinary lives: a hundred years ago
Virago, 1982
228pp; bibliography
Extracts from interviews with people who
lived at the time, or who remember what they
were told of it by their parents or
grandparents, are arranged thematically. Of
particular value for school use.

18 **ADAMS, Caroline (ed.)**
Across seven seas and thirteen rivers: life stories
of pioneer Sylhetti settlers in Britain
THAP Books, 1987
230pp; bibliography
A history of the beginnings of a Bangladeshi
community in Britain told through the life
stories of ten pioneer seamen.

19 **ADAMS, John**
"Reminiscence in the geriatric ward: an
undervalued resource"
Oral History, vol.12, no.2 (1984), pp.54-9

20 **ADAMS, John**
"Anamnesis in dementia: restoring a personal
history"
Geriatric Nursing, September/October 1986;
Oral History, vol.17, no.2 (1989), pp.62-4

21 **ADAMS, John**
"Ghosts of Christmas past"
Nursing Times, vol.84, no.50, 14 December
1988

22 **ADAMS, John**
"Caring for the casual poor"
Oral History, vol.17, no.1 (1989), pp.29-35
Examines changing policies towards tramps,
the homeless and the destitute, from the last
days of the Poor Law Guardians' workhouses
to the present.

ADAMS, K.J. *see* **HAREVEN, Tamara K.**

23 **ADELMAN, Marcy (ed.)**
Long time passing: lives of older lesbians
Boston: Alyson Press, 1986
265pp
An anthology of manuscripts and extracts
from over 200 recorded interviews.

24 **AFIGBO, A.E.**
"Oral tradition and history in Eastern
Nigeria"
African Notes, vol.3, no.3 & vol.4, no.1

25 **AFRO-CARIBBEAN EDUCATION
RESOURCE PROJECT**
Images and reflections: education and the Afro-
Caribbean child
ACER Project, nd
50pp
A collection of articles and interviews by
teachers, researchers, parents and children
looking at aspects of the Black British
experience: identity, Caribbean influence,
racism, the law, and racial bias in the media,
books and visual materials.

26 **AGE CONCERN (SCOTLAND)**
Reminiscence work with older people in
Scotland: the proceedings of the Exploring
Living Memory Conference held at Edinburgh
University on 19th November 1983
Edinburgh: Age Concern Scotland's
Development Advisory Resource Group and
Edinburgh University's Department of Extra-
mural Studies, 1984
45pp; bibliography

27-40 **AGE EXCHANGE THEATRE COMPANY**
Age Exchange has produced a series of books
based on the reminiscences and current
concerns of older people. Many have been
tied to touring reminiscence theatre
productions of the same name:

27   *Fifty years ago*
Age Exchange, 1983
48pp
Stories of work and home life from the 1930s
including growing up, courting and marriage,
hop picking, the Peace Movement, outings
and entertainment.

28   *All our Christmases*
Age Exchange, 1983
24pp

29   *Of whole heart cometh hope*
Age Exchange, 1983
48pp
Personal recollections by long-standing
members of the Co-operative Women's Guild
to mark the Guild's centenary.

30   *My first job*
Age Exchange, 1984
32pp
An anthology of memories and photographs
from pensioners who started work between
1912 and 1940.

31   *A place to stay: memories of pensioners from
many lands*
Age Exchange, 1984
64pp
Contributors from the West Indies, India, the
Far East, Cyprus, Poland and Italy recall their
homelands, their arrival in Britain and settling
in. In all cases their stories appear in their
mother tongue as well as in English.

32   *What did you do in the war, Mum?*
Age Exchange, 1985
72pp
Women recall their experiences of working in
munitions, in the forces, the Land Army,
administration and the service industries
during the Second World War.

33   *Can we afford the doctor?*
Age Exchange, 1985
80pp
Memories of health care and sickness from the
turn of the century to the present day.

34   *The time of our lives*
Age Exchange, 1986
64pp
Memories of leisure, courting days, cinema-
going and cycling in the 1920s and 1930s.

35   *Many happy retirements*
Age Exchange, 1986
48pp
A handbook which explores personal and
social aspects of retirement which are
considered problematical.

36   *Health remedies and healthy recipes*
Age Exchange, 1987
28pp
Reflections by Caribbean elders on the subject
of health and diet as remembered from
Jamaica and from experiences in Britain.

37   *Lifetimes*
Age Exchange, 1987
68pp
A handbook and sixty printed picture cards
designed to stimulate older people to
remember their lives. Intended for use by
people working with the elderly in both group
and individual contexts.

38   *Good morning children*
Age Exchange, 1988
56pp
Memories of schooldays in the 1920s and
1930s.

39   *On the river*
Age Exchange, 1989
184pp
Memories of living and working by the River
Thames and in London's docks before the
Second World War.

40   *Across the Irish Sea*
Age Exchange, 1989
175pp
Irish experiences of Ireland in the 1920s and
30s, the decision to leave, and memories of
coming to Britain to work in domestic service,
in hospitals, and in the building and hotel
trades.

41   **AGEE, James and EVANS, Walker**
Let us now praise famous men
New York: Ballantine Books, 1966; first
published, 1939
471pp
Part of a larger work entitled *Three Tenant
Farmers*, this volume concerns North
American cotton tenantry through the eyes of
three representative white families.

42 AGIRI, Babatunde
"Oral traditions and the study of the U.S. and Africa"
American Studies International, vol. 17 (Winter, 1979), pp.67-71
Argues African historians are not giving oral sources sufficient weight.

43 ALBEN, John Richard
"Tape recording local history in Morriston"
Morriston Other Times, vol.1, no.2 (July 1977)

44 ALBEN, John Richard
"Tape recording local history in Swansea"
Local Historian, vol.14, no.5 (February 1981)

45 ALBEN, John Richard
Air raids on Swansea
Swansea: Swansea City Council, 1981
A resource pack including two booklets, facsimile documents, photographs and transcripts of recorded interviews with Swansea people about the Second World War. The result of an oral history project into the effects of air raids on a civilian population.

46 ALBEN, John Richard
"Preparations for air raid precautions in Swansea, 1935-9"
Morgannwg: The Journal of Glamorgan History, vol.28 (1984), pp.55-73

47 ALBERTSON, Dean
Roosevelt's farmer: Claude R. Wickard in the New Deal
University Press, 1961
424pp
American political biography written by an Assistant Director of the Oral History Project of Columbia University.

48 ALEXANDER, Maxine (ed.)
Speaking for ourselves: women of the south
New York: Pantheon, 1984
290pp
Forty pieces, many originally published in *Southern Exposure*, about southern American women's lives over the last half century: white and black, debutante and sharecropper, poet and steelworker, mother and daughter, prostitute and beauty queen. Interviews figure prominently.

49 ALEXANDER, Sally
St.Giles Fair, 1830-1914: popular culture and the industrial revolution in nineteenth century Oxford
Oxford: History Workshop, Ruskin College, 1970
History Workshop pamphlets 2
59pp
A small amount of oral testimony is used.

50 ALEYBELEYE, B.
"Oral archives in Africa: their nature, value and accessibilty"
International Library Review, vol.17, no.4 (October 1985), pp.419-24
Contrasts African archives with those in the West and looks at the problems of accessibility common to many African collections.

51 ALLEN, Barbara and MONTELL, William Lynwood
From memory to history: using oral sources in local historical research
Nashville, Tenn.: American Association for State and Local History, 1981
172pp; bibliography
What to look for in interviewing and how to make sense of the stories collected. Includes a case study based on a celebrated triple murder in Tennessee.

52 ALLEN, Charles (ed.)
Plain tales from the Raj: images of British India in the twentieth century
BBC, 1975; Futura, 1979; Deutsch/BBC, 1985
239pp
A collection of transcribed interviews with members of the British rule in India and those who experienced it, based on the BBC Radio Four series of the same name. (*See also* INDIA OFFICE LIBRARY AND RECORDS; MASANI, Zareer)

53 ALLEN, Charles (ed.)
Tales from the Dark Continent
Deutsch/BBC, 1979; Futura, 1980
200pp
The recorded experiences of some fifty Britons who lived and worked in Africa during British colonial rule. (*See also* IMPERIAL WAR MUSEUM; INDIA OFFICE LIBRARY AND RECORDS)

54 **ALLEN, Charles (ed.)**
Tales from the South China Seas: images of the British in South-East Asia in the twentieth century
Deutsch/BBC, 1983; Futura paperback, 1983
320pp
The final part of an imperial trilogy, based on a BBC Radio Four series featuring fifty interviews of experiences from the 1920s and 1930s of British rule in Singapore, Borneo, Sarawak, Penang, Malacca, the Christmas Islands and elsewhere. The oldest contributor was born in 1890 and joined the Malay civil service in 1913.

ALLEN, Jane *see* **PATEL, Bhadra**

55 **ALLEN, Richard B.**
"New Orleans jazz archive at Tulane"
Wilson Library Bulletin, no.40 (March 1966), pp.619-23
The archive was set up in 1958 to collect interviews, discs, sheet music and photographs about jazz greats and non-musicians from the US and abroad.

ALLEN, Richard B. *see also* **SCHAFER, William J.**

ALLERTON, Robert *see* **PARKER, Tony**

56 **ALLNUT, Gillian**
It's the hardest job in the world, doing nothing!
Dudley, Northumberland: Dudley People's Centre, 1989
20pp
Transcripts of reminiscence sessions with seven women aged 79 to 90 in a Northumberland mining community, covering topics like first job, washing, baking and the Co-op.

57 **ALOGOA, E.J.**
"Oral tradition among the Ijo of the Niger Delta"
Journal of African History, vol.7, no.3

58 **ALOGOA, E.J.**
"Dating oral tradition"
African Notes, vol.4, no.1

AMBLESIDE ORAL HISTORY GROUP *see*
CHARLOTTE MASON COLLEGE

59 **AMERICAN INDIAN RESEARCH PROJECT**
Oyate Iyechinka Woglakapi: the people speak for themselves, an oral history collection
Vermillion: American Indian Research Project, 1970-
Several volumes by way of a catalogue of interviews and music from Plains Indians and non-Indians.

60 **ANDERSON, R. Wayne**
"Oral history dissertations, 1977-81"
Oral History Review, vol.10 (1982), pp.133-44
Includes US dissertations on methodology and which make extensive use of oral sources.

61 **ANDERSON, Terri**
"Oral history in sound"
Studio Sound, vol.27, no.3 (March 1985), pp.98-101
A description of the British Library National Sound Archive's oral history project on the recording industry. (*See also* BRITISH LIBRARY NATIONAL SOUND ARCHIVE; STAPLEY, Laurence)

ANDRESEN, Carl Erik *see* **BURCHARDT, Jorgen**

ANGELL, R. *see* **GOTTSCHALK, L.**

62 **APPEL, Benjamin**
The people talk: American voices from the Great Depression
New York: E.P.Dutton, 1940; reprinted Simon and Schuster, 1982
502pp
The author toured the United States from coast to coast in 1939 and 1940 recording what people had to say about their lives. With an introduction by Nathan Glazer.

63 **APPLE RECORDS**
The Beatles' story: a narrative and musical biography of beatlemania
Apple Records, STBO 2222, nd, 2 LP records
Includes interviews with each Beatle, Brian Epstein, George Martin and fans.

64 **ARCHER, Stuart and SHEPLEY, Nigel**
Witnessing history: looking at oral evidence
Cheltenham: Stanley Thornes, 1988
104pp
Written by two classroom teachers and based on eighty interviews about the inter-war period, this book was the first published to be of direct relevance to using oral history in GCSE class projects.

65   ARENSBERG, Conrad M. and KIMBALL, Solon T.
Family and community in Ireland
Oxford University Press, 1968, second edition; first edition, 1940
417pp
An inductive social analysis of rural life in Ireland with extracts from conversations with people from County Clare.

66   ARMITAGE, Susan
"Housework and childrearing on the Frontier: the oral history record"
Sociology and Social Research, vol.63 (April 1979), pp.467-74
Twenty Colorado women talk about housework and childrearing in the 1920s on mountain ranches, mining camps and homesteads. Children were fitted in between chores.

67   ARMSTRONG, Keith and BEYNON, Huw (eds.)
Hello, are you working? Memories of thirties in the North East of England
Whitley Bay, Tyne and Wear: Strong Words/ Erdesdun Publications, 1977
96pp
Sixteen recollections of the Depression in the North East in the 1930s, one of the worst hit areas in England.

68   ARMSTRONG, Keith, PICKLES, Helen and WHITTLE, Tony (eds.)
Missile village: a 'Strong Words' portrait of Gilsland
Whitley Bay, Tyne and Wear: Strong Words/ Erdesdun Publications, 1978
66pp
Post-war changes in a rural village of 400 people on the Cumbria/Northumberland border and the development of the Blue Streak missile research centre, closed in the 1960s.

69   ARMSTRONG, Paul F.
The use of the life history method in social and educational research
Hull: University of Hull Department of Adult Education, 1982
Newland Papers no.7
69pp

70   ARTS IN MEDWAY
The times of our lives: women in Medway from 1900, volume one 1900-1939
Gillingham, Kent: AIM Publications/Arts in Medway, 1989
62pp
A women's history photographic project, launched in 1987, which became a book, showing women's views about life and change in Medway and drawn from over 60 women's testimony. Includes memories of domestic life, shopping, childhood, World War One, work, village life, transport, leisure and school.

71   ASHDOWN, Ellen
"Florida's Black Archives: a substantial past"
Change, vol.11 (April 1979), pp.48-9
The Black Archives Research Center and Museum described.

72   ASHWORTH, M.
The Oxford House in Bethnal Green
Oxford House: 1985
65pp
An account of the pioneering university settlement in the East End of London through oral reminiscence, photographs and documents.

73   ASKHAM, Janet
"Telling stories"
Sociological Review, vol.30 (1982)

74   ATIYA, Nayra
Khul-Khaal: five Egyptian women tell their stories
Virago, 1988; first published New York, 1982
182pp
Five life stories illustrating shared experiences of female circumcision, marriage, belief in the 'evil eye', and illiteracy, which offer an insight into lower class women's lives in urban Egypt.

75   ATKINSON, Elizabeth
"'Strict but not cruel'?: living in children's homes, 1903-1943"
Oral History, vol.15, no.2 (1987), pp.38-45
Based on interviews with fifteen people, many of them ex-pupils of York Blue Coat School which admitted mainly orphans.

76   ATKINSON, Frank
Life and traditions in Northumberland and Durham
Dent, 1977
168pp; bibliography
Incorporates many recollections of local people to portray a sense of regional unity and culture in the North East of England.

76A   ATTMORE, Stephen and MERSON, Elizabeth
Entertainment and transport in 1900
Harlow: Longman, 1983
Into the past series vols. 5-6
24pp
Originally published as separate volumes by the two individual authors.

77   AUBREY, John
Brief lives
Woodbridge: Boydell, 1968
332pp
A modern English version of this late seventeenth century example of oral history, edited by Richard Barber.

78   AUSTIN, Tony
"The spoken word: oral history" in MACKINOLTY, Judy (ed.), *Past Continuous*, *Sydney: History Teachers' Association of Australia, 1983, pp.101-190*

79   AUSTRALIAN BROADCASTING COMPANY
Voices from a vanishing Australia: recollections of the way things used to be
Crows Nest, New South Wales: ABC, 1988

80   "Avon archive"
Library Association Record, vol.83 (March 1981), p.114

81   AYERS, Pat
The Liverpool docklands: life and work in Athol Street
Liverpool: Docklands History Project, nd
81pp
From interviews revealing the realities of dockland life: the growth of Liverpool's north end docks, leisure, making ends meet, inter-war family life and Second World War experiences.

82   AYERS, Pat
Women at war: Liverpool women 1939-45
Liverpool: Liver Press, 1988
The History and Society of Merseyside Series
58pp; bibliography
Based on interviews covering women at work, evacuation, family and how war affected daily life.

83   AYLESBURY PAST PROJECT
Aylesbury remembered: conversations with Aylesbury residents
Aylesbury, Buckinghamshire: Buckinghamshire County Museum/ Community Programme Agency, 1987
73pp
Extracts from interviews with some forty people, recorded in 1986 and 1987 and covering childhood, school and games, doctors and vets, work, food, the world wars, transport, local characters, markets and fairs.

BACK, Kathryn *see* DAVIS, Cullom

84   BADDELEY, Alan, GITTINS, Diana, and HINDLEY, Colin
in MOSS, Louis and GOLDSTEIN, Harvey *see* (eds.)
For consistency of accuracy in memory.

85   BAGGS, Chris
"Video and local studies librarianship - a slight return: a report on a weekend school on 'Video History'"
Audiovisual Librarian, vol.11, no.1 (Winter 1985), pp.47-9

86   BAHRICK, H.P., BAHRICK, P.O., and WITTLINGER, R.P.
"Fifty years of memory for names and faces"
Journal of Experimental Psychology, no.104, 1 March 1975

87   BAILEY, David Thomas
"Divided prism: two sources of black testimony on slavery"
Journal of Southern History, vol. 46 (August 1980), pp.381-404
Compares black autobiographies with 637 New Deal Writers' Projects interviews and finds the two sources disagree.

88 **BAILEY, Derek**
Improvisation: its nature and practice in music
Ashbourne: Moorland, 1980; new edition by
the British Library National Sound Archive
due 1991
154pp; bibliography
Based on interviews with musicians involved
in Indian, flamenco, baroque, organ, jazz and
rock music, it seeks to explore the
practitioner's understanding of improvisation.

BAIRD, Patrick *see* **BLIZZARD, Andrew**

89 **BALDWIN, B.S.**
"Public Library of South Australia's oral
history project, 1903-1908"
Archives and Manuscripts, vol.6 (August 1976),
pp.292-302

90 **BAKER, Mark**
Nam: the Vietnam war in the words of the men
and women who fought there
New York: William Morrow, 1981; Sphere
paperback, 1981
324pp
Interviews with American soldiers from all
ranks for and against the war.

91 **BAKER, Mark**
Cops: their lives in their own words
Abacus, 1987
504pp
Through interviews with over 100 US
policemen and women, the author wanted to
get beyond press hype and sociological studies
by talking to the people themselves about
their lives.

92 **BALLARD, Linda May**
"Collecting oral narrative"
Donegal Annual, 1983
Oral history in Northern Ireland.

93 **BALLARD, Linda May**
"Awk, but maybe it's only a load of aul' lies:
an opinion on oral tradition"
Oral History, vol.14, no.2 (1986), pp.39-45
Compares oral history and 'personal
experience narrative', and examines the
reliability of oral testimony using Northern
Ireland sources.

BALLARD, Linda May *see also* **BUCKLEY,
Anthony D.**

BALLARD, Michael *see* **CUNNINGHAM,
Kitty**

94 **BALLIETT, Whitney**
American musicians: 56 portraits in jazz
New York: Oxford University Press, 1986
415pp
The roots of great and near-great jazz artists.

95 **BANKS, Ann (ed.)**
First person America
New York: Knopf/Random House, 1980
Bibliography
Eighty narratives originally recorded by
members of the New Deal Federal Writers'
Project in the 1930s, some of whom have since
become writers of note. They are grouped by
particular industry.

96 **BANKS, Lynne Reid**
Torn country: an oral history of the Israeli war
of independence
New York: Watts, 1982
400pp
Over sixty interviews were conducted in
English about the 1947-9 Arab-Israeli war and
are arranged by topic.

97 **BARHAM, Jeffrey**
Cambridgeshire at war
Cambridge: Bird's Farm Publications, 1977
67pp
World War Two memories from six local
people.

98 **BARKER, T.C.**
Pilkington Brothers and the glass industry
Allen and Unwin, 1960
296pp
A pioneer of oral history who makes
widespread use of oral history in this company
history of one of Britain's leading glass
manufacturers.

99 **BARKER, T.C. (ed.)**
The long march of everyman
Deutsch/BBC, 1975
301pp
Based on the BBC Radio Four series of the
same name, originally broadcast in 1971-2,
which comprised twenty-six 45 minute
compilations, or 'sound symphonies', of 'vox
pop' drawn from 800 speakers all over Britain
and from the BBC Sound Archives.

100 **BARKOW, Al**
Gettin' to the dance floor: an oral history of
American golf
New York: Atheneum, 1986
282pp

101 BARNES, Annie
Tough Annie: from suffragette to Stepney councillor
Stepney Books, 1980
70pp
Annie in conversation with Kate Harding and Caroline Gibbs recalls the early suffragette movement in East London, the influence of Sylvia Pankhurst, Stepney Labour Party and the Charity Organisation Society.

102 BARNES, J.A. and WEBSTER N.
Police interrogation: tape recording
H.M.S.O., 1980
Royal Commission on Criminal Procedure research study no.8
106pp; bibliography
A survey describing and evaluating the various procedures involved in police interviews.

103 BARNETT, C.R.
"Use of oral history and interviews as research techniques in sport history"
Physical Educator, vol.39 (December 1982), pp.187-9
Includes a short bibliography.

104 BARNETT, Don and NJAMA, Karari
Mau Mau from within: autobiography of Njama Karari and analysis of Kenya's peasant revolt
MacGibbon & Kee, 1966
512pp
Kenyan political history.

BARNETT, Julie *see* **EVANS, Catherine**

105 BARR, Pat
The dust in the balance: British women in India 1905-1945
Hamish Hamilton, 1989
186pp
B sed on interviews with women doctors, teachers, nurses and missionaries, and critical of the myth of women in India as frivolous 'memsahibs'.

106 BARRIOS DE CHUNGARA, Domitila
Let me speak! Testimony of Domitila, a woman of the Bolivian mines
Stage 1, 1978
235pp
The story of the wife of a tin miner, herself an organiser of women tin miners in the Bolivian Andes, from interviews with Moema Viezzer.

107 BARROW, Karen (ed.)
West End as I remember it: memories of the West End area of Leicester by local people who lived and worked there
Leicester: Leicestershire Libraries and Information Service, 1985
28pp
The second title in a series of books based on entries to a competition where local people recorded reminiscences of their community. (*See also* COUCHMAN, Elizabeth)

108 BARRY DOCKS CENTENARY PROJECT
In our own words, in our own pictures
Barry: Valley and Vale, 1989
91pp
The turbulent history of what was once the world's largest coal-exporting port, condensed from over fifty hours of interviews, with personal photographs.

109 BARTLETT, Frederick Charles
Remembering: a study in experimental and social psychology
Cambridge: Cambridge University Press 1967, reprint of 1932 edition
317pp

110 BARTLETT, Liz (ed.)
'They were happy days': memories of growing up in North Kensington
North Kensington Amenity Trust, 1983
24pp
From conversations with eleven members of a reminiscence class called 'Your Past' which met every Wednesday during 1982-3.

111 BARTLETT, Liz and SENIOR, Diana (eds.)
Having a good time: North Kensington memories of days out and time off
North Kensington Amenity Trust, 1985
24pp
Twelve local people talked to the North Kensington Local History Project about holidays, day-tripping to Southend, hiking, cinema, and entertainments at home.

112 BARWICK, Diane, URRY, James and BURNETT, David
"A select bibliography of aboriginal history and social change: theses and published research to 1976"
Aboriginal History, vol.1, no.2 (1977), pp.111-69

113 BASKIN, John
New Burlington: the life and death of an
American village
New York: Norton, 1976
259pp
Interviews with the inhabitants of an Ohio
town before it was destroyed to become a
reservoir.

114 BASSO, Rosanna
"A short-lived myth of a children's strike"
Oral History, vol.16, no.1 (1988), pp.19-24
A school strike in Southern Italy in 1977.

115 BASTIN, Bruce
Red River blues: the blues tradition in the
southwest
Urbana: University of Illinois Press, 1986
379pp
An interview-based sociological study of
traditional blues musicians.

116 BAUM, Willa K.
"Oral history: a revived tradition at the
Bancroft Library"
Pacific North West Quarterly, vol. 58 (April
1967), pp.57-64

117 BAUM, Willa K.
"Oral history, the library and the genealogical
researcher"
Journal of Library History, vol.5 (October
1970), pp.359-71
Considers the usefulness of existing oral
history sources for family historians in the
United States.

118 BAUM, Willa K.
"Building community identity through oral
history: a new role for the local library"
California Librarian, vol.31 (October 1970),
pp.271-84

119 BAUM, Willa K.
"Oral history in the United States"
Oral History, vol.1, no.3 (1972), pp.15-29

120 BAUM, Willa K.
Oral history for the local historical society
Nashville, Tennessee: American Association
for State and Local History, 1974; revised
second edition
63pp; bibliography
An innovative handbook for recording oral
history. The revised second edition contains
updates on equipment.

121 BAUM, Willa K.
Transcribing and editing oral history
Nashville, Tenn.: American Association for
State and Local History, 1977
127pp; bibliography
A manual on the techniques of processing oral
material after the interview, with advice on
indexing and editing, and examples of
transcribed interviews, one of which features
on the accompanying 33rpm record.

122 BAUM, Willa K.
"Therapeutic value of oral history"
International Journal of Aging and Human
Development, vol.12, no.1 (1980/1), pp.49-53
Argues that the convergence of oral historians
and gerontologists on reminiscence must not
obscure their basic differences in approach.

123 BAUM, Willa K.
"Guidebooks for oral history projects"
History News, vol.35 (December, 1980)

124 BAUM, Willa K.
"Oral history: a selective bibliography"
Catholic Library World, vol.55, no.5
(December 1983), pp.226-9
Works of special library relevance.

BAUM, Willa K. *see also* **DUNAWAY, David**
King; FRY, Amelia

125 BAYNHAM, Henry
Men from the Dreadnoughts
Hutchinson, 1976
272pp; bibliography
Based on taped interviews with men from the
non-commissioned ranks of the Royal Navy
around the First World War.

126 BAYNHAM, Mike and MACE, Jane
Doing research, interviews, tapes, transcriptions
and observations: a collection of papers on
research and practice in adult literacy
Lee Community Education Centre/University
of London Goldsmiths' College, 1986
57pp; bibliography

127 BBC RECORDS
Gandhi: man on trial
BBC Records, RESR4, 1969, 1 LP record
Gandhi himself and others assess his life,
including Earl Mountbatten, Jawaharlal
Nehru, Gilbert Murray and Zakir Hussain.
Written by Francis Watson and based on BBC
Third Programme recordings.

128 BBC RECORDS
'I was there...': eyewitness accounts of
momentous occasions. Recordings from the
BBC Sound Archives
BBC Records, REB 78M, 1970, 1 LP record
Direct personal reminiscences of: the Duke of
Wellington's funeral in 1852 (recorded in
1940); the Seige of Paris in 1870 (recorded in
1946); Mafeking in 1899 recalled by Lord
Baden Powell in 1937; the opening of
Tutankhamen's tomb in 1924 recalled by
Howard Carter in 1936; the declaration of the
First World War in 1914 by Harold Nicolson
in 1937; the Reichstag fire in 1933; the Munich
agreement of 1938 by Neville Chamberlain on
his return to Britain.

129 BBC RECORDS
Railways remembered/The end of steam
BBC Records and Tapes, 190(M), 1975, 2 LP
records
Originally issued as two separate records in
1968. Railway nostalgia in sound and words
from BBC archive recordings by the people
who built, operated and used them. Includes
an interview with Mr.Froude, a Great
Western railway guard, recorded in 1935 when
he was 99 years old, in which he recalls
Brunel.

130 BEAGLEHOLE, Ann
A small price to pay: refugees from Hitler in
New Zealand 1936-46
Wellington, New Zealand: Allen and Unwin
N.Z./Historical Branch, Department of
Internal Affairs, 1988
Bibliography
Based on interviews with thirty-two former
refugees.

131 BEAMISH MUSEUM
A day in the life of...
Beamish, County Durham: Beamish, The
North of England Open Air Museum, 1988
Series of four page leaflets, being accounts of
everyday life written in the first person.
Featured are a domestic servant, a co-op
drapery assistant, a pitman and a pitman's
wife.

132 BEAN, Philip and MELVILLE, Joy
Lost children of the empire: the untold story of
Britain's child migrants
Unwin Hyman, 1989
177pp; bibliography
The story of some of the 130,000 children,
some just three years old, who were shipped
from Britain to distant parts of the empire, the
last as recently as 1967. Based on interviews
with child migrants to Canada, Australia and
Zimbabwe, the book accompanied a Granada
Television documentary. (*See also*
HARRISON, Phyllis)

133 BEATON, S.R.
"Reminiscence in old age"
Nursing Forum, vol.19. no.3 (1980), pp.271-83
Reminiscence as encouraging a more positive
view of ageing, with discussion of the different
functions of reminiscence.

134 BECKWITH, Ian
"Joe's Journals: an experiment in
broadcasting total history"
Oral History, vol.6, no.2 (1978), pp.93-101
The role of oral testimony in teaching history,
through twenty short radio programmes
broadcast on BBC Radio Humberside in 1975.

135 BEDDOE, Deirdre
Discovering women's history: a practical
manual
Pandora, 1983
232pp; bibliography
An excellent introductory guide to source
material, including oral history, for people
researching women's lives.

136 BEINART, William
The political economy of Pondoland 1860-1930
Cambridge: Cambridge University Press, 1982
African Studies series no.33
218pp; bibliography
Analyses the ways in which formerly
independent African chiefdoms were
transformed by the development of industrial
capitalism in South Africa, drawing on
interviews carried out in Pondoland during
1976-7.

BELL, Colin *see* **NEWBY, Howard**

11

137   BENISON, Saul
"Reflections on oral history"
American Archivist, vol.28 (January 1965), pp.71-7
Argues the case for oral history's role in augmenting autobiography and urges interviews with lesser-known people. Remarks that oral history tapes should be kept for voice inflection.

138   BENISON, Saul
Tom Rivers: reflections on a life in medicine and science; an oral history memoir
Cambridge, Massachusetts: M.I.T.Press, 1967
682pp
Virus researcher Thomas Rivers talks about his education, medical career and the problems of medical research. Well researched, using documentary sources to provide a framework for the interviews.

139   BENISON, Saul
"Oral history: a personal view" in CLARKE, Edwin (ed.), *Modern methods in the history of medicine, Athlone Press, 1971, pp.286-305*
A useful survey of the problems and practice of interviews in the history of science and medicine, with a helpful bibliography.

140   BENNETT, James
Oral history and delinquency: the rhetoric of criminology
Chicago: University of Chicago Press, 1981
363pp; bibliography
A history of life story work in this field.

141   BENSON, John
The penny capitalists: a study of nineteenth-century working-class entrepreneurs
Dublin: Gill and Macmillan, 1983
172pp; bibliography
Draws on oral collections.

142   BERG, Maclyn *see* **BURG, Maclyn P.**

143   BERRIDGE, V.
"Opium and oral history"
Oral History, vol.7, no.2 (1979), pp.48-58
The use of opium in the light of growing medicalisation of drugs over the past century.

144   BERTAUX, Daniel (ed.)
Biography and society: the life history approach in the social sciences
Sage, 1981
314pp
An important collection of thirteen articles, mainly by sociologists, which introduce readers to life-story interviewing; including the problems and uses of interviews, testing the accuracy of oral accounts, and the value of individual testimony in understanding society.

145   BERTAUX, Daniel
"The bakers of France"
History Today, vol.33 (June 1983), pp.33-7
Based on interviews with apprentices, bakers and their wives. Espouses a broad approach to oral history.

146   BERTAUX, Daniel and BERTAUX-WIAME, Isabelle
"Artisanal bakery in France: how it lives and why it survives" in BECHHOFER Frank and ELLIOTT, Brian (eds.) *The petite bourgeoisie: comparative studies of the uneasy stratum, Macmillan, 1981*

147   BERTAUX-WIAME, Isabelle
"The life story approach to the study of internal migration"
Oral History, vol.7, no.1 (1979), pp.26-32
French oral histories.

148   BETHEL, Elizabeth Rauh
Promiseland: a century of life in a negro community
Philadelphia: Temple University Press, 1981
329pp; bibliography
A detailed study using contemporary records and oral evidence, which has been carefully cross-checked and discussed 'page by page' with the community itself.

149   BEWDLEY MUSEUM
Sound archive catalogue
Bewdley, Worcestershire: Wyre Forest District Council Leisure and Recreation Department, 1989
19pp
The result of two years' work by two MSC workers concentrating on the Kidderminster carpet industry, but also including interviews on basket making, coracle making, rope making, clay pipe manufacturing, timber processing and work on the River Severn.

BEYNON, Huw *see* **ARMSTRONG, Keith**

150 BINGHAM, Walter Van Dyke and MOORE, Bruce Victor
How to interview
New York: Harper, 1959, fourth revised edition; first edition, 1931
272pp
A full discussion of interviewing and sociological methods.

151 BINNEY, Judith and CHAPLIN, Gillian
Nga Morehu: the survivors
Auckland, New Zealand: Oxford University Press, 1986
218pp; bibliography
The life stories of eight Maori women in the first book of its kind. All were brought up in small rural communities associated with the Ringatu faith, a distinct Maori religious movement founded in the nineteenth century.

152 BINNEY, Simon (ed.)
"Cicely Williams: memoirs of a doctor. An interview with Jenny Bienart and Robert King"
Newsletter of the History Workshop Centre for Social History, no.3 (1985), pp.69-80

153 BIRD, Elizabeth
"Jazz bands of North East England: the evolution of a working class cultural activity"
Oral History, vol.4, no.2 (1976), pp.79-88

154 BIRD, Julie
Oral history collections: their importance in the local history library
Polytechnic of North London, School of Librarianship and Information Studies, 1983
Occasional publication no.5
52pp; bibliography
Undergraduate dissertation.

155 BIRD, Stewart, GEORGAKAS, Dan and SHAFFER, Deborah
Solidarity forever: the IWW. An oral history of the Wobblies
Lawrence and Wishart, 1987; first published Chicago, 1985
247pp
A history of the US trade union Industrial Workers of the World.

156 BIRMINGHAM MUSEUMS AND ART GALLERY
I was there: Birmingham and the Great War
Birmingham: Birmingham Museums and Art Gallery/West Midlands Oral History Group, 1982
Cassette tape of extracts from fifty interviews with some of the 150,000 Birmingham men and women that served in the First World War, and with those on the home front in the armaments factories and hospitals.

157 BIRMINGHAM MUSEUMS AND ART GALLERY
The boatman's garden
Birmingham: Birmingham Museums and Art Gallery/West Midlands Oral History Group, 1983
Cassette tape of recollections of boat people working on canals throughout the Midlands and south to London covering tunnels, horses, disputes, illness, schooling, the IRA, the Second World War and nationalisation. The Second World War revived the canal trade but by the 1950s it had virtually ceased.

158 BISHOP, N.
"Description of family harmony in oral histories of grandmother-grandaughter bonding"
Gerontologist, vol.20, no.5 (1980)

159 BISHTON, Derek and HOMER, Brian (eds.)
Talking blues: the black community speaks about its relationship with the police
AFFOR (All Faiths For One Race), 1980, fifth edition
48pp
A collection of interviews with young people from Birmingham who relate experiences of racially motivated police harassment.

160 BLACKWELL, Ron
Low Moor Chemical Works explosion, 1916
Coventry: Lanchester Polytechnic, 1986
133pp
Oral testimonies of one of Bradford's worst industrial accidents and its impact on the community.

161 BLAIKIE, Roberta
As time goes by
Edinburgh: Community History Project/Community Service Volunteers Scotland, nd
12pp
Memories and reminiscences of residents of Silverlea Residential Home, Edinburgh.

162   **BLAIKIE, Roberta**
Forthland House: memories from residents at Forthland House Residential Home
Edinburgh: Community History Project/ Community Service Volunteers Scotland, nd
20pp
Memories and reminiscences of residents of Forthland Residential Home.

163   **BLAIKIE, Roberta and TELFER, Glenn**
Way to the past
Glasgow: Community Service Volunteers, 1987
24pp
An introduction to oral history and reminiscence work.

164   **BLAIR, May**
Once upon the Lagan: the story of the Lagan canal
Belfast: Blackstaff Press, 1981
126pp
Based on extensive interviews with the lock-keepers, lightermen, bank-rangers and haulers who worked the Lagan Navigation in Northern Ireland.

165   **BLAKE, David M.**
"Oral archives at the India Office Library and Records" in GAUR, Albertine (ed.) *South Asian Studies*, British Library, 1986, pp.128-34

166   **BLIZZARD, Andrew and BAIRD, Patrick**
Five ways into Birmingham's past
Birmingham: Birmingham City Council, 1989
60pp; bibliography
Five ways of doing local history research: reading, visual, architectural, family and oral.

BLOCH, Howard *see* **MILLER, Les**

167   **BLOOM, Jonathan and BUHLE, Paul (eds.)**
Guide to the Oral History of the American Left
New York: New York University Libraries, 1984
58pp
A catalogue of interviews carried out by the OHAL project established in 1976 at Tamiment Library at New York University to research US labor and radicalism. Includes films and videos.

BLOOMFIELD, Barbara *see* **SAMUEL, Raphael**

168   **BLYTHE, Ronald**
Akenfield: portrait of an English village
Allen Lane, 1969; Harmondsworth: Penguin, 1972
336pp; bibliography
Based on intimate conversations in 1967 with inhabitants of Charsfield, an isolated village in rural Suffolk, including farmers, a blacksmith, a vet and a gravedigger.

169   **BLYTHE, Ronald**
The view in winter: reflections on old age
Allen Lane, 1979; Harmondsworth: Penguin, 1981
321pp; bibliography
Based on several dozen rural old people's memories of war, work, family and community.

BOANAS, Guy *see* **SAMUEL, Raphael**

170   **BODER, David P.**
I did not interview the dead
Urbana: University of Illinois Press, 1949
Includes eight selected conversations with Holocaust survivors recorded in the summer of 1945 using a magnetic wire recorder.

171   **BOGDAN, Robert (ed.)**
Being different: the autobiography of Jane Fry
Wiley Inter-Science, 1974
235pp
Derived from 100 hours of interviews recorded between April and June 1972, this is the life of someone with the organs of a man but who dresses and lives as a woman. It also discusses the autobiography as a method of understanding lives.

172   **BOLTON, G.C.**
A fine country to starve in
Nedlands, Perth: University of Western Australia Press, 1972
278pp; select bibliography
Drawn from interviews revealing people's reactions to the Western Australian Depression of the 1930s.

173 BOLTON ORAL HISTORY PROJECT
Growing up in Bolton 1900-1940
Bolton: Bolton Metropolitan Borough
Department of Education and Arts, 1983
An educational and reminiscence pack of 35
photographs, 38 documents, 40 pages of
transcripts, 13 pages of notes, two sixty-
minute cassettes and a bibliography. The main
topics covered are home and neighbourhood,
leisure and school, work and social change,
drawn from some 300 hours of recorded
interviews.

174 BONFIELD, Lynn A.
"Conversation with Arthur M. Schlesinger, Jr.:
the use of oral history"
American Archivist, vol.43 (Fall 1980),
pp.461-72
Schlesinger discusses his use of oral testimony
in his book about the Kennedy family,
including release forms, access and other local
history projects.

175 BOOTH, Gill
Diamonds in brown paper
Sheffield: Sheffield City Libraries, 1988
65pp
The working lives of 'buffers': women who
work polishing cutlery and silver in Sheffield.
A handful remain whilst at one time there
were thousands of them, noted for their 'brats'
and brown paper leggings.

176 BORNAT, Joanna
"Home and work: a new context for trade
union history"
Oral History, vol.5, no.2 (1977), pp.101-123
Women and the General Union of Textile
Workers in the first twenty years of the
century, from interviews carried out in West
Yorkshire's Colne Valley.

177 BORNAT, Joanna
"Women's history and oral history: an outline
bibliography"
Oral History, vol. 5, no. 2, (1977), pp.124-35
A useful bibliography covering sociological,
anthropological and autobiographical works.

178 BORNAT, Joanna
"Review article: Exploring Living Memory -
the uses of reminiscence"
Ageing and Society, vol.5 (1985), pp.333-7
(*See also* EXPLORING LIVING MEMORY)

179 BORNAT, Joanna (ed.)
Memories of the twenties and thirties
Help the Aged, 1985
Ten work cards.

180 BORNAT, Joanna
"Reminiscence, the state of the art"
New Age, no. 30, Summer 1985, pp.14-17

181 BORNAT, Joanna
"Oral history as a social movement:
reminiscence and older people"
Oral History, vol.17, no.2 (1989), pp.16-25
An excellent retrospective overview.

182 BORNAT, Joanna
"Oral history and reminiscence: a social
context for sound archives"
Phonographic Bulletin, no.55 (November
1989), pp.26-31

BORNAT, Joanna *see also* **JONES, Derek;**
THOMPSON, Paul

183 BORNEMAN, Patricia (ed.)
Directory to Montana oral resources
Helena, Montana: Montana Oral History
Association, 1985
82pp

184 BOROUGHS AND HORSEMARKET
LIVING MEMORY PROJECT
In living memory: life in the Boroughs
Northampton: Northampton Arts
Development, 1987
136pp
Memories of an area of working class housing
in Northampton demolished to make way for
new development.

185 BOSSIN, Bob
Settling Clayoquot
Victoria, British Columbia: Sound and Moving
Image Division, Provincial Archives of British
Columbia, 1981
Sound Heritage series no.33
76pp
Interviews with settlers of Tofino, on the west
coast of Vancouver Island. Covers 1870-1950s,
using mainly oral testimony and other primary
sources.

186 BOSTLE, Eileen
"Local history and reminiscence therapy"
Local Studies Librarian, vol.4, no.1 (Summer
1985), p.13

187 BOSTON, J.S.
"Oral tradition and the history of Igala"
Journal of African History, vol.10, no.1 (1969)

188 BOTKIN, B.A. (ed.)
Lay my burden down: a folk history of slavery
Chicago: Chicago University Press, 1945
285pp
A compilation of extracts from interviews with
former slaves collected between 1936 and 1938
under the New Deal WPA Writers' Project.

189 BOURNE VALLEY DAY CENTRE FOR THE
ELDERLY
*Hard times but good times: a book of memories
and photographs*
Salisbury: Bourne Valley Day Centre for the
Elderly/Mobile Arts, 1986
41pp
Rural Wiltshire recalled by twenty-nine older
people.

190 BOYD, Lois A. and BRACKENRIDGE, R.
Douglas
"Oral history: an introduction"
Journal of Presbyterian History, vol.56 (Spring
1978), pp.3-9
Describes a project by the Presbyterian
Historical Society and includes (pp.10-78) five
full interview transcripts.

191 BOYLIN, W., GORDON, S.K. and
NEHRKE, M.F.
"Reminiscence and ego integrity in
institutionalised elderly males"
Gerontologist, vol.16 (1976), pp.114-8
Argues that men who reminisce most
frequently achieve high scores on scales
measuring ego integrity.

192 BOZZOLI, Belinda (ed.)
*Town and countryside in the Transvaal:
capitalist penetration and popular response*
Johannesburg: Ravan, 1983
*History Workshop 2, held at University of
Witwatersrand, February 1981*
446pp
Recent social history and political struggle,
focussing on the history of ordinary people.

BRACKENRIDGE, R. Douglas *see* BOYD,
Lois A.

193 BRADFORD HERITAGE RECORDING
UNIT
From mill to microchip: Bradford in the making
Bradford: Bradford Heritage Recording Unit,
1986
32pp
Photographs and oral history of social and
industrial change in a West Riding city.

194 BRADFORD HERITAGE RECORDING
UNIT
Domestic life, 1910 to 1950
Bradford: Bradford Heritage Recording Unit,
1986
A slide/tape pack featuring a cassette of oral
history extracts and sixteen slides about
housing conditions and cooking, washing and
sanitary arrangements in the Bradford and
Shipley area. Aimed for use in schools and as
reminiscence material.

195 BRADFORD HERITAGE RECORDING
UNIT
Destination Bradford: a century of immigration
Bradford: Bradford Library and Information
Service, 1987
96pp; bibliography
Oral history and photographs drawn from one
of the largest archives in England covering the
experiences of successive groups of migrants
to Bradford: Irish, German, Italian, Jewish,
Ukrainian, Yugoslav, Polish, Latvian,
Lithuanian, Estonian, West Indian, Asian,
Chinese and Vietnamese. Suitable for use in
schools.

196 BRADFORD HERITAGE RECORDING
UNIT
School-life, 1900-1945
Bradford: Bradford Heritage Recording Unit,
1987
A slide/tape pack featuring a cassette of
memories, songs and sounds, and thirty-four
slides covering starting school, assembly,
lessons, clothing, discipline, meals, games and
leaving. Produced for use in schools and with
older people.

197 **BRADFORD HERITAGE RECORDING UNIT**
Catalogues
Bradford: Bradford Heritage Recording Unit, 1986-8
Five subject catalogues covering the archive's oral history and sound recordings: textiles, people of European origin, people of Asian and Afro-Caribbean origin, health care and miscellaneous. Each features detailed synopses of interviews. Transcripts and listening copies are available through Bradford Central Reference Library.

198-203 BRADFORD HERITAGE RECORDING UNIT
Cassette publications: each features extracts from the wider archive and in some cases accompanied exhibitions.
Bradford: Bradford Heritage Recording Unit, 1984-8

198 *Bradford voices*
An introductory tape with memories of the textile industry and experiences of arriving and settling in Bradford as related by Ukrainians, Italians, Poles and Yugoslavs.

199 *Bradford textiles*
Oral testimony of working in textiles from 1900 until the industry's recent decline.

200 *Destination Bradford*
A selection from interviews with first and second generation migrants charting the common experiences of people of differing origin: first impressions, finding work and housing, language, religion, building the community and the future.

201 *Childhood experiences of immigration*
A child's-eye view of upheaval and arrival in Bradford: first impressions, school, politics, pressures of the community and the question of identity.

202 *Bradford 'Pals' in the First World War*
Memories and songs from survivors of the 16th and 18th volunteer 'Pals' battalions of the West Yorkshire Regiment: joining up, training, overseas service and trench warfare on the Western Front ending at the Somme in 1916.

203 *'When we were young...'*
Oral history, songs, chants and hymns about childhood, Sunday school, holidays, courtship and marriage.

BRADFORD HERITAGE RECORDING UNIT *see also* **HOWARTH, Olive; PERKS, Robert; SMITH, Tim**

204 **BRADHURST, Jane**
Document of our day: the opinions of women of the pre-Pill generation on men, marriage and motherhood
Canberra: Australia Free Press, 1986
93pp
Extracts from in-depth interviews with forty white middle-class Australian women all in their forties and fifties from Sydney, Canberra and Goulbourn. Commissioned by the Australian Film Commission and aimed at use in schools and colleges.

205 **BRADLEY, Ian**
Breaking the mould
Oxford: Robertson, 1981
172pp; bibliography
A dozen interviews were carried out with the 'Gang of Four' (Roy Jenkins, David Owen, Shirley Williams and Bill Rodgers) and their personal assistants for this instant history of the origins of the Social Democratic Party.

206 **BRADMAN, E.**
''Education and attitude of early medical libraries to their work''
Journal of Library History, *vol.15 (Spring 1980), pp.167-82*
A discussion of the United States' Medical Library Association oral history project.

207 **BRAGG, Melvyn**
Speak for England: an essay on England 1900-1975 based on interviews with inhabitants of Wigton, Cumberland
Secker & Warburg, 1976; Coronet, revised edition 1978; reprinted Sceptre, 1987
464pp
A large number of people aged 8 to 80 from all walks of life from the author's home town were interviewed.

208 BRANAGHAN, K.E.
An oral history of St.Andrew's Church,
Birchills, Walsall 1887-1987
Walsall: St.Andrew's Church, 1988
38pp
Recollections of church goers about church
life, clergy and changes in the area.

BRANDENBURGER, Caroline *see* **SILVER,**
Rachel

209 BRANSON, Noreen
London squatters 1946
Communist Party History Group, 1984
28pp
The proceedings of a CPHG conference held
in May 1984 which featured first-hand
accounts of one of the biggest squats this
century by homeless families after the war
who moved into empty army camps, flats and
houses.

210 BRAVO, Anna
"Italian women in the Nazi camps - aspects of
identity in their accounts"
Oral History, vol.13, no.1 (1985), pp.20-27

211 BRAVO, Anna
"Solidarity and loneliness: Piedmontese
peasant women at the turn of the century"
International Journal of Oral History, vol.3
(June 1982) pp.76-91
Forty married women were interviewed about
rites of passage.

212 BRAYBON, Gail and SUMMERFIELD,
Penny
Out of the cage: women's experiences in two
world wars
Pandora, 1987
280pp; bibliography
Originally published as two separate volumes.
The oral material used was drawn from the
Imperial War Museum's War Work collection
and the Oral History Project on women's war
work at Southampton Museum (for World
War One) and Mass Observation, television
programmes and the Age Exchange project
"What did you do in the war, Mum?" (for
World War Two).

213 BRECHER, Jeremy
History from below
New Haven, Conn.: Advocate Press/
Commonwork, 1986
54pp; bibliography
A guide for non-professionals who want to
explore the history of their community,
workplace, union or organisation. Includes
how to carry out and present interviews,
collect documents, antidotes to anxiety in an
interview, and release forms.

214 BRECHER, Jeremy, LOMBARDI, Jerry and
STACKHOUSE, Jan
Brass Valley: the story of working people's lives
and struggles in an American industrial region
Philadelphia: Temple University Press, 1982
284pp

215 BRENNAN, P.L. and STEINBERG, L.D.
"Is reminiscence adaptive? Relations among
social activity level, reminiscence and morale"
International Journal of Ageing and Human
Development, vol.18, no.2, (1983-4) pp.99-110

216-   **BRISTOL BROADSIDES**
223   Bristol Broadsides is a collectively run
community publisher which has been involved
in people's history and autobiography for
some years.

216   *Up Knowle West*
Bristol: Knowle West TV Workshop/Bristol
Broadsides, 1977
28pp
Four accounts by older residents of their lives
before moving to the Knowle West estate in
the 1930s.

217   *Bristol as we remember it*
Bristol: Bristol Broadsides, 1978
28pp
Recollections of the Barton Hill area of
Bristol from the people that lived and worked
there. It takes the form of a dialogue and
covers childhood days, going to work, the
cotton factory, war and entertainment.

218   *Looking back on Bristol*
Bristol: Bristol Broadsides (Co-op) Ltd/Bristol
Co-operative Press, 1978
32pp
Recollections of people living on Hartcliffe
council housing estate, showing that "people
who live out on the estates have a history that
is worth recording".

219 *Fred's people*
Bristol: Bristol Broadsides, 1980
44pp
Lively and frank written and tape recorded experiences of young people telling about school, work unemployment, home and social life.

220 *St.Paul's people talking*
Bristol: Bristol Broadsides (Co-op) Ltd., 1983
56pp
St.Barnabas is an infants and junior school in the middle of St.Pauls, Bristol, and some of the school's older pupils interviewed the people that lived around them, reflecting the cultural and ethnic diversity of the area. Included are the local midwife, the school caretaker, a baker and the lollipop lady.

221 *Bristol lives*
Bristol: Bristol Broadsides, 1987
228pp
Thirty-two stories of Bristol from 1892 to the present by people who have built, repaired, healed, washed, cooked and entertained for Bristol.

222 *Bristol reflections*
Bristol: Bristol Broadsides, 1988
144pp
A collection by Bedminster Writers' Workshop of local people's memories of South Bristol in the 1920s and 30s.

223 *More Bristol lives*
Bristol: Bristol Broadsides, 1988
224pp
A collaboration with BBC Radio Bristol of stories from ordinary Bristolians.

BRITISH LIBRARY INDIA OFFICE LIBRARY AND RECORDS *see* **INDIA OFFICE LIBRARY AND RECORDS**

224 **BRITISH LIBRARY NATIONAL SOUND ARCHIVE**
Directory of recorded sound resources in the United Kingdom
The British Library, 1989
174pp; short bibliography
Compiled by Lali Weerasinghe and Jeremy Silver, this unique guide provides details of 489 collections arranged in county order, many of which hold oral history material. There is information on holdings, access and opening hours, related publications and an extensive subject index. The best, though incomplete, guide to local oral history projects and archives in Britain.

225 **BRITISH LIBRARY NATIONAL SOUND ARCHIVE**
Developments in Recorded Sound: a catalogue of oral history interviews
The British Library, 1989
60pp; short bibliography
Synopses of some 100 interviews, carried out by the National Sound Archive between 1983 and 1987, with artists, engineers and managers about the history of the recording industry, covering matters technical, commercial, legal and inter-personal.(*See also* ANDERSON, Terri; STAPLEY, Laurence)

226 **BRITTAN, Samuel**
Steering the economy
Harmondsworth: Penguin, 1971, third edition; first published in 1964 as The Treasury under the Tories 1951-64; second edition first published in 1969
374pp
Relies heavily on oral evidence for some vivid portraits of Chancellors and officials.

227 **BROADFOOT, Barry (ed.)**
Ten lost years 1929-1939: memories of Canadians who survived the Depression
Toronto: Doubleday, 1973
390pp
A Canadian version of Terkel's *Hard Times* based on the testimony of hundreds of anonymous interviewees recalling the years 1929-39. Not the definitive oral history work on the Depression but useful for material on unemployment.

228 BROADFOOT, Barry
Six war years 1939-1945: memories of
Canadians at home and abroad
New York: Doubleday, 1974
417pp
Covers memories of enlistment, training,
building the Alaska Highway and the
animosity between the English and French.

229 BROADFOOT, Barry
The pioneer years 1895-1914: memories of
settlers who opened the west
New York: Doubleday, 1976
403pp
Recollections from pioneering homesteaders
arranged by topic.

230 BROADFOOT, Barry
Years of sorrow, years of shame: the story of
Japanese Canadians in world war 2
Toronto, Canada and Garden City, New York:
Doubleday, 1977
370pp
The experiences of Canadians of Japanese
background during the 1940s.

231 BRODIE, Louise
"Museum on the move"
BASC News, no.4 (1989)
Oral histories of London's docklands, as used
by the Museum of London's mobile exhibition
trailer.

232 BRODY, Hugh
Inishkillane: change and decline in the West of
Ireland
Faber, 1986; first published 1973
226pp; bibliography
Deals with the effects of capitalism on the
Irish countryside drawing on five years' living
and working there in the 1960s.

233 BROMILOW, Anne and POWER, Jim
Looking back: photographs and memories of life
in the Bolton area 1890-1939
Bolton: Bolton Metropolitan Borough
Department of Education and Arts, 1983
92pp
Verbatim extracts from the Bolton Oral
History Project's extensive collection,
covering childhood, neighbourhood, leisure,
work and streetlife in a Lancashire town.

234 BROOKS, Courtney G., GRIMWOOD, James
M. and SWENSON, Loyd S.
Chariots for Apollo: a history of manned lunar
spacecraft
Washington, DC: NASA, 1979
538pp

235 BROOKS, Margaret
"An introduction to fieldwork problems"
Phonographic Bulletin, no.30 (July 1981),
pp.15-19
What makes a good interview, from the
experiences of the Imperial War Museum's
oral history programme.

236 BROOKS, Margaret
"The Department of Sound Records at the
Imperial War Museum"
Oral History, vol.17, no.2 (1989), pp.56-7

237 BROOMHILL, Ray
"Using oral sources in writing a social history
of the unemployed during the Depression in
South Australia" in CAMPBELL, Joan
(1975)

238 BROOMHILL, Ray
Unemployed workers: a social history of the
Great Depression in Adelaide
Brisbane: University of Queensland Press,
1978
220pp; bibliography
The impact of unemployment based on
interviews carried out in Adelaide between
June and December 1973.

239 BROSE, Hanns-Georg
"Coping with instability: the emergence of
new biographical patterns"
Life Stories, no.5 (1989), pp.3-26

BROTCHIE, Janet *see* THORNTON, Susan

240 BROWN, Courtney
"Oral history and the oral tradition of Black
America: the Kinte Foundation"
Oral History Review, vol.1 (1973), pp.26-8
Considers black scholars' hostility to the
written page.

241 BROWN, Cynthia Stokes
Like it was: a complete guide to writing oral
history
New York: Teachers and Writers
Collaborative, 1988
129pp; bibliography
Planning, interviewing, transcribing, editing
and publishing oral histories and biographies.

242 BROWN, James Seay (ed.)
Up before daylight: life histories from the Alabama Writers' Project, 1938-1939
Alabama: University of Alabama Press, 1982
261pp; bibliography
Twenty-eight life histories grouped by geographical area.

243 BROWN, Lyle
"Methods and approaches in oral history: interviewing Latin American elites"
Oral History Review, vol.1 (1973), pp.77-86

244 BROWN, Robert F.
The new New Englanders
Worcester, Mass.: Commonwealth Press, 1980
Based on interviews with new arrivals to Southbridge, Massachusetts.

245 BRUCE, Stuart and McMORLAND, Alison (eds.)
Memories of the Edwardian era
Firebird Trust, 1988
The result of a project in Bridlington begun in 1987 in which elderly people's memories were taped at Edwardian concert evenings. These reminiscences were then edited into blank verse.

246 BRUFORD, Alan
"The archive of the School of Scottish Studies"
Oral History, vol.2, no.2 (1974), pp.18-22
Edinburgh University's School of Scottish Studies has been prominent in encouraging oral history in Scotland and holds a large archive of recordings.

247 BRYAN, Beverley, DADZIE, Stella and SCAFE, Suzanne
The heart of the race: Black women's lives in Britain
Virago, 1985
250pp; bibliography
A record of the lives of Afro-Caribbean women in Britain over the past forty years, drawn from interviews and covering their treatment by the welfare state, housing, health, self-image, racism and the Black community.

248 BRYANT, V.J.M.
"Talking to octogenarians: a key to their memories"
Local Historian, vol.10, no.4, (1972), pp.183-5
Advocates short visits rather than long interviews, and the use of memory joggers.

249 BUCHAN, David
The ballad and the folk
Routledge & Kegan Paul, 1972
326pp
A historical analysis of the ballad and oral tradition.

250 BUCHAN, David (ed.)
Scottish tradition: a collection of Scottish folk literature
Routledge & Kegan Paul, 1984
265pp; bibliographies
Includes transcripts of tales rather than formalised versions.

251 BUCKLEY, Anthony D.
A gentle people: a study of a peaceful community in Northern Ireland
Holywood, Co. Down: Ulster Folk and Transport Museum, 1982
184pp
Includes a chapter based on oral history.

252 BUCKLEY, Anthony D.
"Neighbourliness: myth and history"
Oral History, vol.11, no.1 (1983), pp.44-51
About Kearney in Northern Ireland.

253 BUCKLEY, Anthony D., BALLARD, Linda M. and HARKNESS, Clifford
Collecting oral history: a guide for teachers and amateur historians
Holywood, Northern Ireland: The Ulster Folk and Transport Museum, 1985; second edition, 1987
20pp; bibliography
A short beginner's guide, with the emphasis on the technical side of recording and conservation.

254 BUCKNELL ORAL HISTORY GROUP
Bucknell talking
Bucknell, Shropshire: Bucknell Oral History Group, 1989
57pp
Extracts from taped interviews about village life from 1900 onwards covering every aspect of daily life from school and sport to church and chapel to farming, transport and the Women's Institute. The project began in 1982 financed by West Midlands Arts.

BUFERD, Norma B. *see* COOPER, Patricia

255 BUHLE, Paul
"Radicalism, the oral history contribution"
International Journal of Oral History, vol.2, no.3 (1981)
On labour biography.

256 BUHLE, Paul (ed.)
"Working lives: an oral history of Rhode
Island labor"
Rhode Island History, *vol.46, no.1 (February,
1987)*
The subject matter dates from the 1890s in this
excellent example of a complex local history.
Transcription has preserved the flavour of the
spoken word and a useful bibliographical
essay is included.

BUHLE, Paul *see also* **BLOOM, Jonathan**

257 BULKIN, Elly
"An old dyke's tale: an interview with Doris
London"
Conditions Six, *vol.2, no.3 (Summer 1980)*
Lesbian oral history.

258 BULL RING ARCHIVES
*The Bull Ring Archives: a photographic and oral
history record*
Birmingham: The Bull Ring Archives, 1989
12pp
A prospectus for a photographic and oral
history project about Birmingham's Bull Ring
market prior to its phased demolition from
1990.

259 BULLOCK, Paul (ed.)
*Watts: the aftermath: an inside view of the
Ghetto, by the people of the Watts*
New York: Grove, 1969
285pp
Work began a year before the Los Angeles
Watts race riot of August 1965 and thirty
interviews, carried out before and after, are
arranged thematically. Pseudonyms are used
to protect the interviewees who discuss illegal
activities.

260 BULMER, Martin (ed.)
Sociological research methods: an introduction
*Basingstoke, Macmillan, 1984, second edition;
first edition, 1977*
351pp; bibliography
Includes chapters on sociology and the
interview, and asking questions.

261 BULMER, Martin
"Sociology and history: some recent trends"
Sociology, *vol.8, no.1, pp.137-150*
Oral history in the context of the
rapprochement of history and sociology.

262 BUNDY, Colin
"Oral history and teaching"
*Teaching History vol.4, no. 16, (Nov. 1976),
pp.366-8*
A report on an Oral History Society
conference in Manchester.

263 BUNDY, Colin and HEALEY, Dermot
"Aspects of urban poverty"
Oral History, *vol.6, no.1 (1978), pp.79-97*
Working class poverty in Manchester and
Salford.

BUNK, Steve *see* **LAWRENCE, Neil**

**264 BURCHARDT, Jorgen and ANDRESEN, Carl
Erik**
"Oral history, people's history and social
change in Scandinavia"
Oral History, *vol.8, no.2 (1980), pp.25-9*

BURCHARDT, Natasha *see* **THOMPSON,
Paul**

BURFORD, Alan *see* **GRIFFITHS, Helen**

265 BURG, Maclyn P.
"An oral historian in Moscow: some first-hand
observations"
Oral History Review, *vol.2 (1974), pp.10-23*
The author found that Soviet historians and
ethnographers tended to use pencil and paper
rather than tape recorders, and transcripts
were rare. He describes his own problems
trying to interview Second World War Russian
Army officers and offers some insights into
Soviet attitudes to oral history.

266 BURGESS, Robert G. (ed.)
Field research: a sourcebook and field manual
Allen Unwin, 1982
286pp; bibliography
Includes two chapters on oral sources:
'Conversations in field research' and
'Historical documents and field research' with
contributions from Raphael Samuel on 'Local
history and oral history' and Burgess on
'Personal documentation, oral sources and life
histories'.

267 BURGOS, Martine
"Life stories, narrativity, and the search for
self"
Life Stories, *no.5 (1989), pp.27-38*

268 BURMAN, Rickie
"Participating in the past? Oral history and community history in the work of Manchester Studies"
International Journal of Oral History, vol.5, no.2 (1984)

269 BURMAN, Rickie
"The Jewish woman as breadwinner: the changing value of women's work in a Manchester immigrant community"
Oral History, vol.10, no.2 (1982), pp.27-39

270 BURMAN, Rickie (ed.)
"Growing up in Manchester Jewry: the story of Clara Weingard"
Oral History, vol.12, no.1 (1984), pp.56-63
From interviews recorded by Rosalyn Livshin.

BURNETT, David *see* BARWICK, Diane

271 BURNETT, John (ed.)
Destiny obscure: autobiographies of childhood, education and family from the 1820s to the 1920s
Allen Lane, 1982; Harmondsworth: Penguin, 1984
345pp
For the later period covered, oral and written autobiography is used in combination.

272 BURTON, M.
"Reality orientation for the elderly: a critique"
Journal of Advanced Nursing, vol.7 (1982)

273 BUSCH, Glenn
Working men
Wellington, New Zealand: National Art Gallery, 1984
115pp
The lives of working men in New Zealand through taped interviews and photographs.

274 BUSH, Julia (ed.)
Moving on: Northamptonshire and the wider world
Northampton: Nene College, 1989
A multi-cultural resource unit comprising a book (120pp); a video of life story interviews with Northampton families from Ireland, Jamaica, Bangladesh and Vietnam (58 minutes); a set of twenty photographs; a set of 98 documents and transcripts; and a 'Teaching Ideas' booklet for teachers. Each unit relates to Northamptonshire's role in Empire and the experience of migrants to the county.

275 BUSHELL, Alma (ed.)
Yesterday's daughters: stories of our past by women over 70
Melbourne, Victoria: Nelson, 1986
221pp

276 BUTCHER, David
The driftermen
Reading: Tops'l Books, 1979
152pp; select bibliography
An account of the North Sea herring fishery between 1910 and 1960 based on interviews from Lowestoft.

277 BUTCHER, David
The trawlermen
Reading: Tops'l Books, 1980
152pp; select bibliography
An account of the trawling voyages made by Lowestoft men in both steam and sailing boats between 1910 and 1960.

278 BUTCHER, David
Living from the sea
Sulhamstead, Reading: Tops'l Books, 1982
152pp; select bibliography
Life in the fishing communities of Lowestoft and Great Yarmouth earlier in the century, based on interviews.

279 BUTCHER, David
"Pay attention to your elders: a personal account of recording local history"
Exploring Local History, Nov. 1984

280 BUTCHER, David
Following the fishing
Newton Abbot: Tops'l Books/David & Charles, 1987
128pp; select bibliography
An account of the industries which derived from and served fishing between 1910 and 1960, based on interviews in Lowestoft and Great Yarmouth.

281 BUTLER, David and STOKES, Donald
Political change in Britain
Macmillan, 1974, second edition; first edition, 1969
500pp
The first edition was based on an analysis of interviews gathered on a sample basis in 1963, 1964 and 1966. The second edition adds material from 1969 and 1970. Both assess the changing fortunes of the main political parties.

282   BUTLER, David and PINTO-DUSCHINSKY, Michael
The British general election of 1970
Macmillan, 1971
493pp; bibliography
Based on extensive interviews between January 1968 and October 1970, the book examines events during 1966-9: the Labour Party's decline, recovery, the campaign itself and the outcome.

283   BUTLER, David and KAVANAGH, Dennis
The British general election of February 1974
Macmillan, 1974
354pp; bibliography
Based on 300 interviews with those centrally concerned with the campaign, the emphasis is very much on the unusual nature of the election and the self-conscious strategies pursued by the parties.

284   BUTLER, David and KAVANAGH, Dennis
The British general election of October 1974
Macmillan, 1975
368pp; bibliography

285   BUTLER, David and KAVANAGH, Dennis
The British general election of 1979
Macmillan, 1980
443pp; bibliography
The election which brought Margaret Thatcher and the Conservative Party to power. Sources include almost 400 interviews.

286   BUTLER, David and KAVANAGH, Dennis
The British general election of 1983
Macmillan, 1984
388pp; bibliography
Over 300 people professionally involved in politics were interviewed in an election which saw the emergence of 'Thatcherism' as a set of ideas and attitudes.

287   BUTLER, David and KAVANAGH, Dennis
The British general election of 1987
Macmillan, 1988
379pp; bibliography
Drawing on interviews with key participants begun in 1984, the book examines Britain's first genuine three party election for fifty years, covering the parties' campaign strategies, the media treatment of the campaign and the role of opinion poll agencies.

288   BUTLER, Robert
"The life review: an interpretation of reminiscence in the aged"
Psychiatry, vol.26 (February 1963), pp.65-76
One of the first argued cases to recognise the universal necessity in older people to review their lives, and the value this has.

289   BUTLER, Robert
Why not survive? Being old in America
New York: Harper and Row, 1975
496pp; bibliography
A synthesis of what oral history can offer gerontologists.

290   BUTLER, Robert
"The life review: an unrecognized bonanza"
International Journal on Aging and Human Development, vol.12, no.1 (1980-1), pp.35-8
Argues that by listening to patients' reflections on the past doctors can increase understanding and expand clinical practice.

291   BUTLER, Robert and LEWIS, Myrna I.
Aging and mental health: positive psychosocial and biomedical approaches
St.Louis: C.V.Mosby and Company, 1977; third edition, 1982
483pp; bibliography
A general account of mental health work with older people which includes Butler's thinking on life review.

BUTLER, Robert *see also* LEWIS, Myrna I.

292   BY WORD OF MOUTH: SCOTTISH ORAL HISTORY GROUP NEWSLETTER
No.1, 1981-
Produced twice yearly and includes news, articles, reports on conferences and reviews on aspects of oral history in Scotland. The SOHG has a strong following in the Edinburgh and Glasgow area, and holds many of its meetings at Edinburgh University's School of Scottish Studies which has long been a focus for oral history activity in Scotland.

293   BYERLY, Victoria
Hard times cotton mill girls: personal histories of womanhood and poverty in the south
Ithaca, New York: ILR Press, New York State School of Industrial and Labor Relations, Cornell University, 1986
223pp
Women's labour history 1900-1980.

294 **CAEDMON RECORDS**
Five British sculptors speak
Caedmon TC1181, 1965, 1 LP record
Barbara Hepworth, Reg Butler, Henry
Moore, Kenneth Armitage and Lynn
Chadwick talk freely about their lives and
work. Recorded in July and August 1963 by
Warren Forma.

295 **CAEDMON RECORDS**
The Truman tapes: Harry S. Truman speaking
frankly with Ben Gradus
Caedmon TC2085, 1970, 2 LP records
From recordings made in 1963 and 1964 for a
television series. Covers his presidential
career from Potsdam, the atom bomb and the
Marshall Plan to the McCarthy era, the Berlin
Crisis and Korea.

296 **CALDER, Angus and SHERIDAN, Dorothy
(eds.)**
Speak for yourself: a mass observation
anthology, 1937-1949
Cape, 1984; Oxford: Oxford University Press,
1985
259pp; bibliography
A selection from Tom Harrison's Mass
Observation Archive housed at Sussex
University Library, covering people's attitudes
to the Second World War, sex and much else.

297 **CAMARGO, Aspasia, DA ROCHA LIMA,
Valentina, and HIPPOLITO, Lucia**
"The life history approach in Latin America"
Life Stories, no.1 (1985), pp. 41-54

298 **CAMERON, James**
Yesterday's Witness: a selection from the BBC
series
BBC, 1979
155pp
Extracts from scripts of over seventy BBC
documentaries in the 'Yesterday's Witness'
series including memories of the great blizzard
of 1891, one of the first women typists, the
battle of Cable Street, the Spanish Civil War,
conscientious objectors in the First World
War, life on a narrow boat, being a nurse in
the Tsar's army, the Jarrow march and
Burston school strike. (*See also* PEET,
Stephen)

299 **CAMPBELL, Ann M.**
"The oral history collection of Columbia
University"
The American Archivist, vol.37 (January 1974)

300 **CAMPBELL, Fiona**
"Apparat: a computer cataloguing system for
sound recordings"
Archives and Manuscripts: The Journal of the
Australian Society of Archivists, vol.8, no.2
(December 1980), pp.33-40
A description of the system used to prepare
finding aids for the Imperial War Museum's
oral history collection.

301 **CAMPBELL, James**
Gate fever: voices from a prison
Weidenfeld & Nicolson, 1986; Sphere, 1987
179pp
The record of a year spent listening to male
inmates of Lewes Prison, Sussex, compiled
from notes, tape-recordings and memory.

302 **CAMPBELL, Joan (ed.)**
Oral history 74: papers presented
Bundoona, Victoria: La Trobe University,
1974
116pp
Papers from the first Australian conference.

303 **CAMPBELL, Joan (ed.)**
Oral history 75: papers presented at the second
oral history conference
Bundoona, Victoria: Department of History,
La Trobe University, 1975
Australian conference proceedings - includes
papers on political and social reasons for bias
in collecting Australian folksong, and the
social history of the unemployed during the
Depression.

304 **CANADIAN ORAL HISTORY
ASSOCIATION JOURNAL**
Vol.1, 1975/6-
Published annually.

305 **CANT, Bob and HEMMINGS, Susan (eds.)**
Radical records: thirty years of lesbian and gay
history, 1957-1987
Routledge, 1988
266pp
An anthology of personal accounts, some oral
history based, covering gay involvement in
Left politics, resistance, gay rights, 'coming
out' experiences and the Gay Liberation
Front.

**305A-F CANTERBURY URBAN STUDIES CENTRE
ORAL HISTORY UNIT**

305A *Homes sweet homes: living in Canterbury 70*
years ago
Canterbury, Kent: Canterbury Urban Studies
Centre, 1985

305B *Living in St. Stephen's 60-80 years ago*
Canterbury, Kent: Canterbury Urban Studies
Centre, nd

305C *Working in Canterbury 70 years ago*
Canterbury, Kent: Canterbury Urban Studies
Centre, 1987

305D *Shopping in Canterbury 70 years ago*
Canterbury, Kent: Canterbury Urban Studies
Centre, 1988

305E *Blean 70 years ago: Leslie's life*
Canterbury, Kent: Canterbury Urban Studies
Centre, 1989
An oral biography of Leslie Wanstall.

305F *Living in Northgate 60 years ago*
Canterbury, Kent: Canterbury Urban Studies
Centre, 1990
Interviews with residents in one area of
Canterbury.

306 CAPLOW, Theodore
*Middletown families: fifty years of change and
continuity*
Minneapolis, 1982
436pp; bibliography
A repeat of Robert and Helen Lynd's studies
of Middletown fifty years before, and based on
interviews carried out during 1976-81 with a
grant from the National Science Foundation.
(*See also* LYND, Robert and Helen)

307 CARLSON, C.M.
"Reminiscing: toward achieving ego integrity
in old age"
*Social Casework: The Journal of Contemporary
Social Work*, vol.65, no.2 (February 1984),
pp.81-9
Interviews with elderly people living in the
community convinced the author that
reminiscence encourages the maintenance of
self-esteem.

308 CARR, Ian
Music outside: contemporary jazz in Britain
Latimer New Dimensions, 1973
179pp; discography
Includes interviews made in 1972 with Trevor
Watts, Jon Hiseman, Evan Parker, Chris
MacGregor, Mike Gibbs, John Stevens and
Mike Westbrook.

309 CARR, Mona
*A guide to resources for reminiscence work in
Kensington and Chelsea*
Kensington and Chelsea Community History
Group, 1988
8pp
A useful handlist of books, videos, contact
addresses and publishers.

310 CARSON, Pam
Recording oral history
Wellington, New Zealand: Continuing
Education Unit, Radio New Zealand, 1985
2 sixty minute cassettes
From the broadcast of the same title with
information on getting started, interview
techniques and equipment. (*See also* IRVINE,
Kathryn)

311 CARSWELL, Jeanne, JOHNSON, Rachel and
KIRRANE, Siobhan (eds.)
*Ours to defend: Leicestershire people remember
World War 2*
Leicester: Leicester Oral History Archive/
Mantle Oral History Project, 1989
79pp
The hidden history of air raids, rationing and
warwork, GIs, evacuees, children at war and
POWs drawn from two extensive oral history
archives which together have amassed 600
interviews since 1983.

312 CARTER, Ian
"Oral history and agrarian history: the North
East"
Oral History, vol.2, no.1 (1974), pp.34-44
Interviews with farmworkers in the north-east
of Scotland.

313 CARTER, Ian
*Farm life in north-east Scotland, 1840-1914: the
poor man's country*
Edinburgh: Donald, 1979
258pp; bibliography
An analysis of peasant farming incorporating
personal accounts.

314 CARTER, Jan
*Nothing to spare: recollections of Australian
pioneering women*
Harmondsworth: Penguin, 1981; 1983
237pp; bibliography
Based on well-documented interviews with
fourteen women from varied backgrounds,
providing a rich and fascinating account of
their lives.

315   CARTER, Ruth and KIRKUP, Gill
Women in engineering: a good place to be?
Macmillan, 1990
Women in Society Series
194pp; bibliography
Based on interviews with women engineers in
Britain and the United States, it examines the
balance between work and mothering, how
women react in a traditionally male
environment, what influenced them to follow
a non-traditional career, and how they relate
engineering to feminism.

316   CARVER, Vida and LIDDIARD, Penny (eds.)
An ageing population: a reader and sourcebook
Sevenoaks, Kent: Hodder and Stoughton;
Milton Keynes: Open University Press, 1978
434pp; bibliographies
Published to accompany an Open University
course. Includes a useful article by Malcolm
Johnson entitled "That was your life: a
biographical approach to later life".

317   CASH, Joseph H. and HOOVER, Herbert T.
To be an Indian: an oral history
New York: Holt, Rinehart & Winston, 1971
239pp
Interviews with American Indians of the
Northern Plains from the Doris Duke Indian
History Project covering four main themes:
spiritual life, reservation life, the Depression
and World War Two, and life in the 1950s and
1960s.

CASH, Joseph H. *see also* **HARRIS, Ramon I.**

CASSIDY, Jules *see* **STEWART-PARK,
Angela**

318   CASTLE, Jo
Reminiscence is fun
Brighton: Pavillion, 1989
18pp
A practical and straightforward training
package for elderly care staff wishing to use
reminiscence.

319   CATFORD REMINISCENCE GROUP
*Were they the good old days? Pensioners'
reflections*
Catford Reminiscence Group, 1987
42pp
Memories of south-east London.

320   CATMULL, Mick and LING, Geraldine
"Memories are made of this..."
New Age, Summer 1981

321   CAUNCE, Stephen
"East Riding hiring fairs"
Oral History, vol.3, no.2 (1975), pp.45-52
The recruitment, at Martinmas fairs, of farm
and domestic labourers in Yorkshire in the
first quarter of the century.

322   CENTERPRISE TRUST
*Working lives: a people's autobiography of
Hackney. Volume one, 1905-1945*
Centerprise Publishing Project, 1976
127pp
Contributions from an embroiderer, casual
worker, First World War soldier, tailor,
school-teacher, cabinet maker, shoe-worker,
demolition worker, lighterman, leather
worker.

323   CENTERPRISE TRUST
*Local publishing and local culture: an account
of the Centerprise Publishing Project 1972-1977*
Centerprise Trust Ltd, 1977
22pp; bibliography
The record of a group which believes in the
availability of working class literature to a
working class audience: "essential for anyone
contemplating or currently involved in oral
history". The Trust has produced several
publications in the field of working class
history.

324   CENTERPRISE TRUST
Working lives: volume two, 1945-1977
Centerprise Publishing Project, 1977
224pp
The second volume brings the story up-to-date
with thirteen accounts of work.

325   CENTERPRISE TRUST
*The Island: the life and death of an East London
community, 1870-1970*
Centerprise Trust, 1979
72pp
The 'Island' was a neighbourhood of five
streets in Hackney, East London which
existed from 1870 to its demolition in 1970 and
had its own dairy, pig farm, stables,
blacksmiths, grocery and provisions stores.
Over fifty people who lived and worked there
relate their memories and experiences. Part of
the People's Autobiography of Hackney.

326   **CENTRE FOR CONTEMPORARY CULTURAL STUDIES**
Making histories: studies in history writing and politics
Hutchinson/University of Birmingham Centre for Contemporary Cultural Studies, 1982
379pp
Chapter six, 'Popular memory: theory, politics, method' by the Popular Memory Group looks at the whole nature of oral history and the issue of subjectivity.

327   **CHAMBERLAIN, Mary**
Fenwomen: a portrait of women in an English village
Quartet, 1975; Virago, 1977
186pp
An innovative and challenging book based on the recollections of East Anglian village women, from very young to very old, which span 150 years.

328   **CHAMBERLAIN, Mary**
Old wives tales: their history, remedies and spells
Virago, 1981
182pp; bibliography
Women as healers in the community, based on interviews with women at elderly people's homes in Lambeth, London, and in Suffolk.

329   **CHAMBERLAIN, Mary**
Growing up in Lambeth
Virago, 1989
182pp; bibliography
Using a wealth of oral material, it tells of childhood and adolescence, marriage and motherhood, keeping house, and of the ingenious ways working class people coped with poverty.

330   **CHAMBERLAIN, Mary and RICHARDSON, Ruth**
"Life and death"
Oral History, vol.11, no.1 (1983), pp.31-43
The role of women in recent society as 'healers': health remedies, midwifery, abortions and 'laying out' of dead bodies.

CHAPLIN, Gillian *see* **BINNEY, Judith**

331   **CHAPLIN, Sid**
Durham mining villages
Durham: University of Durham, Department of Sociology and Social Administration, 1972
Working papers in sociology no.3
34pp
This study of 1920s Durham villages is a good example of using informal oral recollection when constructing social history.

332   **CHAPMAN, Stanley**
Jesse Boot of Boots the Chemists: a study in business history
Hodder and Stoughton, 1974
221pp
A business history of the family firm that originated in Nottingham, including interviews with four family members, twelve current directors and managers, and twenty seven retired employees.

333   **CHARLOTTE MASON COLLEGE and AMBLESIDE ORAL HISTORY GROUP**
The Lake District at war
Ambleside, Cumbria: Charlotte Mason College and Ambleside Oral History Group, 1988
27pp booklet and sixty minute audio cassette
A teaching pack of eye witness accounts of the Second World War covering black-out, evacuation, rationing, women at work, enemy action, growing food and conscientious objection. Drawn from Ambleside's archive of over 200 hours of tapes on all aspects of Lake District history.

334   **CHARLTON, Thomas L.**
"Oral history guidebooks"
Family Heritage, vol.1 (August, 1978)
A guide to US publications.

335   **CHARLTON, Thomas L.**
Oral history for Texans
Austin, Texas: Texas Historical Commission, 1981
85pp; bibliography
An overview of the movement in Texas by the director of the Baylor University oral history programme.

336   **CHARLTON, Thomas L.**
"Videotaped oral histories: problems and perspectives"
American Archivist, vol.47, no.3 (Summer 1984), pp.228-36
Raises the difficulties of compatability of hardware and tape, differing formats, camera angles and legal aspects.

337 CHESNEAUX, Jean
Pasts and futures, or, What is history for?
Translated from the French
Thames and Hudson, 1978
150pp
On the social purposes and manipulation of history.

CHILDS, Keith *see* RENDELL, Brian

338 CHINN, Carl
They worked all their lives: women of the urban poor in England, 1880-1939
Manchester: Manchester University Press, 1988
166pp; bibliography
Centering on vivid and detailed interviews with Birmingham people, many of them part of the author's own large working class family, Chinn encompasses issues from infant mortality to charwomen's wages, and regions from London to Middlesbrough. He argues that women of the urban poor exercised tremendous control over their communities through a hidden matriarchy.

339 CHISNALL, Edward H.
More stories from the bell in the tree: thirty stories from Glasgow's past
Glasgow: Collins/Radio Clyde, 1984
146pp

340 CHRISP, Peter and GIBBS, Richard (eds.)
The Blitz
Evacuation
Children at war
Brighton: University of Sussex, 1987
Mass Observation Teaching Packs
Individual attitudes rather than stereotypes are explored. They may be freely copied for classroom use.

341 CHURCH OF JESUS CHRIST OF LATTER-DAY SAINTS
A guide to the oral history program of the historical department
Salt Lake City, Utah: Church of Jesus Christ of Latter day Saints, 1975
47pp
A catalogue of the collection and a description of how the project operates.

342 CINCINNATI WOMEN WORKING
Stitches, whistles, bells and wires: an oral history of Cincinnati's working women, 1904-1981
Cincinnati: Cincinnati Women Working, 1981

343 CLARE, Leo La
"Oral history in Canada: an overview"
Oral History Review, vol.1 (1973), pp.87-91
Notes that most oral history is done by non-academics, that little is transcribed, and that most is non-elite.

344 CLARE, Leo La
"Oral history: what's in a name? The Canadian Oral History Association"
Phonographic Bulletin, no.13 (1975), pp.22-25

345 CLARK, E. Culpepper, HYDE, Michael and McMAHAN, Eva
"Communication in the oral history interview: investigating problems of interpreting oral data"
International Journal of Oral History, vol.1 (1980), pp.28-40

346 CLARK, Helen, INESON, Antonia, MORETON, Ginnie and SIM, Judith
"Oral history and reminiscence in Lothian"
Oral History, vol.17, no.2 (1989), pp.35-42
Includes the background to the People's Story Museum in Edinburgh, one of Britain's first oral history-based museums, and a project on health provision.

347 CLARK, Paul Frederick
Those other camps: an oral history analysis of Japanese enemy alien internment during world war two
Ann Arbor, Michigan: University Microfilms International, 1980
Three microfiches
206pp; bibliography

348 CLARKE, J.F.
"An interview with Sir Will Lawther"
Bulletin of the Society for the Study of Labour History, no.19 (Autumn 1969), pp.14-21
On the inter-war coal industry, the 1926 General Strike and post-war nationalisation.

349 CLARKE, J.F and ROWE, D.J.
"Local records for labour history: tape recordings"
North East Group for the Study of Labour History Bulletin, no.2 (October 1968), pp.10-12

350 CLAY, John
Men at midlife
Sidgwick and Jackson, 1989
160pp
Sixty-five interviews with men aged 35-50, interlaced with the author's comments as a psychotherapist.

351 CLAYTON, Ian (ed.)
Running for clocks and dessert spoons
Castleford, West Yorkshire: Yorkshire Art
Circus, 1988
70pp
Stories of soccer for women, boxing, cycling,
long distance swimming and pub games build a
picture of sport and leisure in a small town.

352 CLAYTON, Ian (ed.)
Mobile memories: looking back and forward
Castleford, West Yorkshire: Yorkshire Art
Circus, 1989
88pp
Produced in association with Age Concern, a
mix of nostalgia and attitudes to modern ways.

CLAYTON, Ian *see also* **LEWIS, Brian**

353 CLEAVER, Elizabeth
"Oral history at Thurston Upper School"
Oral History, vol.13, no.1 (1985), pp.11-13

354 COALVILLE 150 GROUP
*Coalville remembered: reminiscences of old
Coalville*
Coalville, Leicestershire: Coalville 150 Group/
Coalville Publishing Co. Ltd., 1989
82pp
Memories produced as a result of a
competition to mark the town's 150th birthday
in 1983.

355 COATTS, Margot
A weaver's life: Ethel Mairet 1872-1952
Bath: Crafts Council/Crafts Study Centre, 1983
136pp; bibliography
The story of a self-taught weaver, spinner and
dyer through the taped reminiscences of her
colleagues made in 1981-3.

356 COCHRANE, Clive
"Public libraries and the changing nature of
oral history"
*Audiovisual Librarian, vol.11, no.4,
pp.201-206*
Discusses the relationship between libraries
and oral historians and radio archives.

357 COCHRANE, Clive
"The place of oral history in libraries"
*An Leabharlann: The Irish Library, vol.3, no.2
(1986), pp.43-51*
Presents the results of a phone survey to assess
the impact of oral history in Northern Ireland
libraries. They indicated interest but little
practical activity, often through lack of
resources.

358 COCHRANE, Ken
*Towards a new past: toil and trouble: an oral
history of industrial unrest in the Estavan-
Bienfait coalfields*
Regina: Department of Culture and Youth/
Government of Saskatchewan, 1975

359 COHEN, David William
*The historical tradition of Busoga: Mukama and
Kintu*
Oxford: Clarendon, 1972
Oxford studies in African affairs
218pp
A historical reconstruction based on a
collection of testimonies recorded in Busoga
in 1966-7, concentrating on migration.

360 COHEN, David William
*Womunafu's Bunafu: a study of authority in a
nineteenth century African community*
Guildford: Princeton University Press, 1977
216pp; bibliography
A study of the pre-colonial Busoga District of
Uganda based on several hundred interviews
carried out in the area during 1966-7 and
1971-3.

361 COLEMAN, Peter
"Assessing self-esteem and its sources in
elderly people"
Ageing and Society, vol.4 (1984), pp.117-35

362 COLEMAN, Peter
"The past in the present: a study of elderly
people's attitudes to reminiscence"
Oral History, vol.14, no.1 (1986), pp.50-9
A discussion of changing attitudes to
reminiscence and various studies including his
own.

363 COLEMAN, Peter
*Ageing and reminiscence processes: social and
clinical implications*
Colchester: John Wiley, 1986
172pp; detailed bibliography
An important study of the role and
significance of reminiscence in old age. Based
on fifteen years' clinical experience and
features useful case studies.

364 COLEMAN, Peter
"Issues in the therapeutic use of reminiscence
with elderly people" in HANLEY, Ian (1986)

365 COLES, Robert
Children of crisis
Boston: Little and Brown, 1964-1977
Five volumes: volume 1, Children of crisis: a
study of courage and fear; volume 2, Migrants,
sharecroppers, mountaineers; volume 3, The
south goes north; volume 4, Eskimos, Chicanos,
Indians; volume 5, Privileged ones: the well-off
and rich in America
A study of children and stress based on
transcribed conversations. Volume one
concerns the desegregation movement in the
south of the United States; volume two looks
at rural depopulation.

366 COLES, Robert
Uprooted children: the early life of migrant farm
workers
New York: Harper and Row, 1970
121pp

367 COLES, Robert
The old ones of New Mexico
Albuquerque: University of New Mexico Press,
1973
74pp
Five extended reflective interviews from a civil
rights radical.

368 COLES, Robert and COLES, Jane Hallowell
Women of crisis: lives of struggle and hope
New York: Delacorte, 1978
291pp; bibliography
Interviews with five women including a
migrant, an Eskimo and a Chicano.

369 COLES, Robert and COLES, Jane Hallowell
Women of crisis II: lives of work and dreams
New York: Delacorte, 1980
237pp
The life stories of five American women: a
bank teller, a civil rights worker, a Pueblo
Indian, a nurse and an advertising executive.

370 COLLEDGE, Dave and FIELD, John
"'To recondition human material...': an
account of a British labour camp in the 1930s.
An interview with William Heard"
History Workshop, no.15 (Spring 1983),
pp.152-66
One experience of unemployment in the
1930s.

371 COLLINS, James, FITZGERALD, Oscar,
ZIMMERMAN, Robert and FRANK, Benis
"Taped interview and the documentation of
Viet Nam combat operations"
Oral History Review, vol.2 (1974)

372 COLMAN, Gould
"Oral history: an appeal for more systematic
procedures"
American Archivist, vol.28 (1965), pp.79-83
Argues for accuracy of transcription, careful
noting of breaks in recording, and
establishment of rapport between interviewer
and interviewee.

373 COLMAN, Gould
"Oral history at Cornell"
Wilson Library Bulletin, vol.40 (1966),
pp.624-8
Agricultural history at Cornell University.

374 COLMAN, Gould
"Theoretical models and oral history
interviews"
Agricultural History, vol.49 (July 1967),
pp.255-66

375 COLUMBIA RECORDS
John Fitzgerald Kennedy...as we remember him
Columbia Records Legacy Collection, L2L
1017, 1965
2 LP record set and illustrated book (242pp)
A sound biography from childhood to the
White House with testimony from Kennedy's
family, friends and associates, including
Lyndon Johnson, Richard Nixon and Lord
Harlech.

376 COLUMBIA UNIVERSITY ORAL HISTORY
RESEARCH OFFICE
Annual reports
Published reports from 1948, printed from
1961, of one of the United States' most
important oral history projects. (*See also*
MASON, Elizabeth B.)

376A COMMON VOICE: LEICESTERSHIRE'S
ORAL HISTORY JOURNAL
No.1, 1988–
An occasional publication produced by
Leicester Oral History Archive and the
Mantle Oral History Project, Coalville,
featuring news, conference reports and short
articles.

377 COMMONWORD
Now then
Manchester: Commonword, 1988
96pp
Memories of living and working in Manchester
since 1945.

378 CONNELL, Kenneth H.
Irish peasant society: four historical essays
Oxford: Clarendon, 1968
167pp
For family history, illicit distillation, ether
drinking in Ulster, illegitimacy before the
Famine, Catholicism and marriage after the
Famine. Makes extensive use of material
collected by the Irish Folklore Commission.

379 COOK, J.B.
"Reminiscing: how it can help confused
nursing home residents"
*Social Case Work: The Journal of
Contemporary Social Work*, *vol.65, no.2
(1984), pp.90-3*

380 COOK, John W. and KLOTZ, Heinrich
Conversations with architects
New York: Praeger, 1973
272pp
Eight contemporary American architects are
interviewed and they talk openly about their
ideas and theories.

381 COOK, Patsy A. (ed.)
*Directory of oral history programs in the United
States*
*Sanford, N.C.: Microfilming Corporation of
America/Oral History Association, 1982*
138pp

382 COOPER, Lee B.
"Oral history, popular music and Les
McCann"
*Social Studies, no.67 (May/June 1976),
pp.115-8*
Urges the use of oral history in music history
through a study of jazz lyricist McCann.

383 COOPER, Patricia and BUFERD, Norma
Bradley
The quilters: women and domestic art
Garden City, New York: Doubleday, 1977
157pp
An oral history about a group of women in
Texas and New Mexico who make quilts, from
tape recordings begun in the spring of 1973.

384 COPELAND, Peter
"Video recording formats: a guide for sound
archivists"
BASC News, no.3 (1988)
An excellent survey of the field.

385 COPELAND, Peter
"Notes on the Copyright, Designs and Patents
Act 1988"
BASC News, no.4 (1989)
The 1988 Act dramatically changed the status
of clearance and copyright forms widely used
by British oral historians.

COPELAND, Peter *see also* THOMPSON,
Paul (1989)

386 CORDER, J.
"The good old days take on a new life, or old
stagers"
*Health and Social Services Journal, vol.89,
no.4650, 13 July 1979, pp.874-5*
Describes the work of a community
reminiscence theatre group in old people's
homes.

387 CORKHILL, D. and RAWNSLEY, Stuart
*The road to Spain: anti-fascists at war
1936-1939*
Dunfermline: Borderline, 1981
164pp
Edited interviews with Spanish Civil War
International Brigaders: an innovative use of
oral history techniques in political historical
research.

388 CORNWELL, Jocelyn
*Hard-earned lives: accounts of health and illness
from East London*
Tavistock Publications, 1984
223pp; bibliography
A study of people's perception of the meaning
of health and illness based on twenty-four life
story interviews carried out in three stages and
covering work, family life, housing, doctors
and health services in East London over eighty
years.

389 CORNWELL, Jocelyn and GEARING, Brian
"Biographical interviews with older people"
Oral History, vol.17, no.1 (1989), pp.36-43
A review of some of the problems of
biographical interviewing.

390 COSTA, P. and KASTENBAUM, R.
"Some aspects of memories and ambitions in
centenarians"
*Journal of Genetic Psychology, vol.110 (1967),
pp.3-16*

391 COTTLE, Thomas J.
Black testimony: voices of Britain's West Indians
Philadelphia: Temple University Press, 1980; first published, Wildwood House, 1978
184pp
Interviews with mainly members of the London black communities.

392 COUCH, W.T. (ed.)
These are our lives
Chapel Hill, 1939
For rural black history: an early example of oral history as community history from the US New Deal Federal Writers' Project.

393 COUCHMAN, Elizabeth (ed.)
Belgrave as I remember it: memories of the Belgrave area of Leicester by local people who lived and worked there
Leicester: Leicestershire Libraries and Information Service, 1984
Features a selection of winning entries in a local competition organised jointly by Age Concern Leicester and Leicester Libraries. (*See also* BARROW, Karen)

394 COULTER, Jim, MILLER, Susan and WALKER, Martin
State of seige: miners' strike 1984 - politics and policing in the coal field
Canary Press, 1984
241pp
Based on first-hand interviews in the mining communities, it comprises three chronological reports on the role of the police in the 1984 strike. The first two parts were originally published separately in pamphlet form.

395 COWDEN, Mandy
Ageing, sociability and reminiscence
Dundee: Dundee Oral History Committee, 1989
25pp; bibliography
A brief account of factors which influence the nature and quality of lifestyle of older people. Split into three sections: social contacts, finances and life review, it includes direct experiences. (*See also* DUNDEE ORAL HISTORY PROJECT)

396 CRAIG, Ann L.
The first agraristas: an oral history of a Mexican agrarian reform movement
Berkeley and London: University of California Press, 1983
312pp; bibliography

397 CRAWFORD, Fred Roberts
"The Holocaust: a never ending agony"
Annals of the American Academy of Political and Social Science, no.450 (1980), pp.250-5
As part of a project, 'Witness to the Holocaust', the author interviewed eighty American and Allied servicemen, nurses and Red Cross workers who had first-hand experience of Nazi concentration camps.

398 CREGEEN, Eric
"Oral tradition and agrarian history in the West Highlands"
Oral History, vol.2, no.1 (1974), pp.15-33

399 CREGEEN, Eric
"Oral sources for the social history of the Scottish Highlands and Islands"
Oral History, vol.2, no.2 (1974), pp.23-36

400 CREGEEN, Eric
"Sound archives in the United Kingdom: field recording programmes and practices: oral history"
Phonographic Bulletin, no.29 (1981), pp.9-14

401 CRESCIANI, Gianfranco
Fascism, anti-fascism and Italians in Australia, 1922-1945
Canberra: Australian National University Press, 1980
261pp; bibliography

402 CRICK, Bernard
George Orwell: a life
Secker and Warburg, 1980
543pp
An example of the use of oral testimony in recent literary biography. In this case the author carried out seventy-five interviews.

403 CROAL, Jonathan
Don't you know there's a war on?: the people's voice 1939-45
Hutchinson, 1988
232pp; bibliography
Thirty-five personal accounts of the home front during the Second World War. Descriptions of dislocated family life, interrupted education, evacuation, the pressures of rationing, the blackout and 'making do'. Includes some people who went to prison for their beliefs.

404 CROCKER, Andrew and JEFFREY, David
"Developing practice in caring for confused elderly people"
Social Work Education, vol.4, no.3 (Winter 1985)
pp.7-11
Includes a list of sources of training material.

405 CROOK, Rosemary
"'Tidy Women': women in the Rhondda between the wars"
Oral History, vol.10, no.2 (1982), pp.40-6
Women and family life in a South Wales mining community during a period of upheaval.

CROSS, L. *see* MERRIAM, S.

406 CROSSICK, Geoffrey (ed.)
The lower middle class in Britain 1870-1914
Croom Helm, 1977; reprinted 1978
213pp
Includes three chapters which make extensive use of Essex University's 'Family Life and Work Experience' oral history archive: Hugh McLeod, 'White collar values and the role of religion'; Richard Price, 'Society, status and jingoism: the social roots of lower middle class patriotism, 1870-1900'; and Thea Vigne and Alun Howkins, 'The small shopkeeper in industrial and market towns'.

407 CROUCH, David and WARD, Colin
The allotment: its landscape and culture
Faber and Faber, 1988
322pp
Several interviews from Essex University's oral history archive are included relating to allotments.

408 CROUSE, Timothy
The boys on the bus
New York: Random House, 1973
383pp; bibliography
Written by a political journalist who gained prominence criss-crossing the United States interviewing scores of people to gauge the mood of the American electorate over a period of years.

409 CROWL, Philip A.
"The Dulles Oral History Project: mission accomplished"
American Historical Association Newsletter, *vol.5 (1967), pp.6-10*

410 CROWTHER, Nicci (ed.)
I can remember…
Edward Arnold, 1976
48pp
Twelve interviews transcribed for use in secondary schools with information on how to make an oral history recording. Based on the author's work in a London comprehensive.

CROWTHER-HUNT, Lord *see* KELLNER, Peter

411 CUMMINGS, Paul
Artists in their own words: interviews
New York: St.Martin's, 1979
242pp
Extracts from twelve interviews carried out over more than a decade for the Archives of American Art.

412 CUNNINGHAM, Kitty and BALLARD, Michael
Conversations with a dancer
New York: St.Martin's, 1980
Interviews recorded over several years with Ballard, a soloist with the Murray Louis Dance Company in the United States, covering teaching, choreography and touring.

413 CURTIN, Patricia Romero
"Laboratory for the oral history of slavery: the Island of Lamu on the Kenya coast"
American Historical Review, vol.88, no.4 (October 1983), pp.858-82

414 CURTIN, Philip D.
"Field techniques for collecting and processing oral data"
Journal of African History, vol.9, no.3 (1968)

415 CURTIN, Philip D.(ed.)
Africa remembered: narratives by West Africans from the era of the slave trade
Madison: University of Wisconsin Press, 1967
363pp
Mainly written childhood memories and dictated reminiscences from those that escaped.

416 CURTISS, Richard D., SHUMWAY, Gary L. and STEPHENSON, Shirley E.
A guide for oral history programs
Fullerton, California: California State University and Southern California Local History Council, 1973
347pp; bibliography
Articles from a range of authors on agreements, cataloguing, editing, transcription etc., with content listings of the eight major oral history projects at California State University.

417 CUTLER, William W.
"Accuracy in oral history interviewing"
Historical Methods Newsletter, vol.3, no.3 (June 1970), pp.1-7
Cautions that inaccuracies of memory and bias can lead to distortion.

418 CUTLER, William W.
"Oral history: its nature and uses for educational history"
History of Education Quarterly, vol.11 (1971), pp.184-94

419 CUTTING-BAKER, Holly, KOTKIN, Amy and YOCOM, Margaret
Family folklore interviewing guide and questionnaire
Washington, DC: US Government Printing Office, 1978

DA ROCHA LIMA, Valentina *see* CAMARGO, Aspasia

DADZIE, Stella *see* BRYAN, Beverley

420 DALLAT, Cahal and GIBSON, Faith
"The Playback Project: a walk into history"
Oral History, vol.15, no.2 (1987), pp.46-57
Details of an enormously successful DHSS-funded oral history/reminiscence competition in Northern Ireland, aimed at schools and youth groups with the intention of inter-generational bridge-building. It attracted 400 project entries involving 4000 young people aged four to nineteen. Prizes were awarded on an area basis.

421 DALLAT, Cahal and GIBSON, Faith
Rooms of time: memories of Ulster people
Antrim, Northern Ireland: Greystone Books, 1988
206pp; bibliography
An excellent anthology of verbatim interview extracts drawn from the Playback Project (see above) and covering home, delivery men and corner shops, work, health, school, play, leisure, transport and the two world wars.

422 D'ALPUGET, Blanche
Robert J. Hawke: a biography
Harmondsworth: Penguin, 1985; first published Melbourne: Schwartz, 1982
426pp
A biography of Australia's Labour prime minister: his battle with alcohol and his political ascent, based on accounts from Hawke himself and colleagues.

DALTON, Mike *see* McFARLAND, Elaine W.

423 DAMER, Sean
Rent strike!: the Clydebank rent strike of the 1920s
Glasgow: Clydebank District Library, 1982
A Clydebank people's history pamphlet
28pp
Based on interviews with the participants involved in the campaign against the 1920 Rent Act and the abandonment of war-time rent control: an example of working-class organisation and solidarity.

424 DANCE, Helen Oakley
Stormy Monday: the T-Bone Walker story
Baton Rouge: University of Louisiana Press, 1986
285pp
An oral biography of blues and jazz guitarist T-Bone Walker.

425 DANIELS, Robin
Conversations with Cardus
Gollancz, 1976
288pp
The result of three years of tape recorded interviews with Neville Cardus, critic and writer about classical music and cricket, which were completed only three weeks before his death.

426 **DANIELS, Robin**
Conversations with Menuhin
Macdonald, 1979
192pp
Interviews with the violinist, each around an hour, recorded over a six to nine month period.

427 **DANZIGER, Danny**
All in a day's work
Fontana, 1987
252pp
Fifty people talk about their jobs: what it entails, their feelings about it, their disappointments and ambitions. Includes a car salesman, chimney sweep, criminal, diver, dustman, funeral director, gamekeeper, kissogram, monk, peer, plumber, photographer, prostitute, taxidermist, tax inspector and zookeeper.

428 **DANZIGER, Danny**
Eton voices
Harmondsworth: Viking Penguin, 1988
290pp
Interviews with over forty old Etonians, from the former prime minister Lord Home to the film director Hugh Hudson, about one of Britain's most famous public schools: its tough regime, harsh conditions and abysmal food, beatings, homosexuality, and its influence on their lives.

DARGUE, Coral *see* **GREIG, John**

429 **DAVEY, Dolly**
A sense of adventure
S.E.1 People's History Project, 1980
37pp
A transcript of an interview with Dolly Davey, who was born in 1913 in Yorkshire, but spent most of her life in London's Waterloo.

430 **DAVID, Kati**
A child's war: world war two through the eyes of children
Peterborough: Ryan, 1989
210pp
The eyewitness accounts of eight girls and seven boys, all aged between five and ten during the war, from Austria, Belgium, Czechoslovakia, Denmark, England, Estonia, France, Germany, Holland, Hungary, Italy, Poland, Rumania and the USSR. Drawn from two and a half years' interviewing of 200 people in twenty-three countries.

431 **DAVIDOFF, Leonore and WESTOVER, Belinda (eds.)**
Our work, our lives, our words: women's history and women's work
Macmillan, 1986
189pp; bibliography
A collection of articles based on life-stories of women born between 1880 and 1914 in the context of rapid social change. Covers attitudes to trade unionism, the Women's Auxiliary Army Corps in the First World War, and jobs in East Anglian farm labouring, Colchester tailoring, Yorkshire textiles, London teaching and shorthand typing, and the civil service.

432 **DAVIDSON, Jim**
Sideways from the page: the Meanjin interviews
Melbourne: Fontana, 1983
415pp
Interviews with Australian writers including Frank Moorhouse and Margaret Attwood.

433 **DAVIES, E.G.**
Recollections: a record of memories and experiences in St.Neots and other places 1912-1947
St.Neots, Cambridgeshire: E.G.Davies, 1988
168pp

434 **DAVIES, Margaret Llewellyn (ed.)**
Life as we have known it by Co-operative working women
Virago, 1977; first published Hogarth, 1931
142pp
Working class women talk about their lives before the First World War. Includes an introduction by Virginia Woolf.

435 **DAVIES, R.U.**
Watchdogs' tales: the District Audit Service - the first 138 years
HMSO, 1987
250pp
A collection of memoirs of a service established to prevent fraud and abuse of public money, latterly in local authorities.

436 **DAVIES, Sonja**
Bread and roses: Sonja Davies, her story
Auckland, New Zealand: ANZ Book Co., 1984
309pp
A tape-recorded biography of one of New Zealand's leading Labour politicians and the founder of the New Zealand Association of Child Care Centres.

437   DAVIES, Stuart
"Museums and oral history"
Museums Journal, vol. 84, no. 1 (June/July 1984)

438   DAVIS, Cullom, BACK, Kathryn and MACLEAN, Kay
Oral history: from tape to type
Chicago: American Library Association, 1977
141pp; bibliography
A guide to interviewing, transcribing, editing and indexing which includes instructional exercises, glossary and rules of style for editing.

439   DAVIS, Francis
In the moment: jazz in the 1980s
New York: Oxford University Press, 1986
258pp
Interviews with Philadelphia rising stars.

440   DAVIS, J.C.
"Slovene laborer and his experience of industrialisation, 1888-1976"
East European Quarterly, *no.10 (Spring 1976), pp.2-20*
Changes in a rural village and the impact of war in one area of Yugoslavia.

441   DAVIS, Madeline and KENNEDY, Elizabeth L.
"Oral history and the study of sexuality in the lesbian community: Buffalo New York 1940-1960"
Feminist Studies, vol.12, no.1 (1986)

DAVIS, O.L. *see* MEHAFFY, George L.; SITTON, Thad

442   DAVIS, Rib (ed.)
Memories of Shirebrook: a collection of reminiscences
Matlock: Derbyshire Library Service, 1985
60pp
Nine people's memories of life in Shirebrook and surrounding mining villages on the Nottinghamshire/Derbyshire border. Long extracts with indications of dialect.

443   DAVIS, Ronald
Oral history collection on the performing arts
Dallas, Tex.:Southern Methodist University, 1981

444   DE GRAEVE, Rie
"Sound records in Flanders: teething problems!"
Phonographic Bulletin, no.37 (November 1983), pp.16-17
Outlines a project at the University of Ghent oral history archive on schools and teachers in Flanders 1900-1940.

DE VORKIN, David H. *see* WEART, Spencer R.

445   DEAN, Peter (ed.)
A step back in time
Luton: Luton College of Higher Education Access Course, 1989
60pp
A variety of transcribed interviews with Luton people of varying backgrounds.

446   DEERING, Mary Jo and POMEROY, Barbara
Transcribing without tears: a guide to transcribing and editing oral history interviews
Washington D.C.: George Washington University, 1976

447   DEGH, Linda
People in the tobacco belt: four lives
Ottawa, Canada: National Museums of Canada, 1975
Canadian Centre for Folk Culture Studies, paper 13
277pp; bibliography
Life histories of four Hungarian immigrants to Canada recorded in 1971.

448   DEL TREDICI, Robert
The people of Three Mile Island
San Francisco: Sierra Club Books, 1980
127pp
Thirty-seven edited interviews are used to analyse the nuclear power station crisis.

449   DELCROIX, Catherine, GUYAUX, Anne and RODRIGUEZ, Evangelina
"Mixed marriage as a life-long cultural encounter"
Life Stories, no.5 (1989), pp.49-63

450   DENNIS, N., HENRIQUES, P. and SLAUGHTER, C.
Coal is our life
Eyre and Spottiswoode, 1956; reprinted Tavistock, 1969
255pp
Based on interviews in the Yorkshire mining community of Ashton in the early 1950s.

451 DENOON, Donald and LACEY, Roderic (eds.)
Oral tradition in Melanesia
Port Moresby: University of Papua New Guinea, 1981
270pp
A collection of papers from a lecture course on oral history at the University of Papua New Guinea covering regional and methodological aspects.

452 DENZIN, Norman K. (ed.)
Sociological methods: a sourcebook
McGraw-Hill, 1978, second edition; first edition, 1970
434pp; bibliography
For interviewing techniques.

453 DENZIN, Norman K.
"Interpreting the lives of ordinary people: Sartre, Heidegger, Faulkner"
Life Stories, no.2 (1986)

454 DERRICK, Deborah
Illegitimate: the experience of people born outside marriage
National Council for One Parent Families, 1986
77pp
Based on 230 letters of personal testimony from people born outside marriage and their mothers. Revealing of the stigma and isolation felt by many of the four million such people in Britain.

455 DEWE, Michael
"Local studies and the new technology: the British experience"
Information Development, vol.3, no.1 (January 1987), pp.23-9
Traces the development of local studies collections in the UK including the advent of oral history.

456 DEXTER, Lewis Anthony (ed.)
Elite and specialized interviewing
Evanston, Illinois: Northwestern University Press, 1970
205pp
A useful guide for the novice interviewer which includes a section on oral history interviewing.

457 DHARMACHAKRA
Tapes on Buddhism
Cambridge: Dharmachakra, 1988, fourth edition
32pp
A listing of 169 titles of lectures, talks and recordings relating to Buddhism in the UK.

458 DICK, Ernest J.
"Oral history in Canada: an archivist's commentary"
Archivaria, no.4 (1977), pp.34-42
A good summary of the development of oral history archives in Canada.

459 DICK, Ernest J.
"Selection and preservation of oral history interviews"
Drexel Library Quarterly, vol.15 (October 1979), pp.35-8
Examines the criteria for the selection by libraries of oral history material: technical quality, background information, uniqueness, and completeness. Ideal tape and storage conditions are outlined. This issue is a special on managing oral history collections in the library.

460 DICKINSON, Bob
"In the audience: Lancashire music halls"
Oral History, vol.11, no.1 (1983), pp.52-61

461 DILLARD, Joey Lee
Black English: its history and usage in the United States
New York: Random House, 1972
361pp

462 DIXON, Elizabeth I.
"The implications of oral history in library history"
Journal of Library History, vol.1 (1966), pp.59-62

463 DOBROFF, Rose
"A time for reclaiming the past"
Journal of Gerontological Social Work, vol.7, nos. 1/2 (1984)
A special double issue on the uses of reminiscence.

464 DODGSON, Elyse
Motherland: West Indian women to Britain in the 1950s
Heinneman Educational, 1984
124pp; bibliography
An educational sourcebook in which twenty-three life stories of West Indian women who have now settled in South London are used as the basis for youth drama.

465 DODGSON, Elyse
"From oral history to drama"
Oral History, vol.12, no.2 (1984), pp.47-53
The processes behind the Motherland project at Vauxhall Manor School, London.

DODSWORTH, Steven *see* EVANS, Catherine

DODWELL, F. *see* ST.HILL DAVIES, E.

466 DOLCI, Danilo
Sicilian lives
New York: Pantheon Books, 1982
The Pantheon Village Series
303pp
Thirty-nine interviews gathered over several years. Translated by Justin Vitiello.

467 DOLLARD, John
Caste and class in a southern town
Garden City, New York: Doubleday, 1957, third edition; first edition, 1937
466pp

468 DONOUGHUE, Bernard and JONES, George
Herbert Morrison: portrait of a politician
Weidenfeld and Nicolson, 1973
696pp
Based heavily on oral evidence, some 300 interviews, after Morrison's personal and government papers were burned by his wife.

469 DONSETT-DAVIES, John
"The past brought to life"
Community Care, 18 December 1986, pp.22-3

470 DORFMAN, Gerald A.
Government versus trade unionism in British politics since 1968
Macmillan, 1979
179pp
Research for the book involved over forty interviews with political and trade union leaders, TUC staff and civil servants between 1969 and 1977.

471 DORIAN, Nancy C.
The tyranny of tide
Ann Arbor: Karoma, 1985
A study of the fishing communities of East Sutherland based on the personal account of Lizzie Sutherland with material on women in the whitefish and herring industry: childhood, dress, customs and beliefs.

472 DORSON, Richard M. (ed.)
Folklore and folklife: an introduction
University of Chicago Press, 1972
561pp
On recording tradition-bearers.

473 DORSON, Richard M. (ed.)
Folklore research around the world: a North American point of view
Kennikat, 1973; first published 1961
197pp
Includes a chapter on the study of African oral art.

474 DOUGLAS, Louise
"A guide to local, family and oral history publications: select bibliographies"
Oral History Association of Australia Journal, vol.4 (1981-2), pp.86-95

475 DOUGLAS, Louise and SPEARRITT, Peter
Australia 1938 oral history handbook
Canberra: Australian National University, 1981
92pp
Published as part of *Australia 1788-1988: a bicentennial history.*

476 DOUGLAS, Louise and SPEARRITT, Peter
"Talking history: the use of oral sources"
in MANDLE, W. and OSBORNE, G. (eds.),
New history: studying Australia today, Sydney:
Allen and Unwin, 1982, pp.51-68

477 DOUGLAS, Louise, ROBERTS, Alan and THOMPSON, Ruth
Oral history: a handbook
Sydney, Australia: Allen and Unwin, 1988
217pp; bibliography
Australia's most outstanding manual with practical guidelines for individuals and groups covering interviewing, equipment, legal, copyright and ethical considerations, preservation, transcription, uses in education, interpretation and the reliability of oral testimony. Included is a sample questionnaire, an overview of the development of oral history in Australia, and a useful contact list.

478 DOUGLAS-HOME, Charles
Evelyn Baring: the last proconsul
Collins, 1978
344pp
For this biography of Baring, Governor of
Kenya 1952-9, the author interviewed about
one hundred colonial officials, soldiers,
diplomats and politicians.

479 DOUGLASS, David
Pit life in County Durham: rank and file
movements and workers' control
Oxford: History Workshop, Ruskin College,
1972
History Workshop pamphlet no.6
92pp

480 DOUGLASS, Enid H.
"Oral history and public history"
Oral History Review, vol.8 (1980), pp.1-5
The value of oral history for non-academic
historians studying public and private
institutions.

481 DOWNING, M.J.
"Company paternalism and the butty system:
conversations with Gresswell residents"
Bulletin of the Society for the Study of Labour
History, no.46 (Spring 1983), pp.21-9
The anatomy of a Derbyshire pit village on the
Nottinghamshire border in which the Bolsover
Colliery Company controlled housing, the
Workmen's Institute and even the Boys' and
Girls' Brigades.

482 DRYDEN, Jean E (ed.)
Voices of Alberta: a survey of oral history
completed in Alberta up to 1980
Edmonton: Alberta Culture, Historical
Resources Division, 1981
460pp

483 DUDGEON, Piers (ed.)
Village voices: a portrait of change in England's
green and pleasant land 1915-1990: a 75th
anniversary celebration of rural Britain by the
W.I. - Britain's foremost women's movement
Sidgwick and Jackson, 1989
176pp
Based on first-hand interviews with
countrywomen aged sixteen to a hundred and
one, it traces the history of the Women's
Institute from its beginnings in Llanfairpwell
to today's movement of 333,000 members in
9000 institutes. It covers the W.I.'s role as an
educator and as a pressure group on such
issues as women's independence, divorce
reform and the environment.

484 DUFFIN, Patricia
"Reminiscence: at the sharp end"
Oral History, vol.17, no.1 (1989)

485 DUFTY, David
Historians at work: investigating and recreating
the past
Sydney: Hicks, Smith and Sons, 1973

486 DUNAWAY, David King
How can I keep from singing: Pete Seeger
Harrap, 1985; originally New York: McGraw-
Hill, 1981
386pp; bibliography and discography
A biography of one of America's leading
political folksingers based on 110 interviews
with Seeger and his associates and family.
Covers his blacklisting during the McCarthy
period and his trade union and political
activities.

487 DUNAWAY, David King
"Field recording oral history"
Oral History Review, vol.15, no.1 (Spring
1987), pp.21-42
A survey of field recording for people with
some experience, with discussion of some of
the dynamics and ethics involved.

488 DUNAWAY, David King
Huxley in Hollywood
Bloomsbury, 1989
458pp
A study of the writer Aldous Huxley, from
interviews with those who knew him.

**489 DUNAWAY, David King and BAUM, Willa K.
(eds.)**
Oral history: an interdisciplinary anthology
Nashville: American Association for State and
Local History/Oral History Association, 1984,
1987
436pp; bibliographies
Thirty seven previously published articles on
the theory and interpretation of oral history.
Topics include local, ethnic, family and
women's history; oral history and related
disciplines e.g. folklore, gerontology; oral
history and schools and libraries. Authors
include Paul Thompson, William Moss, Jan
Vansina, David Lance, Saul Benison, Alex
Haley, Eliot Wigginton and Barbara
Tuchman.

490 DUNDEE ORAL HISTORY PROJECT
Oral history learning pack
Dundee: Dundee Oral History Project, 1985
10pp booklet and cassette tape; bibliography
An anthology for use in schools covering
booth boxing, disease, women's war work in
the Second World War, bookmaking and
Arbroath fishing.

491 DUNDEE ORAL HISTORY PROJECT
Oral history learning pack 2: school life
Dundee: Dundee Oral History Project, 1985
14pp booklet and cassette tape; bibliography
An anthology for use in schools about
schooling in Dundee between the wars.

492 DUNDEE ORAL HISTORY PROJECT
A guide to reminiscence
Dundee: Dundee Oral History Project, 1987,
second edition; first edition, 1986
40pp; bibliography
A pack of practical ideas for using
reminiscence, with tips on equipment,
materials, conducting a group, cataloguing
and ideas for developing the results. Includes
a loose A4 supplement of a 'suggested
schedule' of thirty topics for use with groups.

493 DUNDEE ORAL HISTORY PROJECT
Oral history learning pack 3: street life
Dundee: Dundee Oral History Project, 1986
10pp booklet and cassette tape
For use in schools, the pack covers retail
trade, the Greenmarket, holidays, street
games and cinema.

494 DUNDEE ORAL HISTORY PROJECT
Oral history learning pack 4: homelife
Dundee: Dundee Oral History Project, 1986
10pp booklet and cassette tape
For use in schools, it covers housing
conditions, community relations, diet and
clothing in Dundee between the wars.

495 DUNDEE ORAL HISTORY PROJECT
The world's ill divided
Dundee: Dundee Oral History Project, 1987
20pp; bibliography
Accompanied DOHP's *Open Space* television
programme shown on BBC 2 on 29 July 1987.
Outlines the practical work and theoretical
basis of the project.

496 DUQUENIN, Anthea
"Who doesn't marry and why"
Oral History, vol.12, no.1 (1984), pp.40-47
Based on interviews with elderly working class
women from one small textile town in Devon
who never married.

497 DURANT, Ruth
Watling: a survey of social life on a new housing
estate
P.S. King, 1939
128pp
Residents began moving onto the estate in
Hendon in 1927: the survey looks at how far it
had grown into a community and what role the
community centre had played.

498 DYER, Geoffrey
"Oral archives"
Journal of the Society of Archivists, vol.6, no.3
(April 1979), pp.157-8

499 DYK, Walter (ed.)
Son of Old Man Hat: a Navaho autobiography
Lincoln: University of Nebraska Press, 1967;
first published 1938
378pp
An account of the early years of Left Handed,
a Navaho Indian born in 1868, as narrated by
him to an interpreter and translator. An
outstanding example of the American
anthropological tradition.

DYKE, Mel *see* **LEWIS, Brian**

500 EAST BOWLING HISTORY WORKSHOP
'Don't look back love' and other stories of the
second world war 1939-45
Bradford: East Bowling History Workshop,
1989
98pp
Memories and experiences of East Bowling
people at home and in the services during the
Second World War.

501 EBER, Dorothy Harley
When the whalers were up north: Inuit
memories from the eastern Arctic
Montreal: McGill-Queen's University Press,
1989
187pp

ECHLIN, Shirley *see* **MERSON, Elizabeth**

EDENSOR, Tim *see* **KELLY, Mij**

502 EDGE, David O. and MULKAY, Michael J.
Astronomy transformed: the emergence of radio astronomy in Britain
Wiley, 1976
496pp
A rare example of an oral history-based examination of scientific study in Britain.

503 EDGE, Y., LIDDINGTON, Jill and SEDDON, J. (eds.)
Hurrah for a life in the factory
Manchester: Manchester Studies, 1983
A teaching pack on the cotton industry based on interviews.

504 EDMOND, Lauris (ed.)
Women in wartime: New Zealand women tell their story
Wellington, New Zealand: Government Printing Office Publishing, 1986
278pp
Testimony from both world wars.

505 EDWARDS, A.
Flawed words and stubborn sounds: a conversation with Elliott Carter
New York: W.W.Norton, 1971
128pp
Six taped interviews with the contemporary classical composer recorded between 1968 and 1970.

506 EDWARDS, Alison and WYNCOLL, Keith
"The Crystal Palace is on fire": memories of the 30th November 1936
Crystal Palace Foundation, 1986
58pp
Based on interviews with local people and employees: includes a BBC transcript of the broadcast commentary describing the fire.

507 EDWARDS, Bertram
The Burston school strike
Lawrence and Wishart, 1974
213pp
The strike began in 1914 with the dismissal of two teachers at the village school in south Norfolk and ended with the opening of a strike school in 1917. This account is based on interviews with participants.

508 EDWARDS, P.J. and MARSHALL, Jean
"Sources of conflict and community in the trawling industries of Hull and Grimsby between the wars"
Oral History, vol.5, no.1 (1977), pp.97-121

509 EELES, Graham and KINNEAR, Jill
"Archivists and historians: friends, strangers or enemies?"
Journal of the Society of Archivists, vol.9, no.4 (October 1988), pp.188-9; Oral History, vol.17, no.1 (1989), pp.54-5
A plea for closer co-operation.

510 EGERTON, John
Generations: an American family
Lexington, Kentucky: University Press of Kentucky, 1983
263pp
An excellent example of an oral approach to family history in which the search for one family, whose history was sufficiently diverse to be typical and representative of a majority of Americans, led to the Ledford family of Kentucky.

EILAH, Mohammed Abu El *see* **NORRIS, Andrew**

511 ELDER, Gladys
The alienated: growing old today
Writers and Readers Publishing Co-operative, 1977
143pp; bibliography
Personal accounts of being elderly in Britain: the collapse of self-esteem and the poor condition of health and housing.

512 ELDRED-GRIGG, Stevan
Oracles and miracles: a novel
Auckland, New Zealand: Penguin, 1987
262pp
Based on taped interviews, this novel concerns twin sisters growing up in working class Christchurch during the 1930s and 1940s.

513 ELINOR, Gillian, RICHARDSON, Sue, SCOTT, Sue and WALKER, Curt (eds.)
Women and craft
Virago, 1987
191pp
Concentrates on the process rather than the product and covers domestic craft work, the issue of craft versus art and selling craft products.

514 ELLE, Lawrence
Not so long ago: oral histories of older Bostonians
Boston: Senior Resource Cooperative Project of the Mayor's Office of Community Schools, 1980
Bostonians born between 1895 and 1915.

515 ELLIOT, Jeffrey M. (ed.)
Conversations with Maya Angelou
Virago, 1989
246pp
Two dozen interviews from British and US
magazines and newspapers about Angelou's
work and life as a poet, writer, dancer,
composer, singer, teacher and black activist.

ELLIOTT, Brian *see* STRAW, Pat

516 ELLIS, Stanley
Tape recording of local dialect
National Council of Social Service for the
Standing Conference for Local History, 1971
Bibliography

517 ELLIS, Stanley
"The Survey of English Dialects and social
history"
Oral History, vol.2, no.2 (1974), pp.37-43
The survey was one of the most extensive and
influential ever carried out in Britain. The
tapes are now held by the North West Sound
Archive.

518 ELLSWORTH, Scott
Death in a promised land: the Tulsa race riot of
1921
Baton Rouge: Louisiana State University
Press, 1982
159pp; bibliography
Documentary evidence of the riot has been
suppressed, so oral testimony has been of
particular importance in this study.

519 ELLWOOD, Sheelagh M.
"Not so much a programme more a way of
life: oral history and Spanish Fascism"
Oral History, vol.16, no.2 (1988), pp.57-66
Based on thirty-two interviews with Falange
militants.

520 ELSE, Anne (ed.)
Listen to the teacher: an oral history of women
who taught in New Zealand, c.1925-1945
Wellington: Society for Research on Women in
New Zealand, 1986
157pp
The stories of thirty women teachers born
between 1900 and 1918: thematic chapters
deal with different aspects of teaching
between 1925 and 1945.

521 ELSWICK LOCAL HISTORY GROUP
Richardson's leather works: the workers' story
Newcastle-upon-Tyne: Elswick Local History
Group, 1985
53pp
One of the best known and established
factories in Newcastle's West End closed in
November 1971: this is verbatim memories
from ex-workers.

522 EMMETT, Isabel
A north Wales village: a social anthropological
study
Routledge & Kegan Paul, 1963
Dartington Hall Studies in Rural Sociology
154pp; bibliography
A study of the Welsh speaking parish of Llan,
based on observations whilst living there
between July 1958 and September 1962.

523 EPSTEIN, E.R. and MENDELSOHN, Rona
Record and remember: tracing your roots
through oral history
New York: Sovereign/Simon and Schuster,
1978
119pp
For family history research: includes interview
outlines and advice on processing interviews.

524 EPSTEIN, Helen
Children of the Holocaust: conversations with
sons and daughters of survivors
New York: G.P.Putnam's Sons, 1979; Bantam
Books, 1980
308pp; bibliography
Herself the daughter of a survivor, the author
gathered hundreds of first-hand stories to
investigate the impact of the extermination of
European Jewry by the Nazis on the second
generation. The project grew out of another
project which interviewed 200 survivors.

525 ERICSON, Stacy
A field notebook for oral history
Boise: Idaho State Historical Society, 1981

526 ESH, Shaul
Yad Washem studies on the European Jewry
catastrophe and resistance
Jerusalem: Yad Washem, 1960
Yad Washem is Israel's leading library of the
Holocaust.

527 ETHNIC COMMUNITIES ORAL HISTORY PROJECT
The Irish in exile: stories of emigration
Ethnic Communities Oral History Project, 1988
Hammersmith & Fulham Community History Series No.1
24pp
Seven Irish people living in London tell their story: of the Ireland they left behind, and their impressions and experiences of the England to which they came. Extracts from many of the life history recordings used in the compilation of this, and subsequent booklets in the series, are available in cassette form.

528 ETHNIC COMMUNITIES ORAL HISTORY PROJECT
Passport to exile: the Polish way to London/Paszport na wygnanie: Polska droga do Londynu
Ethnic Communities Oral History Project, 1988
Hammersmith & Fulham Community History Series No.2
40pp
Edited by Sav Kyriacou and the Polish Reminiscence Group, five people tell of the different routes taken by Poles coming to Britain: of their childhood memories and wartime experiences through battlefields and prison camps. Published in dual language.

529 ETHNIC COMMUNITIES ORAL HISTORY PROJECT
In exile: Iranian recollections
Ethnic Communities Oral History Project, 1989
Hammersmith & Fulham Community History Series No.3
40pp
Five Iranians living in London talk about why they came, their life at home, the journey, life in Britain as they see it, their feelings, reflections, perceptions and expectations. A dual language publication.

530 ETHNIC COMMUNITIES ORAL HISTORY PROJECT
The Motherland calls: African-Caribbean experiences
Ethnic Communities Oral History Project, 1989
Hammersmith & Fulham Community History Series No.4
36pp
Seven African-Caribbeans living in London tell their stories.

531 ETHNIC COMMUNITIES ORAL HISTORY PROJECT
The forgotten lives: Gypsies and travellers on the Westway Site
Ethnic Communities Oral History Project, 1989
24pp
Gypsies and travellers have lived in and around Hammersmith for centuries, and tell their stories.

532 EVANS, Catherine, DODSWORTH, Steven and BARNETT, Julie
Below the bridge
Cardiff: National Museum of Wales, 1984
147pp
A photo-historical survey of Cardiff's Butetown dock area carried out between 1982 and 1983 by an MSC scheme for the Welsh Industrial and Maritime Museum, and featuring a wealth of oral testimony.

533 EVANS, Christopher
Pioneers of computing
Hugo Informatics Enterprises, nd
Ten tapes (about five hours in length)
Interviews with the British computer elite of the 1940s and 1950s.

534 EVANS, Christopher
The making of the micro: a history of the computer
New York: Von Nostrand Reinhold, 1981
113pp; bibliography
A popular history including interviews with computer pioneers which have been deposited with the Science Museum in London.

535 EVANS, Dilys M.
"A small oral history project in four rural Cumbrian primary schools"
Teaching History, no.57 (October 1989), pp.25-7

536 EVANS, George Ewart
Ask the fellows who cut the hay
Faber, 1956; second edition, 1965
262pp; bibliography
Recollections of a group of old people in the East Suffolk village of Blaxhall about declining hand-tool methods of farming and domestic crafts, including shepherding, sheep shearing, bread, beer and cheese making, bacon curing, harvesting, bell ringing, poaching and smuggling. An important book by one of Britain's pioneers of oral history.

537   EVANS, George Ewart
The horse in the furrow
Faber, 1960; 1967
292pp; bibliography
Horses and horsemen in Suffolk farming: the
horseman's day, the farmer, ploughing,
grooms, blacksmiths, harness-makers and
folklore associated with horses.

538   EVANS, George Ewart
The pattern under the plough: aspects of the
folk-life of East Anglia
Faber, 1966; 1971
269pp; bibliography
Concentrates on house and home and the
farm.

539   EVANS, George Ewart
The farm and the village
Faber, 1969; second edition 1974
181pp; bibliographies
An introduction to the history of farming in
East Anglia, aimed at the younger reader and
covering the early history up to the turn of the
century before wide-scale mechanisation.
Includes oral testimony from a horseman,
harness-maker, tailor, blacksmith, miller and
millwright.

540   EVANS, George Ewart
Where beards wag all: the relevance of the oral
tradition
Faber, 1970; second edition, 1977
296pp; bibliography
Explains the importance of the oral tradition
on which his books are based and includes
material from East Anglia on the wheelwright
and foundry, the saddler, ploughing and
farming, the auctioneer, the cattle trade,
village dialect, the church, the school, and
migrant brewery labour to Burton-on-Trent.

541   EVANS, George Ewart
"Flesh and blood archives: some early
experiences"
Oral History, vol.1, no.1 (1970), pp.3-4

542   EVANS, George Ewart
Tools of their trade: an oral history of men at
work, c.1900
New York: Taplinger Publishing Company,
1970
296pp; bibliography

543   EVANS, George Ewart
Oral tradition
Saffron Walden: Suffolk Federation WEA,
1973
16pp
The Harry Clement memorial lecture
delivered on 16 June 1973.

544   EVANS, George Ewart
"Approaches to interviewing"
Oral History, vol.1, no.4 (1973), pp.56-71

545   EVANS, George Ewart
The days that we have seen
Faber, 1975
224pp
A rural social history of a Suffolk village in
which Evans demonstrates the possible time
span of historically valuable oral evidence.
Includes material on fishing.

546   EVANS, George Ewart
"I am a tape recorder: 'oral history'"
Encounter, vol.47 (November 1976), pp.70,
72, 74-8
Outlines his recording techniques and
compares British with US technique.

547   EVANS, George Ewart
From mouths of men
Faber, 1976
202pp; bibliography
The culmination of Evans' studies in local
history, looking at 'the town' and 'mining'.
Includes interviews with domestic servants,
Welsh miners, a Yorkshire wool manufacturer
and a discussion of some of the fore-runners of
oral historians; plus material on costume and
clothing, and changes in university education
and business methods.

548   EVANS, George Ewart
Horse power and magic
Faber, 1979
222pp; bibliography
More history of the horse and farming (see
The horse in the furrow above) in which Evans
describes how horses were still in use on farms
in East Anglia in the 1970s, of the attraction of
heavy horses, the skills of horse tamers and
horsemen's tales.

548A   EVANS, George Ewart
The strength of the hills: an autobiography
Faber, 1983
180pp

549 **EVANS, George Ewart**
Spoken history
Faber, 1987
255pp
A conspectus of all Evans' oral history work in which he describes his pioneering work and argues that historians ought to widen their brief to study people as well as documents.

550 **EVANS, George Ewart and THOMSON, David**
The leaping hare
Faber, 1972; 1974
262pp
Examines the role of the hare in human myth and experience using various sources including folk material and interviews with gamekeepers and poachers.

551 **EVANS, Mari (ed.)**
Black women writers: arguments and interviews
Pluto, 1985
528pp
Interviews and critical evaluation of US Black women writers like Maya Angelou, Alice Walker, Paule Marshall and Toni Morrison, whose work is available in Britain.

EVANS, Walker *see* **AGEE, James**

552 **EVEREST, Allan S.**
Rum across the border: the prohibition era in Northern New York
Syracuse: Syracuse University Press, 1978
172pp
The Canadian-US border of New York in the 1920s and 1930s through the accounts of border officials, bootleggers and lawyers.

553 **EWEN, Elizabeth**
Immigrant women in the land of dollars: life and culture on the Lower East Side, 1890-1925
New York: Monthly Review Press, 1985
New Feminist Library
303pp; bibliography
The story of Jewish and Italian women who came to live in New York's Lower East Side through interviews with two generations: mothers born in the 'old world' and daughters born in the new. Together they relate their first impressions, experiences of work, making ends meet, home and community, health, and assimilation.

554 **EXELL, Arthur**
"The experience of being interviewed"
Oral History, vol.14, no.2 (1986), pp.66-7

555 **EXPLORING LIVING MEMORY**
Exploring living memory 1984 report
Exploring Living Memory, 1985
30pp
A report on a festival of local, community and oral history and reminiscence in the London area, held at the Royal Festival Hall in February 1984.

556 **EXPLORING LIVING MEMORY**
Exploring living memory 1985
Exploring Living Memory, 1985
12pp
A report on the February 1985 festival which featured over ninety displays from oral history and reminiscence groups from all over London.

557 **FADIMAN, J.**
An oral history of tribal warfare: the Meru of Mt. Kenya
Athens: Ohio University Press, 1982
185pp; bibliography
Based on 100 interviews with warriors.

558 **FAIERS, Carol**
"Persistence and change in farming methods in a Suffolk village"
Oral History, vol.4, no.2 (1976), pp.52-62
The value of oral history in the study of farming methods, based on interviews in Haughley about farming up to the 1930s.

559 **FALK, J.M.** *see* **LIEBERMAN, M.A.**

560 **FALLOT, Roger D.**
"The impact on mood of verbal reminiscing in later adulthood"
International Journal of Human Development, no.10 (1979), pp.385-400
Questions the age-specific nature of the mood change brought about by reminiscing.

561 **FARADAY, Annabel and PLUMMER, Kenneth**
"Doing life histories"
The Sociological Review, vol.27, no. 4 (Nov. 1979) pp.773-798
The sociologist's experience of interviewing.

562 **FARRELL, Edmund**
"Oral histories as living literature"
English Journal, no.71 (April 1982), pp.87-92

FARRELL, James *see* **FARRELL, Terrance**

563 FARRELL, Robert
Benwhat and Corbie Craigs: a brief history
Cumnock, Strathclyde: Cumnock and Doon
Valley District Council/Manpower Services
Commission, 1983
24pp; bibliography
An oral history of two Scottish mining
communities.

**564 FARRELL, Terrance, FARRELL, James and
TOMLIN, David**
"A glancing view of childhood: Bow Bridge
Island Council Estate 1947-1962"
Oral History, vol.16, no.1 (1988), pp.25-33
This study of a post-war London housing
estate made the Bow Group winners of the
London Weekend Television History of
London competition.

565 FEIERMAN, Steven
The Shambaa Kingdom
University of Wisconsin Press, 1974
235pp; bibliography
Chapter five for the pre-colonial African
economy from oral testimony.

FENICHEL, C.H. *see* **MORANTZ, Regina
Markell**

566 FERGUSON, Ted
Sentimental journey: an oral history of train
travel in Canada
Toronto: Doubleday Canada, 1985
246pp

567 FERRIS, Paul
Dylan Thomas
Hodder and Stoughton, 1977
399pp
An example of the use of oral evidence in a
recent literary biography of Wales' foremost
twentieth century writer. It includes 200
interviews with people in the Swansea area.

568 FESTING, Sally
Fishermen: a community living from the sea
Newton Abbot: David and Charles, 1977
206pp; bibliography
Based on interviews with East Anglian
fishermen.

569 FESTING, Sally
"The temptations of the tape recorder"
The Times Educational Supplement, 2
December 1977

570 FIDO, Rebecca and POTTS, Maggie
"'It's not true what was written down':
experiences of life in a mental handicap
institution"
Oral History, vol.17, no.2 (1989), pp.31-4
An innovative article using the memories of
the mentally ill themselves.

571 FIELD, Clive
"A sociological profile of English Methodism
1900-1932"
Oral History, vol.4, no.1 (1976), pp.73-95
Based on a mixture of questionnaires and
interviews. Includes a useful bibliography on
religious Methodism.

FIELD, John *see* **COLLEDGE, Dave**

572 FIELDING, P.A.
"An exploratory investigation of self-concept
in the institutionalised elderly and a
comparison with nurses' conceptions and
attitudes"
International Journal of Nursing Studies, no.16
(1979), pp.345-56

573 FIELDS, Karen
"What one cannot remember mistakenly"
Oral History, vol.17, no.1 (1989), pp.44-53
The effects of memory changes on oral
history.

574 FIGLIO, Karl
"Oral history and the unconscious"
History Workshop, no.26 (Autumn 1988),
pp.120-32
Part of a special issue on psychoanalysis and
history.

575 FILIPPELLI, R.L.
"Oral history and the archives"
American Archivist, vol.39, no.4 (October,
1976), pp.479-83
Argues that oral history transcripts should be
handled in the same way as original
manuscripts.

576 FINNEGAN, Ruth
"A note on oral tradition and historical
evidence"
History and Theory, vol.9, no.2 (1970),
pp.195-201

577 FINNEGAN, Ruth
Oral literature in Africa
Oxford: Oxford University Press, 1976; first
published Clarendon, 1970
558pp; bibliography
An introduction to the unwritten literature of
Africa: its social as well as literary aspects.

578 FISHER, Josey G. (ed.)
The persistence of youth: oral testimonies of the
Holocaust
Westport and London: Meckler, 1990
175pp
Drawn from the Holocaust Oral History
Archive of Gratz University.

579 FISHER, Ray
"A tremendous sort of feeling: an interview by
Howard Glasser, October 3, 1973"
Sing Out!, no.22 (January/February 1973),
pp.2-8

580 FISHMAN, William Jack
East End Jewish radicals, 1875-1914
Duckworth, 1975
336pp; bibliography
Based on a variety of unpublished
autobiographical material including the
reminiscences of 'old survivors'.

FITZGERALD, J.M *see* **LAWRENCE, R.**

FITZGERALD, Oscar *see* **COLLINS, James**

581 FITZGIBBON, Constantine
The Blitz
Allan Wingate, 1957
272pp
One of the first post-war books to use eye-
witness accounts of the Blitz from individual
Londoners, complemented by Henry Moore's
war sketches.

582 FITZPATRICK, Jim and REID, Stuart
"Indexing a large scale oral history project"
Oral History, vol.15, no.1 (1987), pp.54-7
The experience of indexing from a National
Library of Australia project entitled 'The
Cultural Context of Unemployment: An Oral
Record', which interviewed unemployed
young people.

583 FLEETWOOD, Jenni (ed.)
Leiston looks back, 1925-1950
Leiston, Suffolk: Leiston High School, 1989
88pp
Sixteen pupils aged nine to thirteen started
interviewing in October 1988 under the
guidance of the editor as writer-in-residence.

584 FLEMING, Denis
The Manchester fighters
Manchester: Neil Richardson, 1986
64pp
A celebration of the famous Manchester
fighters of the 1920s and 1930s: boxing booths,
the Collyhurst Stable, Belle Vue, managers
and money.

585 FLETCHER, William P.
Recording your family history: a guide to
preserving oral history with videotape,
audiotape, suggested topics and questions,
interview techniques
Berkeley, California: Ten Speed Press, 1989
Bibliography

586 FLOWER, Robin
The western island, or, The Great Blasket
Oxford: Clarendon, 1944; reprinted Oxford
University Press, 1978
143pp
A study of the lives of the peasantry and
labourers of the West of Ireland, based
entirely on oral sources.

587 FLYNN, Tony
The history of Salford cinemas
Manchester: Neil Richardson, 1987
44pp
Recorded recollections with cinema goers to
over thirty Salford cinemas.

588 FOGERTY, James E.
"Filling the gap: oral history in archives"
American Archivist, vol.46, no.2 (Spring 1983),
pp.148-57
Looks at the way oral history can make up for
deficiencies in written sources by providing
background and new perspectives.

589 FOLEY, John Miles (ed.)
Oral traditional literature: a festschrift for Albert
Bates Lord
Columbus, Ohio: Slavica, 1981
461pp
For oral history in non-literate societies.

590 FOLGUERA, Pilar
"City space and the daily life of women in
Madrid in the 1920s"
Oral History, vol.13, no.2 (1985), pp.49-56

591-600 FOLKWAYS RECORDS

591   *1,2,3, and a zing, zing, zing: street games and songs of the children of New York City*
New York: Folkways Records, 1953
One twenty-five minute record and booklet
A collection from West Midtown, Manhattan featuring children aged from 4 to 17 from Black, Puerto Rican, French and mixed race backgrounds.

592   *The sit-in story: the story of the lunch-room sit-ins*
New York: Folkways Records FH5502, 1961
One LP record
Participants, including Martin Luther King, talk about a series of sit-ins in canteens and restaurants in the American south in 1960 to protest against racial segregation.

593   *The House Committee on Un-American Activities: hearings in San Francisco, May 1960. Excerpts from the actual hearings, interviews outside the court-room and from eyewitness accounts*
New York: Folkways Records FD5530, 1961
One LP record

594   *Bertolt Brecht before the Committee on Un-American Activities. An historical encounter*
New York: Folkways Records FD5531, 1963
One LP record
The actual recording of Brecht's appearance on 30 October 1947.

595   *An interview with Henry Miller*
New York: Folkways Records FL9724, 1964
One LP record

596   *Excerpts from interviews with Dock Boggs, legendary banjo player and singer*
New York: Folkways Records FH5458, 1965
One LP record
Boggs talks about learning the banjo and playing in a band for a living.

597   *Born to live: Hiroshima*
New York: Folkways Records FD5525, 1965
One LP record
A radio documentary compiled and edited by Studs Terkel in which he interviews Hiroshima survivors and talks to a variety of people about the atomic age including Simone de Beauvoir, Pete Seeger, Sean O'Casey, Bertrand Russell and Arthur C.Clarke.

598   *Interview with Sir Edmund Hillary: mountain climbing*
New York: Folkways Records FX6102, 1974
One LP record
Hillary talks about the dangers of mountaineering, equipment and techniques, the Everest Expedition, the abominable snowman, women mountaineers and climbing personalities.

599   *Interviews with Phil Ochs*
New York: Folkways Records FH5321, 1976
One LP record
In which he talks about the music industry in the early 1960s, Bob Dylan, the Kennedy Assassination, the Woody Guthrie Memorial Concert, Vietnam and West Coast music.

600   *Interview with Antonio Salemme, sculptor and painter*
New York: Folkways Records FX6004, 1978
Two LP records
Interviewed by Peter O'Brien.

601   FONTANA, Bernard
"American Indian oral history"
History and Theory, vol.8 (1969), pp.366-70

602   FORD, Amos A.
Telling the truth: the life and times of the British Honduran Forestry Unit in Scotland (1941-44)
Karia Press, 1984
96pp
The author was himself a member of the unit.

603   FORD, Janet and SINCLAIR, Ruth
Sixty years on: women talk about old age
Women's Press, 1987
168pp
Aims to overturn stereotypes about old age through interviews with fourteen women aged between sixty and ninety living in the West Midlands who talk about difficulties adjusting to old age, overcoming problems of loneliness and immobility, and trying to retain independence and a sense of purpose.

604   FOREST HILL SCHOOL
South east London in the second world war: reminiscences of residents gathered by the boys of Forest Hill School
Forest Hill School, 1987
26pp

605   FOREST HISTORY
Journal of the Forest History Society, Santa Cruz, (US)
Special issue vol.16, no.3 (1972) on oral history.

606   FORMAN, Charles
Industrial town: self-portrait of St.Helens in the 1920s
Cameron and Taylor, 1978; St.Albans, Hertfordshire: Granada Publishing, 1979
272pp
A collection of some seventy accounts covering every aspect of life in a North West mining community between the wars.

607   FORMAN, Deborah
"Inheriting the Holocaust"
Boston, no.73 (November 1981), pp.156-9, 213-7
Outlines the work of One Generation After, an organisation which has interviewed survivors and their children. Four families feature here.

608   FORONDA, Marcelino A.
"Oral history in the Philippines: trends and prospects"
International Journal of Oral History, vol.2, no.1 (February 1981), pp.13-25
A review of a number of mainly academic-based projects which all face the common problem of lack of funding.

609   FOSTER, Janet and SHEPPARD, Julia
British Archives
Macmillan, 1989; first edition, 1982
834pp
Includes information on oral archives but now superseded by the British Library National Sound Archive's *Directory of Recorded Sound Resources*.

610   FOSTER, Nikki
"Old Times"
New Society, 2 January 1987
A view of an old people's home run more for the benefit of its staff than its residents.

611   FOTHERGILL, Robert A.
Private chronicles: a study of English diaries
Oxford University Press, 1974
214pp; bibliography
A study of the diary as a genre of personal testimony.

FOX, Anne Valley *see* KEEN, Sam

612   FOX, John J.
"Bibliographic update"
Oral History Review, vol.5 (1977), pp.48-57
Updates Waserman's 1975 revision for US oral history publications.

613   FOX, John J.
"Window on the past: a guide to oral history"
Choice, vol.17 (June 1980), pp.495-508
A large bibliography covering US guides, manuals and catalogues.

FOXFIRE *see* WIGGINTON, Eliot (ed.)

614   FRANCIS, Hywel
"Welsh miners and the Spanish Civil War"
Journal of Contemporary History, vol.53, no.3 (1970)

615   FRANCIS, Hywel
"South Wales" in SKELLEY, Geoffrey (ed.), *The General Strike, 1926, Lawrence and Wishart, 1976*

616   FRANCIS, Hywel
"The background and motives of Welsh volunteers in the International Brigades, 1936-1938"
International Journal of Oral History, vol.2, no.2 (June 1981), pp.84-108
In this study of Welsh involvement in the Spanish Civil War oral history was used due to the paucity of written sources.

617   FRANCIS, Hywel
"The voice of an immigrant into the South Wales coalfield: Dick Cooke"
Oral History, vol.9, no.2 (1981), pp.42-8
Part of the South Wales Coalfield History Project which interviewed 176 people.

618   FRANCIS, Hywel
Miners against fascism: Wales and the Spanish Civil War
Lawrence and Wishart, 1984
304pp
An account of South Wales miners' response to and involvement in the war in Spain, and the socio-political background.

619   FRANCIS, Hywel and HOWELLS, Kim
"The politics of coal in South Wales 1945-8"
Llafur, vol.3, no.3 (1978), pp.74-85
Based on the Social Science Research Council Coalfield Research Project which used oral history video recording to complement traditional sources and focussed on the changeover from private to public ownership after the war.

620 FRANCIS, Hywel and SMITH, David
The Fed: a history of the South Wales miners in the twentieth century
Lawrence and Wishart, 1980
530pp; bibliography
A model trade union history based on extensive interviewing.

FRANK, Benis *see* COLLINS, James

621 FRANK, Peter
"Women's work in the Yorkshire inshore fishing industry"
Oral History, vol.4, no.1 (1976), pp.57-72

FRANKEL, R. *see* LESSER, J.

622 FRANKENBERG, Ronald
Village on the border: a social study of religion, politics and football in a North Wales community
Cohen & West, 1957
163pp; bibliography
An anthropological study of the author's own village in North Wales where most of the inhabitants work in the nearby English town.

623 FRASER, Ronald (ed.)
Work: twenty personal accounts
Harmondsworth: Penguin Books in association with New Left Review, *1968; 1969*
298pp

624 FRASER, Ronald
In hiding: the life of Manuel Cortes
Allen Lane, 1972; Harmondsworth: Penguin, 1982
238pp
Manuel Cortes, the last Republican mayor of a small Spanish village before it fell to Franco forces during the Civil War, emerged in 1969 after thirty years hiding from the regime. This is a direct account of his and his family's experiences from interviews which started three months after he emerged.

625 FRASER, Ronald
The pueblo: a mountain village on the Costa del Sol
Allen Lane, 1973
285pp
A study of the people of Tajos in the Malaga Province based on the author's time living there in 1957.

626 FRASER, Ronald
Blood of Spain: the experience of the civil war, 1936-1939
Allen Lane, 1979; Harmondsworth: Penguin, 1981
628pp; bibliography
A detailed view of the period through personal testimony from participants in five areas recorded in Spain and France between June 1973 and May 1975. The focus is on the everyday existence of those not directly involved in the fighting. (*See also* KELLY, Jim)

627 FRASER, Ronald
In search of a past: the Manor House, Amnersfield, 1933-1945
Verso, 1984
187pp
The author's autobiography, compiled from his own recollections and interviews with servants who worked at the manor when he was a child. Good on the influence of inner consciousness and subjectivity.

628 FRASER, Ronald (ed.)
1968: a student generation in revolt
Chatto & Windus, 1988
370pp; bibliography
A study of the student rebellions of the 1960s in the United States, West Germany, France, Italy, Britain and Northern Ireland based on interviews conducted in 1984-5. Nine oral historians contribute making it the first large scale international oral history of its kind.

629 FREEDMAN, Lawrence
Britain and the Falklands war
Basil Blackwell, 1988
Making Contemporary Britain series
188pp; bibliography
Makes use of interviews carried out by MORI polls in April to June 1982 and aims to present a balanced account.

630 FREEMAN, James M.
Untouchable: an Indian life history
Allen & Unwin, 1979
421pp; bibliography
The oral autobiography of Muli, a lower caste Indian, as told to Freeman.

631 **FRIEDLANDER, Peter**
The emergence of a UAW local, 1936-1939: a study in class and culture
Feffer and Simons, 1976
155pp
On unionisation and strikes: based mainly on the oral testimony of the local's president, Edmund Kord. The introduction also discusses oral history's role in Marxist philosophy of history, and the role of oral history theory in field work.

632 **FRIENDS OF THE PEOPLE'S PALACE**
Barrapatter: an oral history of Glasgow's Barrows: compiled from tapes kept at the People's Palace Museum
Glasgow: Friends of the People's Palace, 1983
32pp
A well-known market in Glasgow's East End, presented in the local people's own words.

633 **FRIENDSHIP GROUP**
A potpourri of tales
Edinburgh: Community Printshop, Drummond High School, 1989
17pp
Memories in poetry and prose of the Dalry area of Edinburgh.

634 **FROGGATT, Alison**
"Keeping the home fires burning: women's lives in the First World War"
New Age, Spring 1984
Draws on interviews made in Airedale, West Yorkshire.

635 *Frontiers: a Journal of Women's Studies*
Vol.2, no.2, 1977: Special issue on women's oral history
Includes resource section with bibliography, in an issue which "reflects the strengths and weaknesses of American oral history".

636 **FROST, Debbie and TAYLOR, Kay**
"Life story books: this is my life"
Community Care, 7 November 1986

637 **FROSTICK, Elizabeth**
"The use of oral evidence in the reconstruction of dental history at Beamish Museum"
Oral History, vol.14, no.2 (1986), pp.59-65

638 **FRY, Amelia**
"The nine commandments of oral history"
Journal of Library History, vol.3 (January 1968), pp.63-73
A spoof with some serious points about the art of interviewing.

639 **FRY, Amelia**
"Persistent issues in oral history"
Journal of Library History, vol.4 (July 1969)

640 **FRY, Amelia**
"Reflections on ethics"
Oral History Review, vol.3 (1975), pp.16-28
A review of the Oral History Association's guidelines.

641 **FRY, Amelia and BAUM, Willa K.**
"A Janus look at oral history"
The American Archivist, vol.32 (October 1969), pp.319-26
The origins of oral history in the United States and a summary of its problems and challenges.

642 **FRY, Gladys-Marie**
Night riders in black folk history
Knoxville: University of Tennessee Press, 1975
252pp
Through extensive interviews with descendants of slaves who migrated to the Washington DC area in the post Civil War period, together with a broad use of the slave narrative collected by the WPA, the author puts forward a Black 'folkview' of the various supernatural and 'bogey' figures used to terrorise the Blacks.

643 **FRY, P.S.**
"Structured and unstructured reminiscence training and depression among the elderly"
Clinical Gerontology, 1983, pp.15-37
Shows that structured reminiscence yields better results.

644 **FULCHER, Ernest A. (ed.)**
A century of Woodford memories
Woodford, Essex: Woodford and District Historical Society, 1986
68pp

645 **FYFE, Judith and MANSON, Hugo**
The gamble: the campaign diary of the Challengers
Auckland, New Zealand: Australia and New Zealand Book Company, 1984
175pp
The story of an election campaign based on daily tape recordings with five leading politicians, the challengers in one of New Zealand's most unusual and unpredictable elections this century.

646 **FYFE, Judith and MANSON, Hugo**
Oral history and how to approach it
Wellington, New Zealand: New Zealand Oral
History Archive, 1989
12pp
Guidelines for oral history recording.

647 **GALLACHER, Cathryn A. and TRELEVEN,**
Dale E.
"Developing an online database and printed
directory and subject guide to oral history
collections"
Oral History Review, vol.16, no.1 (Spring
1988), pp.33-68
Gallacher worked at Avon County Library in
Bristol; Treleven is director of the UCLA
Oral History Program.

648 **GALLAGHER, Dorothy**
Hannah's daughters: six generations of an
American family, 1876-1976
New York: Thomas Cromwell, 1976
343pp
The oral history of a white working class
family in the states of Michigan and
Washington based on six weeks of
conversations in 1974.

649 **GANNAGE, Charlene**
Double day double bind: women garment
workers
Toronto, Ontario: Women's Press, 1986
253pp; bibliography
Women, many of them migrant workers, from
a small garment shop in Toronto talk frankly
about their work and unionisation.

650 **GANT, Robert**
"Extreme weather conditions in the Honddu
Valley: oral evidence and the documentary
record"
Gwent Local History, no.57 (1984), pp.23-7

651 **GANT, Robert**
"Oral history and local meteorology"
Oral History, vol.14, no.2 (1986), pp.67-9

652 **GARDNER, Joel**
"Oral history: the visual element"
Phonographic Bulletin, no.23 (April 1979),
pp.4-8
Video recording at the UCLA Oral History
Program began as early as 1973.

653 **GARDNER, Joel**
Oral history for Louisiana
Baton Rouge: Louisiana State Archives and
Records Service, 1981
28pp

654 **GARDNER, Joel**
"A bibliography on oral history"
ALA Bulletin, no.48 (1985), pp.24-7

655 **GARNER, Van H.**
Oral history: a new experience in learning
Dayton: Pflaum, 1975

656 **GARRETT, Annette**
Interviewing, its principles and methods
New York: Family Service Association of
America, 1982, third revised edition
186pp
How to become an effective and sensitive
interviewer - written for social workers, but
useful for oral historians.

657 **GARWOOD, John**
Chorley Pals 'Y' Company, 11th (Service)
Battalion, East Lancashire Regiment: a short
history of the company in the Great War,
1914-1919
Manchester: Neil Richardson, 1989
56pp
Includes recollections.

658 **GATEHOUSE PROJECT**
Just lately I realise
Manchester: Gatehouse Project, 1985
23pp
Memories of five people's childhoods in
Tobago and Jamaica, and coming to Britain in
the 1950s and 1960s.

659 **GATEHOUSE PROJECT**
Day in day out: memories of North Manchester
from women in Monsall Hospital
Manchester: Gatehouse Project, 1985
39pp
A selection of taped conversations in wards 10
and 14 at Monsall Hospital with women aged
seventy to ninety, many of them recovering
from falls and strokes. They discuss their
childhood, work, home life, the war and
leisure.

660 **GATEHOUSE PROJECT**
Then and now: a resource pack for reminiscence
work with the elderly
Manchester: Gatehouse Project, 1986
A pack of material including sample workshop
plans, listening skills, using your local library,
resource list and bibliography, and places to
visit in the Manchester area, plus a report on
two reminiscence projects in north
Manchester.

GEARING, Brian *see* **CORNWELL, Jocelyn**

661 GENOVESE, Eugene D.
Roll, Jordan, roll: the world the slaves made
Deutsch, 1975; first published New York:
Pantheon, 1974
825pp
A monumental study of American slavery
drawing on a variety of slave narrative and
testimony, including interviews with ex-slaves
carried out by the Federal Writers' Project of
the New Deal Works Project Administration
in the 1930s.

GEORGAKAS, Dan *see* **BIRD, Stewart**

662 GERARD, David
Librarians speaking
Aberystwyth, Wales: College of Librarianship
Wales, 1979
Sixteen tapes of conversations with eminent
librarians covering the changes in the
profession over the last half-century as well as
details of their working lives. Librarians from
adult education, Oxford colleges and public
libraries are all represented.

663 GERASSI, John
The premature antifascists: North American
volunteers in the Spanish Civil War, 1936-39, an
oral history
New York: Praeger, 1986
275pp; bibliography

664 GERSHON, Karen
We came as children: a collective autobiography
of refugees
Gollancz, 1966; Papermac reprint, 1989
178pp
Testimony from 240 of the 10,000 children,
mainly Jewish, who fled to Britain from Nazi
repression in the winter and spring of 1938/9.
Known as the 'Kindertransporte', many never
saw their parents again.

GIBBS, Richard *see* **CHRISP, Peter**

665 GIBSON, Colin (ed.)
Our Ollerton: a collection of photographs and
memories
Newark: Newark and Sherwood District
Council Recreation and Tourism Department,
1986
60pp
A series of unattributed recollections of a
Nottinghamshire mining community.

666 GIBSON, Douglas M.
"Oral history: a publisher's perspective"
Canadian Oral History Association Journal,
vol.4, no.2 (1980), pp.1-8
A discussion on selecting and editing oral
histories for publication, and of some of the
ethical questions raised.

667 GIBSON, Faith
Do you mind the time?
Help the Aged, nd
A Northern Ireland version of *Recall* (see
HELP THE AGED) featuring four
sequences, each of forty slides and an eight
page booklet of background notes and cue
questions to encourage reminiscence amongst
older people. The emphasis is on four aspects
of Ulster life: city, country, family and social
life.

668 GIBSON, Faith
Using reminiscence: a training pack
Help the Aged, 1989
A pack comprising a tape/slide programme of
forty coloured slides with commentary
depicting reminiscence groups in a hospital
and residential home; a 48 minute VHS video
film with transcript showing the operation of a
weekly reminiscence group in a residential
home; and a manual explaining the theoretical
ideas underlying reminiscence work with
individuals and groups (with a guide to
resources).

GIBSON, Faith *see also* **DALLAT, Cahal**

669 GILBERT, G.N.
"Being interviewed: a role analysis"
Social Science Information, vol.19 (1980)

670 GILBERT, Kevin
Living black: blacks to Kevin Gilbert
Allen Lane, 1977
305pp
Testimony from Australian blacks.

671 GILBERT, Martin
The Holocaust: the Jewish tragedy
Fontana, 1987; first published Collins, 1986
959pp
A monumental history of the Nazi destruction
of European Jewry drawn from many sources
including the disturbing testimony of
survivors.

672 GILDING, Bob
The journeyman coopers of East London: workers' control in an old London trade
Oxford: Oxford History Workshop, Ruskin College, 1971
History Workshop pamphlet 4
86pp

673 GILES, L.C. (ed.)
Liphook remembers
Liphook, Hampshire: Bramshott and Liphook Preservation Society, 1987
48pp

GILHOOLY, Mary see HANLEY, Ian

674 GILL, Anton
The journey back from hell: conversations with concentration camp survivors
Grafton, 1988
494pp; bibliography
Interviews with over 120 survivors from fourteen countries, including political prisoners and resistance fighters as well as Jews, examining how the horrific experiences have affected them emotionally, psychologically and politically.

GILLIS, Frank J. see STONE, Ruth M.

675 GILLIS, John R.
For better, for worse: British marriages, 1600 to the present
Oxford: Oxford University Press, 1985
417pp; bibliography

676 GILMOUR, Andrew
My role in the rehabilitation of Singapore: 1946-1953
Singapore: Institute of Southeast Asian Studies, 1973
Oral History Pilot Study no.2
The transcript of an interview with the British Colonial Secretary involved in Singapore's post-war economic reconstruction.

677 GINGELL, Maria and WRIGHT, Mel
"From Vietnam to Catford"
Social Services Insight, 9 October 1987, pp.20-2
Lewisham's Vietnamese People's History Group.

678 GIOGLIO, Gerald P.
Days of decision: an oral history of conscientious objectors in the military during the Vietnam war
Trenton, New Jersey: Broken Rifle Press, 1988
338pp
Based on the experiences of twenty-four in-service objectors.

679 GIRLINGTON LOCAL HISTORY GROUP
This and that
Bradford: Girlington Local History Group, 1989
37pp
An anthology of memories of one area of Bradford, West Yorkshire.

680 GITLER, Ira
Swing to Bop: an oral history of the transition to jazz in the 1940s
Oxford University Press, 1985
331pp
Traces the roots of jazz and the role of the big bands of the 1930s and 1940s.

681 GITTINS, Diana
"Married life and birth control between the wars"
Oral History, vol.3, no.2 (1975), pp.53-64
Based on eighteen interviews with Essex women.

682 GITTINS, Diana
"How the coitus was interrupted"
New Society, 30 September 1976

683 GITTINS, Diana
"Women's work and family size between the wars"
Oral History, vol.5, no.2 (1977), pp.84-100

684 GITTINS, Diana
"Oral history, reliability and recollection" in MOSS, L. and GOLDSTEIN, H. (eds.)

685 GITTINS, Diana
Fair sex: family size and structure, 1900-1939
Hutchinson, 1982
240pp; bibliography
An analysis of the dramatic decline in working class family size between 1900 and 1939 in which interviews revealed that changing economic roles for women and their relationship with men were crucial factors.

686 GITTINS, Diana
"Let the people speak: oral history in Britain"
Victorian Studies, Summer 1983, pp.431-441.

687 GLASER, Barney G. and STRAUSS, Anselm L.
The discovery of grounded theory: strategies for qualitative research
Weidenfeld & Nicolson, 1968
271pp
On interviewing and sociological methods.

688 GLASGOW WOMEN'S STUDY GROUP
Uncharted lives: extracts from Scottish women's experiences 1850-1982
Glasgow: Pressgang, 1983
206pp; bibliography
The first major collection of articles to focus entirely on the lives of women in Scotland: each chapter is based on oral testimony or fresh historical research.

GLASSER, R. *see* HAVIGHURST, R.J.

689 GLASSIE, Henry
Passing the time in Ballymenone: culture and history of an Ulster community
Philadelphia: University of Pennsylvania Press, 1982
852pp
Includes material on space and the community, and folklore fieldwork.

690 GLASSON, Michael
City children: Birmingham children at work and play 1900-1930
Birmingham: Birmingham Museum and Art Gallery, 1985
24pp
Oral histories of changing childhood in the inner city terraces and back-to-backs of Britain's second city.

GLASSON, Michael *see also* MULLINS, Samuel

691 GLENN, Evelyn Nakano
Issei, Nisei, war bride: three generations of Japanese American women in domestic service
Philadelphia: Temple University Press, 1986
290pp
Based on over eighty recorded life stories.

692 GLUCK, Sherna
"Interlude or change: women and the World War II experience"
International Journal of Oral History, vol.3, no.2 (June 1982), pp.92-113
Testimony from forty-three women who worked during the war.

693 GLUCK, Sherna
From parlor to prison: five American suffragists talk about their lives, an oral history
New York: Vintage, 1976
The life stories of five rank-and-file suffragists, the oldest aged 104. The women talk about their reasons for joining and the movement's strategies. The original tapes are available at the Los Angeles Feminist History Research Project.

694 GMELCH, Sharon
Nan: the life of an Irish travelling woman
Souvenir, 1986
239pp; bibliography
An oral biography of Nan Donahue, 1930-1985.

695 GOFFEE, Robert E.
"The butty system and the Kent coalfield"
Bulletin of the Society for the Study of Labour History, no.34 (1977), pp.41-55
Based on interviews with three generations of miners in Aylesham covering the system of sub-contracting known as the butty system, trade union activity and the inter-war slump.

GOFFEE, Robert E. *see* SCASE, Richard

696 GOLD, Don
Until the singing stops: a celebration of life and old age in America
New York: Holt, Rinehart and Winston, 1979
338pp
A collection of edited interviews with twenty Americans aged sixty-five and over.

697 GOLDMAN, Harry
"Workers theatre to Broadway hit: the evolution of an American radical revue"
Oral History, vol.10, no.1 (1982), pp.56-66
'Pins and Needles', a left-wing satirical review, was mounted by the International Ladies' Garment Workers' Union on Broadway in 1937. This article features in-depth interviews with the original cast and production crew.

GOLDSTEIN, Harvey *see* MOSS, Louis

698 GOODWIN, Lawrence
"Populist dreams and Negro rights: East Texas as a case study"
American Historical Review, vol.76, no.1 (1971)

699 GOODY, Jack (ed.)
Literacy in traditional societies
Cambridge: Cambridge University Press, 1968
349pp; bibliography
A series of academic essays revealing the characteristics of oral communication.

700 GORDEN, Raymond L.
Interviewing: strategy, techniques and tactics
Homewood, Illinois: Dorsey Press, 1975

GORDON, S.K. *see* **BOYLIN, W.**

701 GORELL, Gill
"Systems theory and family therapy"
see RUTTER, M. and HERSOV, L. (eds.)
Child and adolescent psychiatry: modern approaches
Oxford: Blackwell Scientific, 1985; first published as Child psychiatry, *1976*
960pp; bibliography

702 GORER, Geoffrey
Himalayan village: an account of the Lepchas of Sikkim
Gloucester: Alan Sutton, 1984, second edition; first edition 1938
488pp
A portrayal of the social life of a tribe which had had no previous contact with Europeans, based on life stories and oral testimonies gathered in 1937.

703 GOTTSCHALK, L., KLUCKHOHN, C. and ANGELL, R.
The use of personal documents in history, anthropology and sociology
New York: Social Research Council, 1947
243pp

704 GOUGH, Richard
The history of Myddle
Caliban, 1979; Harmondsworth: Penguin, 1981; Macdonald Futura, 1981; Folio Society, 1983
313pp
Reprint of a history written in the early 1700s, first published in 1834 under the title *Human nature displayed in the history of Myddle*, and now hailed as 'a fore-runner of oral history'. The Penguin edition has a modern introduction.

705 GOULBOURNE, Harry
"Oral history and black labour: an overview"
Oral History, vol.8, no.1 (1980), pp.24-34
Illustrates the value of oral history where written sources are so patchy.

706 GOULD, Fraser
"The Jordanhill Local History Archive Project"
Scottish Library Association News, no.157 (May/June 1980), pp.85-6
An MSC-funded scheme which employed forty people between 1977 and 1979.

707 GOULD, Tony and KENYON, Joe
Stories from the dole queue
Temple Smith/New Society, 1972
192pp
A compilation of extensive tape-recorded conversations about the effects of unemployment and poverty. Kenyon was founder and national organiser of the Claimants and Unemployed Workers' Union.

708 GOW, Neil
"Oral history bibliography"
Australian Historical Association Bulletin, no.1 (March 1976), pp.24-40

709 GRAEF, Roger
Talking blues: the police in their own words
Collins Harvill, 1989
512pp; bibliography
'An emotional mosaic' in which some 500 serving officers of every rank from twelve forces all over Britain and Northern Ireland speak about every aspect of their work and how the 1980s has seen a transformation in policing.

710 GRAFTON, Pete
You, you, you: the people out of step with World War II
Pluto, 1981
169pp
The taped voices of people who didn't 'fit in', particularly blacks, pacifists and conscientious objectors. The book is critical of the myth of comradeship and togetherness.

711 GRAHAM, Stanley
"The Lancashire textile project: a description of the work and some of the techniques involved"
Oral History, vol.8, no.2 (1980), pp.48-52

712 GRAINGER, Bruce
"Information sources for oral history in Canada"
Ontario Library Review, no.62, no.2 (June 1981), pp.124-8
An annotated list and bibliography of associations, periodicals, union catalogues, books and programmes.

713 **GRANATSTEIN, J.L.**
"Oral interviews: York University Oral
History Programme"
Canadian Archivist, vol.2, no.2 (1971), pp.32-6

714 **GRANATSTEIN, J.L.**
"Canadian public figures on tape"
The Canadian Forum, January 1974, pp.39-40

715 **GRANT, David**
*Out in the cold: pacifists and conscientious
objectors in New Zealand during World War
Two*
*Auckland, New Zealand: Reed Methuen
Publishers, 1986*
270pp; bibliography
Drawing on numerous interviews with those
who refused to fight for religious, political and
humanitarian reasons.

716 **GRAY, Nigel**
*The worst of times: an oral history of the Great
Depression in Britain*
Wildwood House, 1985
201pp
Personal recollections of working-class life in
the 1920s and 1930s, reproduced verbatim
from thirty-nine interviews with people from
all over Britain: Aberdeen, Ashton-under-
Lyne, Barnsley, Caerphilly, Forest of Dean,
Lancaster, Leicestershire, London,
Manchester, Rochdale, Salford and South
Shields.

717 **GRAY, Richard**
"History is what you want to say - publishing
people's history: the experience of Peckham
People's History Group"
Oral History, vol.12, no.2 (1984), pp.38-46

718 **GRAYZEL, Susan**
"'Many clear words to say': Afro-American,
oral and feminist history" in ARCHER,
Leonie (ed.) *Slavery and other forms of unfree
labour*, Routledge 1988, pp.251-61
An article about the Black Women Oral
History project set up in 1976 at Radcliffe
College, Cambridge, Massachusetts. (*See also*
HILL, Ruth E.)

719 **GREEN, Jonathon**
*Days in the life: voices from the English
underground, 1961-1971*
Heinemann, 1988
468pp
Verbatim extracts from interviews with 101
varied people about 'alternative society' in
England in the mid and late 1960s: hippies,
squatters, macrobiotics, the New Left, 'Oz',
CND, jazz, mods, drugs, pop art and sex.

720 **GREENE, R.R.**
"Life review: a technique for clarifying family
roles in adulthood"
*Clinical Gerontologist, vol.1, no.2 (Winter
1982), pp.59-67*
Life review as a way of helping older people
adjust to role changes in later adulthood.

GREENER, Peter *see* **SHORT, David**

721 **GREENLEAF, Richard E. and MEYER,
Michael C. (eds.)**
*Research in Mexican history: topics,
methodology, sources and a practical guide to
field research*
Lincoln: University of Nebraska Press, 1973
226pp; bibliographies

722 **GREIG, John, SAVAGE, Bryony, DARGUE,
Coral and KIRKWOOD-SMITH, Lorna**
Leith lives
Edinburgh: Leith Lives, nd
36pp; bibliography
A history of Leith. (*See also* LEITH LOCAL
HISTORY PROJECT)

723 **GRELE, Ronald (ed.)**
Envelopes of sound: the art of oral history
Chicago: Precedent, 1975; second edition, 1985
283pp
Articles on various aspects of oral testimony,
including an interview with Studs Terkel, a
panel discussion, and sections on oral history
as poetry, the interpretation of interviews and
public presentation.

724 **GRELE, Ronald**
"Can anyone over thirty be trusted: a friendly
critique of oral history"
Oral History Review, vol.6 (1978), pp.36-44
Argues that oral history must candidly assess
its role and achievement: that there is danger
in seeing it as a panacea to revitalise history
generally and that oral history tends to
encourage a personalised and self-justificatory
history.

725   **GRELE, Ronald**
"Listen to their voices: two case studies in the interpretation of oral history interviews"
Oral History, vol.7, no.1 (1979), pp.33-42

726   **GRELE, Ronald**
"Oral history and archives"
Phonographic Bulletin, no.37 (November 1983), pp.12-15

727   **GRIFFITH, Kenneth and O'GRADY, Timothy E.**
Curious journey: an oral history of Ireland's unfinished revolution
Hutchinson, 1982
376pp; bibliography
Nine Irish men and women from all parts of Ireland give their personal accounts of the 1916 Easter Rising, the Tan War and the Civil War in the 1920s, and their views on present day Ireland.

728   **GRIFFITHS, Gareth**
"Museums and the practice of oral history"
Social History Curators' Group Journal, Winter 1986 and Oral History, vol.17, no.2 (1989), pp.49-52
A critique of museums' unquestioning enthusiasm for oral history, the dynamics of interviewing and the reliability of memory.

GRIFFITHS, Gareth *see also* **MULLINS, Samuel**

729   **GRIFFITHS, Helen and BURFORD, Alan**
"Thanks for the memories"
Nursing Times, vol.84, no.36 (7 September 1988)

730   **GRIFFITHS, Paul**
New sounds, new personalities: British composers of the 1980s in conversation with Paul Griffiths
Faber, 1985
212pp
Classical composers of a wide variety of styles, but all in their thirties and early forties, were interviewed at work.

731   **GRIFFITHS, Sally**
Prestonfield remembers: an exploring living memory project. Report on methodology
Edinburgh: Workers' Educational Association South-East Scotland District, 1984
23pp; bibliography
(See also PRESTONFIELD REMEMBERS GROUP)

732   **GRIFFITHS, Sally**
Memories and things: linking museums and libraries and older people
Edinburgh: Edinburgh Workers' Educational Association, 1988
32pp
Includes details of a project to provide 'handling boxes' of museum artefacts to stimulate reminiscence, of people's history groups and outreach work. Complements a slide/tape pack of the same name.

733   **GRIFFITHS, Tom**
"The debate about oral history"
Melbourne History Journal, no.13 (1981), pp.16-21
Assesses the debate between traditional historians and oral historians.

GRIMWOOD, James M. *see* **BROOKS, Courtney G.**

734   **GROVE, Valerie**
The compleat woman. Marriage, motherhood, career: can she have it all?
Chatto and Windus, 1987; Hogarth Press, 1988
293pp
Interviews with twenty-five women, all married for over twenty-five years with three or more children and successful professional lives, in which they explain how they have combined family and occupation. Included are Mary Warnock, Fay Weldon and Elizabeth Longford as well as doctors, writers, journalists, academics and politicians.

735   **GRUNEBERG, M.M., MORRIS, P.E. and SYKES, R.M. (eds.)**
Practical aspects of memory: current research and issues. Volume one: memory in everyday life
Chichester: Wiley, 1988
568pp; bibliography
A selection of papers presented at the Welsh Branch of the British Psychological Society's Second International Conference on Practical Aspects of Memory in Swansea in August 1987. It includes a section on autobiographical memory (pp.228-309). Papers from the first conference were published in 1978 by Academic Press.

736   **GUNSON, Neil**
"Proud shoes: black family history in Australia"
Aboriginal History, vol.5, no.2 (1982), pp.147-52

GUYAUX, Anne *see* **DELCROIX, Catherine**

737 GWALTNEY, John Langston (ed.)
Drylongso: a self-portrait of Black America
New York: Random House, 1980
287pp

738 GWALTNEY, John Langston (ed.)
The dissenters: voices from contemporary America
New York: Random House, 1986
321pp

739 GWYNEDD ARCHIVES SERVICE
Recording the past/Recordio'r gorffennol: a report on the first year of the Gwynedd Archives Service Oral History Project
Caernarfon: Gwynedd Archives Service, 1984
28pp
A bilingual report of an MSC-supported project which carried out over 200 recordings in north Wales in its first year and produced education packs on markets, shopping, domestic service, schooling, workhouses and the Poor Law, and Christmas. Includes some extracts from interviews.

740 GWYNEDD ARCHIVES SERVICE
'Sibols': Hirael childhood 1900-1930 in words and pictures
Caernarfon: Gwynedd Archives Service, 1988
63pp
A portrait of a working class area of Bangor in North Wales through the people themselves who recall housing conditions, homelife, school, sickness, play, Sundays, work, floods, neighbourliness and funerals.

741 HACKNEY READING CENTRE
Every birth it comes different
Hackney Reading Centre/Centerprise Publishing Project, 1980
72pp
A collection of accounts of the experience of childbirth by students and tutors at Hackney Reading Centre.

742 HAGGARD, Lilias Rider
I walked by night: being the life and history of the King of the Norfolk poachers written by himself
Oxford University Press, 1982; Woodbridge: Boydell, 1986; first published 1935
184pp
Early oral autobiography.

743 HAIG-BROWN, Celia
Resistance and renewal: surviving the Indian Residential School
Vancouver, Canada: Tillacum Library, 1988
164pp; bibliography
Thirteen interviews with former Canadian Indian students who attended Kamloops Indian Residential School in British Columbia between 1907 and 1967. They discuss leaving home, surviving the daily routine of school life, and their resistance to the system's oppression of native people and culture.

744 HAIGHT, Barbara K
"The therapeutic role of a structured life review process in homebound elderly subjects"
Journal of Gerontology, vol.43, no.2 (1988), pp.40-4

745 HAIMSON, Leopold H. (ed.)
The making of three Russian revolutionaries: voices from the Menshevik past
Cambridge: Cambridge University Press, 1987
515pp
Three life stories with Lydia Dan, Boris Nicolaevsky and George Denite, recorded between 1960 and 1965, about events surrounding the Russian Revolutions of 1905 and 1917.

746 HAINES, Kevin and SHILTON, Clare
Hard times, good times: tales of Portsea people
Horndean, Hants.: Milestone Publications, 1987
96pp; bibliography

747 HALBERSTAM, David
The best and the brightest
Pan, 1972
831pp; bibliography
A John F. Kennedy Library oral history project about the Vietnam War.

748 HALE, S.M.
"The horse buses stopped north of the Rye"
Case Conference, vol.7, no.6 (November 1960), pp.153-5
One of the first published arguments in Britain for the benefits of reminiscence in work with the elderly.

749   **HALEY, Alex**
Autobiography of Malcolm X
Hutchinson, 1966; Harmondsworth: Penguin,
1968
462pp
As an outspoken defender of Muslim
doctrines, Malcolm X formed the
Organization of Afro-American Unity in 1963
as a breakaway from the Black Muslim
movement. The book is a result of interviews
and includes an epilogue covering Malcolm
X's assassination.

750   **HALEY, Alex**
"Black history, oral history and genealogy"
Oral History Review, vol.1 (1973), pp.1-25

751   **HALEY, Alex**
Roots
Hutchinson, 1977
688pp
A milestone book in which one Black
American's quest to discover his origins led
him back to Africa.

752   **HALL, Adrian**
"A Lincolnshire horseman: work and class"
Oral History, vol.5, no.1 (1977), pp.88-96

753   **HALL, Catherine**
"Married women at home in Birmingham in
the 1920s and 1930s"
Oral History, vol.5, no.2 (1977), pp.62-83

754   **HALL, David**
"History via the eye-witness: one use of local
radio for the teaching of contemporary
history"
*Teaching History, vol.3, no.9 (May 1973),
pp.37-40*

755   **HALL, Phoebe**
*Reforming the welfare: the politics of change in
the personal services*
Heinemann Educational, 1976
162pp
In this study of social welfare services in the
1960s, the author used many interviews.

756   **HALL CARPENTER ARCHIVES GAY
MEN'S ORAL HISTORY GROUP**
Walking after midnight: gay men's life stories
Routledge, 1989
238pp
A milestone book in which fourteen gay men
from a wide range of ages and backgrounds
speak openly about their lives: about being
gay before, during and after the Second World
War; about the influences of books, pubs and
clubs; of the impact of the gay liberation
movement and AIDS. Drawn from the Hall
Carpenter Oral History Archive now at the
National Sound Archive.

757   **HALL CARPENTER ARCHIVES LESBIAN
ORAL HISTORY GROUP**
Inventing ourselves: lesbian life stories
Routledge, 1989
228pp
Important verbatim interviews in which fifteen
women talk openly about childhood, family,
lovers, friends, work, lesbian social and
political life. They cover the peace movement,
the Second World War, the lesbian bar scene,
their experiences of butch-femme, the
Women's Liberation Movement and Black
lesbianism. Drawn from the oral history
project that ran from 1985 to 1989.

758   **HALSTEAD, John, HARRISON, Royden and
STEVENSON, John**
"The reminiscences of Sid Elias"
*Bulletin of the Society for the Study of Labour
History, no.38 (Spring 1979), pp.35-48*
An edited interview transcript concentrating
on Elias' involvement in the National
Unemployed Workers' Movement, the
Communist Party and the British Iron and
Steel Trades Union.

759   **HAM, Joan**
Storrington in living memory
Phillimore, 1982
130pp
Personal recollections of life in West Sussex,
1865-1980.

760   **HAMBURGER, Robert**
*Our portion of hell: Fayette County, Tennessee:
an oral history of the struggle for civil rights*
New York: Links Books, 1973
255pp
The author was a Civil Rights Movement
worker in Fayette County, which has a sixty
per cent black population, and recorded the
interviews in 1971-2.

761 HAMILTON, Nigel
Monty: the making of a general 1887-1942
Hamish Hamilton, 1981; Sevenoaks: Sceptre, 1987
832pp; bibliography
Includes verbatim quotations from forty interviews aiming to personalise this account of the life of Montgomery of Alamein.

762 HAMILTON, Sheila
"Interviewing the middle class: women graduates of the Scottish universities"
Oral History, vol.10, no.2 (1982), pp.58-67

HAMMOND, Joyce see WALSALL LIBRARY AND MUSEUM SERVICES

763 HAMOUDA, Naziha
"Rural women in the Aures: a poetry in context"
Oral History, vol.13, no.1 (1985), pp.43-53
Aures is the largest region of Algeria.

764 HAND, Samuel B.
"Some words on oral histories"
Scholarly Publishing, vol.9 (January 1978), pp.171-85
A bibliographical essay which incorporates a history of the movement in the United States.

765 HANDFIELD, F.G.
History on tape: a guide to oral history in Indiana
Indianapolis: Indiana State Library, 1979

766 HANDFIELD, F.G.
"The importance of video history in libraries"
Drexel Library Quarterly, vol.15, no.4 (October 1979), pp.29-34

767 HANLEY, Ian and GILHOOLY, Mary (eds.)
Psychological therapies for the elderly
Croom Helm, 1986
224p
Includes a chapter by Peter Coleman, "Issues in the therapeutic use of reminiscence with elderly people" (pp.41-65).

768 HARDY, Dennis and WARD, Colin
Arcadia for all: the legacy of a makeshift landscape
Mansell, 1984
307pp
A history of the 'plotlands' of south east England in the first four decades of the century drawing on a small number of interviews.

HARDY, Dennis see also WARD, Colin

769 HAREVEN, Tamara K.
Family time and industrial time: the relationship between the family and work in a New England industrial community
Cambridge: Cambridge University Press, 1982
Interdisciplinary Perspectives on Modern History
474pp; bibliography
Examines the role of the family in the adaption of immigrant labourers to factory work in Manchester, USA.

770 HAREVEN, Tamara K. and LANGENBACH, Randolph
Amoskeag: life and work in an American factory-city in New England
Methuen, 1979
397pp
An outstanding history of the Amoskeag Manufacturing Company, once the largest textile factory in the world, up to its closure, using interviews and photographs of workers and management.

771 HAREVEN, Tamara K. and ADAMS, K.J. (eds.)
Aging and life course transitions: an interdisciplinary perspective
Tavistock Publications, 1982
281pp; bibliography
A multi-disciplinary collection of essays looking at life changes as a whole life process rather than as isolated events.

772 HARKELL, Gina
"The migration of mining families to the Kent coalfield between the wars"
Oral History, vol.6, no.1 (1978), pp.98-113

HARKNESS, Clifford see BUCKLEY, Anthony D.

773 HARMS, Robert W.
River of wealth, river of sorrow: the central Zaire basin in the era of the slave and ivory trade, 1500-1891
New Haven and London: Yale University Press, 1981
277pp; bibliography
The transformation of an African society under the impact of an expanding world economy, based on fieldwork in 1975 and 1976 with the Moye fishermen living along the Ubangi River.

HARRIS, Christopher C. see ROSSER, Colin

774 HARRIS, Kenneth
Conversations
Hodder and Stoughton, 1967
286pp
Interviews with a variety of public figures in sport, politics and journalism.

775 HARRIS, Kenneth
Kenneth Harris talking to
Weidenfeld and Nicolson, 1971
150pp
Two volumes of interviews with public figures (mainly politicians) ranging from Bertrand Russell to the Duke of Windsor, originally conducted for press or broadcasting.

776 HARRIS, Mollie
From Acre End: portrait of a village
Chatto and Windus, 1982
153pp
An evocative portrait of Eynsham in the first quarter of the century: a village to the west of Oxford, through the memories of twenty-four people, the oldest born in 1889.

777 HARRIS, Ramon I., CASH, Joseph H., HOOVER, Herbert T., and WARD, Stephen
The practice of oral history, a handbook
Glen Rock, New Jersey: Microfilming Corporation of America, 1975
98pp
Useful guidelines for fieldwork based on the American Indian Oral History Project at the University of South Dakota.

778 HARRIS, Raymond and HARRIS, Sarah
"Therapeutic uses of oral history techniques in medicine"
International Journal on Aging and Human Development, vol.12, no.1 (1980-1), pp.27-34

779 HARRISON, Brian
"Tape recorders and the teaching of history"
Oral History, vol.1, no.2 (1971), pp.3-10

780 HARRISON, Brian
"Oral history and recent political history"
Oral History, vol.1, no.3 (1972), pp.30-48

781 HARRISON, Brian
"For Church, Queen and Family: the Girls' Friendly Society 1874-1920"
Past and Present, November 1973

782 HARRISON, Brian
Separate spheres: the opposition to women's suffrage in Britain
Croom Helm, 1978
274pp; bibliographical note

783 HARRISON, Brian
Prudent revolutionaries: portraits of British feminists between the wars
Oxford: Clarendon, 1987
410pp; bibliography
A portrayal of fourteen prominent women and two men, ranging from non-militant suffragists and militant suffragettes to Labour MPs and the first woman cabinet minister.

784 HARRISON, Helen (ed.)
Selection in sound archives: collected papers from IASA conference sessions
Milton Keynes: International Association of Sound Archives, 1984
Special publications no.5
128pp
Includes articles on oral history archive selection policy by David Lance and Peter Hart of the Imperial War Museum.

785 HARRISON, Mary
"Domestic service between the wars: the experience of two rural women"
Oral History, vol.16, no.1 (1988), pp.48-54

786 HARRISON, Phyllis (ed.)
The home children: their personal stories
Winnipeg, Canada: Watson and Dwyer, 1979
271pp
Moving stories from some of 100,000 British 'home' children sent to work on Canadian farms from the 1870s to the 1930s. They recall the sea voyage, arrival, loneliness and separation, the harsh conditions of work, and discrimination. (*See also* BEAN, Philip)

787 HARRISON, Robert
"A study of oral history librarianship in England and Wales"
Unpublished BA Librarianship Studies thesis, Manchester Polytechnic, 1980

788 HARRISON, Royden and SEYD, Pat
"An interview with Len Youle"
Bulletin of the Society for the Study of Labour History, no.20 (Spring 1970), pp.35-41
Born in 1890, Youle was a leader of the Left in Sheffield.

HARRISON, Royden see also **HALSTEAD, John**

789 HARRISON, Stephen
Yorkshire farming memories: a collection of photographs, recollections and poems
York: York Castle Museum, 1981
Booklet (44pp) and audio cassette
An innovative compilation based on interviews recorded between 1978-1980 with active and retired farmworkers who discuss Martinmas hiring fairs, horses, ploughing, pig killing, food, harvest, leisure, religion, markets and changes in farming methods.

790 HART, Carroll
"The new documentation: oral history and photography"
Drexel Library Quarterly, vol.15, no.4 (October 1979), pp.5-11
The value of photographs in enriching oral testimony, with examples of successful use in Georgia and Michigan.

791 HART, Lorraine and LIBOVICH, Sue (eds.)
Jewish East End education pack
Tower Hamlet Environment Trust, 1988
A schools pack aimed at the 9-16 age range which uses interviews from the Jewish Women in London Archive to give a view of Jewish East Enders' experiences of immigration, homelife, work, politics and anti-semitism.

792 HART, Peter
"Selection policy in the Imperial War Museum's Sound Records Department" *see* HARRISON, Helen

793 HARTLEY, Marie and INGILBY, Joan
Life and tradition in West Yorkshire
Dent, 1976
160pp
Based on first hand accounts of people's lives from the 1890s to World War Two.

794 HARTMAN, Geoffrey H.
"Preserving the personal story: the role of video documentation"
Dimensions: A Journal of Holocaust Studies, vol.1, no.1 (Spring 1985), pp.14-18
An excellent article outlining Yale University's Video Archive for Holocaust Testimonies (which had collected over 1000 interviews by 1988) and raising the particular difficulties of interviewing Holocaust survivors.

795 HARTRIDGE, Digby
"Oral history librarianship"
Rhodesian Librarian, vol.5, no.1 (January 1973), pp.12-18
Based on the oral history programme of the National Archives of Rhodesia. Estimates that forty hours is required for research, checking, transcription etc. for every hour of interview, and urges a methodical single-topic approach to setting up a project.

796 HARTWICH, V.C.
Ale an' athing: aspects of the grocery and licensed trade in Dundee, 1800-1950
Dundee: Dundee Museums and Art Gallery, 1981
32pp

797 HASELER, Stephen
The Gaitskellites: revisionism in the British Labour Party 1951-64
Macmillan, 1969
286pp; bibliography
Includes interview material with MPs gathered in 1964-5 and informal talks with Hugh Gaitskell himself.

798 HASTINGS, Max
The Korean war
Joseph, 1987
476pp; bibliography
Draws on interviews with participants high and low in Korea, Britain and the United States, and takes the view that America's commitment to Korea in June 1950 was right.

HASTINGS, Max *see also* **JENKINS, Simon**

799 HASTINGS MODERN HISTORY WORKSHOP
Hastings voices: local people talking about their lives in Hastings and St.Leonards before the Second World War
Brighton: Hastings Modern History Workshop/Centre for Continuing Education, University of Sussex, 1982
74pp
Based on eight tape-recorded interviews with people from this seaside resort, the oldest born in 1894.

800 HAUSEMAN, C.
"Life review therapy"
Journal of Gerontological Social Work, vol.3, no.2, pp.31-7

801 HAVIGHURST, R.J. and GLASSER, R.
"An exploratory study of reminiscence"
Journal of Gerontology, vol. 27, no. 2 (1972),
pp.235-53

802 HAVLICE, Patricia Pate
Oral history: a reference guide and annotated bibliography
Jefferson, N.C. and London: McFarland, 1985
140pp
Covers 773 books, articles and dissertations on oral history which appeared from the 1950s to late 1983, with descriptive annotations of content and a brief subject index. The emphasis is very much on material published in the United States.

803 HAY, Cynthia
"The pangs of the past"
Oral History, vol.9, no.1 (1981), pp.41-6
Critical of the notion that only pleasant memories are accurately recalled and assesses research on the reliability of memory.

804 HAY, Roy
The use and abuse of oral evidence
Waurn Ponds, Victoria: Deakin University Press, 1986
24pp; bibliography

805 HAY, Roy and McCLAUCHLAN, J.
"The oral history of Upper Clyde Shipbuilders"
Oral History, vol.2, no.1 (1974), pp.45-58

806 HAYDEN, Robert C. (ed.)
A dialogue with the past: oral history accounts of Boston's ethnic neighborhoods and people
Newton, Mass.: Educational Development Center, 1979
Ten interviews with Bostonian immigrants.

807 HAYNES, Debbie and WEST, Kath (eds.)
Bending the truth a little bit: growing up in West Bromwich and thereabouts
West Bromwich, West Midlands: Churchfields School in the Community, 1989
76pp
Memories and experiences of being fourteen years old growing up in one part of the West Midlands, from 1900 to the present day: family, school, play and starting work. The culmination of a year-long school and community project.

HEALY, Dermot *see* **BUNDY, Colin**

808 HEATON, Frank (ed.)
Fred Roberts (1884-1982): recollections
Manchester: Neil Richardson, 1983
48pp
Recorded conversations about childhood (which included a glimpse of Queen Victoria) and working life as a headmaster in the Miles Platting district of Manchester.

809 HEDBLOM, Folke
"Methods and organisation of folklore research in Sweden"
Oral History, vol.2, no.2 (1974), pp.44-58

810 HEBREW UNIVERSITY OF JERUSALEM INSTITUTE OF CONTEMPORARY JEWRY
Oral History Division: catalogue no. 3
Jerusalem: Keter, 1970
311pp
Oral History Division: catalogue no. 4
Jerusalem: Keter, 1975
131pp
No.3 is a complete (to 1968) catalogue of the Division's tapes and transcripts, which cover Jewish communities throughout the world, from the USSR 1917-1935 to Jewish life in Latin America. No.4 contains holdings acquired 1969-1973.

811 HELIAS, Pierre Jakez
The horse of pride: life in a Breton village
Translated from the French
New Haven and London: Yale University Press, 1978; first published in French, 1975
351pp
An autobiographical account of a Brittany childhood.

812 HELP THE AGED
Recall
Help the Aged Education Department, 1981
An innovative series of six tape/slide sequences in three parts, each part with 40 slides, one cassette tape and user's handbook (40pp, available separately). Part one covers childhood and the Great War, part two: youth and living through the thirties, part three: the Second World War and afterwards. Each acts as a starting point from which elderly people are encouraged to reminisce, sharing their memories with each other and with younger people. Recall has become a model for other locally-produced packs all over Britain and has been widely used by social services departments, hospitals and day centres. (*See also* GIBSON, Faith)

813 HELP THE AGED
Side by side: an introductory guide for secondary schools
Help the Aged, 1988
24pp; bibliography
Information and advice for teachers wanting to set up inter-generational school projects: making contact with elderly people, ideas for project work, an evaluation guide, contact and resource lists, plus a number of case studies from schools all over Britain.

814 HELP THE AGED
Side by side: an introductory guide for primary schools
Help the Aged, 1988
24pp; bibliography
A primary school version of the above.

815 HEMMINGS, Susan
A wealth of experience: the lives of older women
Pandora, 1985
181pp
Eighteen women, mainly forty to sixty five years old, talk openly about personal experiences and political changes that have influenced them: the Second World War, contraception, abortion, cancer, the peace movement, the Women's Liberation Movement, and racism.

HEMMINGS, Susan *see also* **CANT, Bob**

816 HENDERSON, M.
"Handling the past"
Social Work Today, 8 March 1983, p.13

817 HENDRY, John
"Reminiscence and the contemporary history of science"
British Journal for the History of Science, *vol.13 (1980)*

818 HENIGE, David
"The problem of feedback in oral tradition: four examples from the Fanti coastlands"
Journal of African History, vol.19 (1973)

819 HENIGE, David
The chronology of oral tradition: quest for a chimera
Oxford: Clarendon, 1974
265pp; bibliography
Stresses the necessity of careful interpretation of the chronological content of oral traditional data in non-calendrical societies, based on his own study of African history.

820 HENIGE, David
Oral historiography
Longman, 1982
150pp; detailed bibliography
A re-evaluation of the collection and interpretation of oral historical data with a special emphasis on Africa. Useful for Third World fieldwork and for a discussion of the distinction between oral history and oral tradition.

821 HENNOCK, E.P.
"Untidy reality: Edwardian Britain and the tape-recorder"
Encounter, vol.46 (March 1976), pp.73-7
A review article of books by Evans, Thompson and Samuel.

HENRIQUES, P. *see* **DENNIS, N.**

822 HEREN, L.
Growing up poor in London
Hamish Hamilton, 1973
208pp
An oral autobiography of growing up in London's East End.

HERSCHER, U. D. *see* **PECK, A. J.**

HERTZOG, Elizabeth *see* **ZBOROWSKI, Mark**

823 HEWINS, Angela (ed.)
The Dillen: memories of a man of Stratford-upon-Avon
Elm Tree, 1981; Oxford: Oxford University Press, 1982
180pp
Transcribed from tapes of interviews with George Hewins. Includes material on labour biography and the small town.

824 HEWINS, Angela
"The RSC's production of 'The Dillen': a personal view"
Oral History, vol.12, no.2 (1984), pp.32-37

825 HEWINS, Angela (ed.)
Mary, after the Queen: memories of a working girl
Oxford: Oxford University Press, 1985
144pp
The story of Mary Elizabeth Hewins, a working class girl who grew up on the outskirts of Stratford after the First World War, based on interviews.

826   **HEYWORTH, Peter (ed.)**
Conversations with Klemperer
Faber and Faber, 1985; original edition,
Gollancz, 1973
149pp
Otto Klemperer, the leading conductor, on
music in central Europe until the advent of
Hitler.

827   **HIBBERT, Joyce**
Fragments of war: stories from survivors of
World War II
Toronto and London: Dundown Press, 1985
267pp; bibliography
Thirty personal accounts of Canadians at war,
many of them volunteers, with experiences as
far apart as India, Britain, Poland and the
Middle East.

828   **HILL, Andy**
"Oral history and multicultural education"
Oral History, vol.16, no.2 (1987), pp.58-66
Oral history projects in a mixed race school in
Erdington on the outskirts of Birmingham.

829   **HILL, Charles C.**
"Oral history and the history of Canadian art"
Canadian Oral History Association Journal,
no.2 (1976-7), pp.31-5
How oral history and art can benefit each
other.

HILL, Frank Ernest *see* **NEVINS, Allan**

830   **HILL, Ruth E.**
"The Black Women Oral History Project"
Behavioral and Social Sciences Librarian,
vol.4, no.4 (Summer 1985), pp.3-14
The origins and development of the project at
the Schlesinger Library, Radcliffe College,
Cambridge, Massachusetts. (*See also*
GRAYZEL, Susan)

831   **HILLFIELDS HISTORY GROUP**
Hillfields in their own words 3: life and work in
the home
Coventry: Hillfields History Group, nd
23pp
Edited transcripts of interviews about
shopping, cooking, washing and housing in the
Hillfields area of Coventry before the Second
World War. Books 1 and 2 in the series are
not based on oral history.

832   **HILLFIELDS HISTORY GROUP**
Hillfields in their own words 4: looking back at
schooldays
Coventry: Hillfields History Group, nd
32pp
Based partially on interviews about schooling
in one area of Coventry.

HINDLEY, Colin *see* **BADDELEY, Alan**

833   **HINDS, Donald**
"The 'island' of Brixton"
Oral History, vol.8, no.1 (1980), pp.49-51
A West Indian experience of living in London.

834   **HINTON, William**
Fanshen: a documentary of revolution in a
Chinese village
Harmondsworth: Penguin, 1972; first
published 1966
757pp
A study of Long Bow in Shansi Province
during 1948 based on extensive interviewing.

835   **HINTON, William**
Shenfan: the continuing revolution in a Chinese
village
Secker & Warburg, 1983
789pp

HIPPOLITO, Lucia *see* **CAMARGO, Aspasia**

836   **HIRSCH, Andrea S.**
"Copyrighting conversations: applying the
1976 Copyright Act to interviews"
The American University Law Review, vol.31
(1982), pp.1071-93
For American copyright.

HIRSCH, Jerrold D. *see* **TERRILL, Tom E.**

837   *History on tape: a guide for oral history in*
Indiana
Indianapolis: Indiana State Library, 1979,
revised edition
19pp; bibliography and glossary of oral history
terms
A brochure with plenty of advice for the
beginner.

838   *History Workshop*
No.8 (Autumn 1979), pp.i-iii
A collective editorial on oral history.

839 HOAR, Victor
The Mackenzie-Papineau Battalion
Toronto: Copp Clark Publishing Company,
1969
285pp
Relies extensively on oral history interviews
collected by the CBC Program Archives
during 1964-5.

840 HOBBS, Sandy
"The folk tale as news"
Oral History, vol.6, no.2 (1978), pp.74-86

HOBBS, Sandy *see also* **THOMPSON, Willie**

**841 HOBSBAWM, Eric and RANGER, Terence
(eds.)**
The invention of tradition
Cambridge: Cambridge University Press, 1983
320pp
On social purposes and the manipulation of
history.

842 HODGKINSON, Jonathan
"Oral history and the history of science"
Oral History, vol.4, no.2 (1976), pp.8-16
Mainly an assessment of the work of David
Edge of Edinburgh University. (*See also*
EDGE, David O.)

843 HOFFMAN, Alice M.
"Oral history in Great Britain" and "Oral
history in the United States"
Journal of Library History, vol.7 (July 1972),
pp.275-77 and 277-85

844 HOGGART, Richard
*The uses of literacy: aspects of working-class
life, with special reference to publications and
entertainments*
Chatto & Windus, 1957
319pp

845 HOLDEN, Len
"'Think of me simply as the skipper':
industrial relations at Vauxhalls 1920-1950"
Oral History, vol.9, no.2 (1981), pp.18-32
Relations between management and workers
in a car factory during a period of industrial
tranquility.

846 HOLDEN, Una P.
Technique for reality orientation
Leeds: St. James University Hospital, 1981

847 HOLDEN, Una P. and WOODS, Robert T.
*Reality orientation: psychological approaches to
the confused elderly*
Edinburgh: Churchill Livingstone, 1982
283pp; bibliography

848 HOLDSWORTH, Angela
*Out of the doll's house: the story of women in
the twentieth century*
BBC, 1988
208pp; bibliography
Based on an eight-part BBC documentary
television series and using personal
recollections of women of all ages and social
backgrounds, the book looks at the
momentous changes in women's lives since the
turn of the century.

849 HOLLERTON, Eric
"Modern techniques and media in local
studies"
*Local Studies Librarian, vol.5, no.2 (Winter
1986), pp.6-8*
Mentions the Nottinghamshire Oral History
Project, 1982-4.

850 HOLMES, Jeremy
"Family and individual therapy: comparisons
and contrasts"
British Journal of Psychiatry, vol.47 (1985)

851 HOLMES, Nigel (ed.)
BBC Radio Cumbria sound archives catalogue
Carlisle, Cumbria: BBC Radio Cumbria, 1982
Two volumes (637pp) and supplement (90pp)
A catalogue of holdings arranged in name and
subject order, including much of local and oral
history interest.

852 HOLWAY, John
Voices from the great Black baseball leagues
New York: Dodd, Mead, 1975
363pp
Eighteen of the great baseball players of the
black segregated league reminisce.

HOMER, Brian *see* **BISHTON, Derek**

**853 HONOR OAK ESTATE NEIGHBOURHOOD
ASSOCIATION**
A street door of our own
*Honor Oak Estate Neighbourhood
Association, 1977*
48pp
Twelve people's accounts of living on a South
London housing estate.

854 HOOD, Lynley
Sylvia: the biography of Sylvia Ashton-Warner
*Auckland, New Zealand: Viking Penguin
(N.Z.), 1988*
264pp; bibliography
A biography of one of New Zealand's greatest
educational innovators and novelists, based
partly on interviews.

855 **HOOPES, James**
Oral history: an introduction for students
Chapel Hill: University of North Carolina
Press, 1979
155pp; bibliography
An excellent introductory handbook covering
the entire interview process from the
interaction of personalities and initial contact
to transcription, with an opening chapter
putting the movement into historical context.

856 **HOOPES, Roy**
*Americans remember the home front: an oral
narrative*
New York: Hawthorn Books, 1977
398pp
Extracted narratives from conversations with
200 American civilians in 1941-5 covering life
in Washington D.C., industry, the experiences
of wives and children, and Truman's
presidency.

857 **HOOPES, Townsend**
The devil and John Foster Dulles
Boston: Little and Brown, 1973
562pp; bibliography
Foreign policy during the Eisenhower years
from the Dulles oral history collection,
Princeton.

HOOVER, Herbert T. *see* **CASH, Joseph H.;
HARRIS, Ramon I.**

858 **HOSTETTLER, Eve**
*Island women: photographs of East End women
1897 to 1983*
Dirk Nishen Publishing, 1988
32pp
Family photographs from the Island History
Trust's outstanding collection, supplemented
by comments from the women themselves
covering childhood, schooling, work, family
life, leisure and old age in a London dockland
commmunity.

859 **HOTHAM SCHOOL SOCIAL HISTORY
GROUP**
*Forty years on: when we look back and
forgetfully wonder what we were like in our work
and play*
Hotham School Social History Group, 1987
10pp
Memories of Joan Morgan, a pupil at Hotham
1947-54.

860 **HOTHAM SCHOOL SOCIAL HISTORY
GROUP**
A regular and punctual pupil
Hotham School Social History Group, 1988
12pp
Continuing the series recording the school's
history: Reginald Edwards tells his story.

861 **HOULIHAN, Marjory**
*A most excellent dish: tales of the Lancashire
tripe trade*
Manchester: Neil Richardson, 1987
44pp
'All you ever wanted to know about tripe' in
the north west: with recollections of cooking
it, selling it and eating it, and traditional
recipes. In 1911 Bolton had seventy-six tripe
shops!

862 **HOWARD, Anthony and WEST, Richard**
The making of the prime minister
Cape, 1965
239pp
Relies heavily on interviews with front and
backbenchers of both parties conducted
between January 1963 and October 1964.

863 **HOWARTH, Ken**
*An introduction to sound recording: for the oral
historian and the sound archivist*
Radcliffe: The North West Sound Archive,
1977
61pp

864 **HOWARTH, Ken**
*Dark days: memories and reminiscences of the
Lancashire and Cheshire coalmining industry
up to nationalisation*
Manchester: Greater Manchester County
Council, 1978; second edition 1985 (with new
introduction)
127pp
Based entirely on taped interviews and
includes a glossary of mining terms.

865 **HOWARTH, Ken**
"Tape recording oral history"
*Museums Journal, vol. 82, no. 2 (Sept 1982),
pp.105-9*
Good basic advice on equipment, techniques
and archiving.

866 HOWARTH, Ken
Remember, remember: tape recording oral history
Hebden Bridge: Pennine Heritage Network, 1984
68pp
An excellent introduction to the techniques of oral history and archival procedures.

867 HOWARTH, Olive (ed.)
Textile voices: mill life this century
Bradford: Bradford Heritage Recording Unit/ Bradford Libraries and Information Service, 1989
84pp
Extracts from BHRU's collection of over two hundred life story interviews with textile workers, trade unionists, owners and managers from what was in living memory the worsted textile capital of the world. It includes sections on home and neighbourhood, women in the mill, the main processes, ancillary trades, leisure activities and the experiences of migrant workers from middle and eastern Europe and Asia, with a useful glossary of textile terminology. (*See also* BRADFORD HERITAGE RECORDING UNIT)

868 HOWELL, Chris
I have heard tell...
Radstock, Bath: the author, 1982
100pp

869 HOWELLS, Kim and JONES, R. Merfyn
"Oral history and contemporary history"
Oral History, vol.11, no.2 (1983), pp.15-20
Based on work with South Wales miners.

HOWELLS, Kim *see also* FRANCIS, Hywel

870 HOWKINS, Alun
"The voice of the people: the social meaning and context of country songs"
Oral History, vol.3, no.1 (1975), pp.50-75

871 HOWKINS, Alun
"Enthusiasms: George Ewart Evans"
History Workshop, no.1 (Spring 1976), pp.254-6

872 HOWKINS, Alun
"Structural conflict and the farmworker: Norfolk, 1900-20"
Journal of Peasant Studies, vol.4, no.3 (1977), pp.217-29
Questions the orthodoxy that farmworkers were 'acquiescent in their bondage'.

873 HOWKINS, Alun
Poor labouring men: rural radicalism in Norfolk, 1872-1923
Routledge & Kegan Paul, 1985
History Workshop Series
225pp; bibliography
An important book based on written and oral sources (the latter especially when covering the Great War and the General Strike). The author is himself an ex-farmworker and established a close relationship with his informants.

874 HOWKINS, Alun
"George Ewart Evans: an appreciation"
Oral History, vol.16, no.2 (1988)
An obituary.

HOWKINS, Alun *see also* VIGNE, Thea

875 HOYLE, N.
"Oral history"
Library Trends, vol.21 (July 1972), pp.60-82
An excellent in-depth survey of activity in the United States.

876 HUDSON, Andrew
"Oral history"
New Library World, no.82 (October 1981), pp.185-6

877 HUDSON, Kenneth
Where we used to work
John Baker, 1980
162pp
Based on interviews with people about their working lives in construction work, the post, gloving, making and selling furniture, biscuit-making, producing newspapers and magazines and making aeroplanes.

878 HUGHES, Helen Macgill (ed.)
The fantastic lodge: the autobiography of a girl drug addict
Barker, 1963
272pp
An outstanding example of the American anthropological tradition.

879 HUGHSTON, G. and MERRIAM, S.
"Reminiscence: a nonformal technique for improving cognitive functioning in the aged"
Journal of Aging and Human Development, no.25 (1982), pp.139-49

880 HUMPHREYS, Hubert (ed.)
Louisiana oral history collections: a directory
Shreveport: Louisiana State University, 1980
174pp

881 HUMPHRIES, Steve
"'Hurrah for England!': schooling and the
working class in Bristol 1870-1914"
Southern History, vol.1 (1979), pp.171-207

882 HUMPHRIES, Steve
"Steal to survive: the social crime of working
class children 1890-1940"
Oral History, vol.9, no.1 (1981), pp.24-33

883 HUMPHRIES, Steve
*Hooligans or rebels?: an oral history of working
class childhood and youth 1889-1939*
Oxford: Blackwell, 1981
279pp; bibliography
Using extensive oral history interviews the
author challenges the established view that
rebellious behaviour was due to indiscipline
rather than social and economic pressures.
Includes chapters on classroom coercion and
rebellion, childhood pranks, school strikes,
social crime, street gangs, juvenile crime and
reformatories.

884 HUMPHRIES, Steve
*The handbook of oral history: recording life
stories*
Inter-Action Imprint, 1984
Creative community projects series
165pp; bibliography
An easy-to-read and practical introduction for
anyone wanting to become involved in or
organise an oral history project, with helpful
advice on equipment, finding interviewees,
interview techniques and ways of making use
of oral history in schools, with older people, in
exhibition form and in broadcasting.

885 HUMPHRIES, Steve
*A secret world of sex. Forbidden fruit: the
British experience 1900-1950*
Sidgwick & Jackson, 1988
224pp
Based on a series of frank interviews with
older people it looks at changing sexual
experiences over the past century, focussing
on sex before marriage and including
illegitimacy, masturbation, sex education,
contraception, seaside and gang sex, back
street abortionists, and homosexuality.

886 HUMPHRIES, Steve and WEIGHTMAN,
Gavin
The making of modern London 1914-1939
Sidgwick & Jackson, 1984
175pp; bibliography
The book of an award-winning London
Weekend Television series of the same name
based extensively on oral sources.

887 HUMPHRIES, Steve and MACK, Joanna
*London at war: the making of modern London
1939-1945*
Sidgwick & Jackson, 1985
176pp; bibliography
Draws on hitherto censored material and
extensive personal testimony from Londoners
themselves.

888 HUMPHRIES, Steve and TAYLOR, John
The making of modern London 1945-1985
Sidgwick & Jackson, 1986
172pp; bibliography
Covers post-war redevelopment, the decline
of London as the hub of empire and
immigration using a range of oral testimonies.

889 HUMPHRIES, Steve, MACK, Joanna, and
PERKS, Robert
A century of childhood
*Sidgwick & Jackson in association with
Channel Four Television Company, 1988*
176pp; bibliography
A social history of twentieth century British
childhood, using extensive oral history
interviews and contemporary photographs,
written to accompany an eight-part Channel
Four documentary series of the same name
broadcast in Spring 1989. Includes chapters on
parents, play, school, gangs and changing
sexual attitudes.

HUMPHRIES, Steve *see also* WEIGHTMAN,
Gavin

890 HUNGRY WOLF, Beverley
The ways of my grandmothers
New York: William Morrow, 1980
256pp
A young Indian woman tape-recorded the
personal and tribal history, domestic skills,
legends and myths of the women of her tribe,
the Blood People of the Blackfoot nation.

891   HUNT, Christine
I'm ninety-five - any objection? Folk history
from the South Island
Auckland, New Zealand: Reed Methuen, 1985
274pp
Men and women speak openly and with
humour about New Zealand at the turn of the
century and describe how it feels to be near
the end of their lives.

892   HUNT, Morton
Sexual behaviour in the 1970s
Chicago: Playboy Press, 1974
395pp
Based on 2026 questionnaires collected in
1972 from twenty-four cities, supplemented
with in-depth recorded interviews with 200
people.

893   HUNTER, Ian
Memory
Harmondsworth: Penguin (Pelican), 1957;
revised edition 1964; reissued 1968
328pp
Covers remembering and forgetting, children
learning to remember, the effects of brain
injury, memory disorders, exceptional
memory abilities and rumour.

894   HUTCHISON, Alison (ed.)
Corrie and Cardenden
Fife: WEA, 1986
32pp
Reminiscences of elderly people.

HUTCHISON, Gerard *see* **O'NEILL, Mark**

**895   HUTCHISON, Pat and McNEILL, Anthony
J.J.**
"Local history from local folk: oral history in
North East Scotland"
Local Studies Librarian, vol.8, no.2 (Autumn
1989), pp.10-13
Details of the Banff, Macduff and District
Oral History Project sponsored by Age
Concern and North East of Scotland Library
Service, which culminated in an exhibition
incorporating sound.

HYDE, Michael *see* **CLARK, E.C.**

**896   HYLAND, Diane T and ACKERMAN, Adele
M.**
"Reminiscence and autobiographical memory
in the study of the personal past"
Journal of Gerontology, vol.43, no.2 (1988),
pp.35-9

897   HYMAN, Herbert Hiram
Interviewing in social research
Chicago: University of Chicago Press, 1954
415pp
A full discussion of interview methods.

898   ILEY, Walter B.
"The village memory"
Local History, vol.9, no.6 (1971), pp.300-303

899   ILIFFE, John (ed.)
Modern Tanzanians: a volume of biographies
Nairobi: East African Publishing House, 1973
258pp

**900-916 IMPERIAL WAR MUSEUM DEPARTMENT
OF SOUND RECORDS**
The IWM's oral history archive is one of the
oldest established, largest and best
documented in Britain, covering all aspects of
war in the twentieth century. A series of
catalogues relating to the sound records
department's holdings have been published.
Each catalogue gives detailed descriptions of
the recordings and have useful indices on
places, names, army units etc., and would also
be a good model for anyone contemplating
cataloguing and indexing a collection of tapes.
(*See also* BROOKS, Margaret; LANCE,
David; WOOD, Conrad)

Oral history recordings:
900   *Western front 1914-1918 (1976)*

901   *War work 1914-1918: medicine and welfare,*
industry and agriculture (1977)

902   *The British Army in India 1919-1939 (1979)*

903   *British involvement in the Spanish Civil War*
1936-1939 (1980)

904   *Military and naval aviation 1914-1918 (1982)*

905   *The British Army in Africa 1919-1939 (1982)*

906   *Lower deck RN 1910-1922 (1982)*

907   *Middle East: British military personnel*
1919-1939 (1982)

908   *Mechanisation of the British Army 1919-1939*
(1982)

909   *Britain and the refugee crisis 1933-1947 (1982)*

910 *The Royal Air Force and the development of air power 1918-1939 (1982)*

911 *The anti-war movement 1914-1918 (1985)*

912 *The anti-war movement 1914-1945 (1985)*

913 *The Invergordon Mutiny 1931 (1987)*

Broadcast recordings:
914 *Thames Television: The World at War 1939-1945*
(second edition 1980)

915 *BBC Radio: Plain Tales from the Raj (1981)*

916 *BBC Sound Archives: world war 1939-1945 (1982)*

917 IMPERIAL WAR MUSEUM DEPARTMENT OF SOUND RECORDS
The first world war remembered: extracts from interviews carried out by the Imperial War Museum
Imperial War Museum, nd
A sixty minute cassette tape: side one covers memories of trench warfare and conscientious objectors. Side two deals with the home front: refugees, nursing, air raids, munitions, the Women's Land Army, and rationing. Thirty one individuals from the IWM's enormous archive of 700 hours of First World War interviews.

918 IMPERIAL WAR MUSEUM DEPARTMENT OF SOUND RECORDS
Life in Nazi Germany: extracts from the museum's collection of recorded interviews
Imperial War Museum, nd
A cassette tape of the experiences of eleven people who lived in Germany between 1933 and 1945, most of whom have subsequently settled in Britain. They touch on the appeal of Nazism, political opposition, censorship and intimidation, school experiences, youth organisations, employment, anti-Semitism and the extermination camps, and civilian wartime experiences.

919 IMPERIAL WAR MUSEUM DEPARTMENT OF SOUND RECORDS
The home front: life in Britain 1939-1945: extracts from the Imperial War Museum's collection of recorded interviews
Imperial War Museum, 1989
A ninety-minute cassette tape drawn from fifteen interviews and covering the outbreak of war, air raid precautions, evacuation, shortages, the threat of invasion, air raids, the war effort, war news, the V1 and V2 flying bombs, and VE day. Tailored for use in schools.

920 INDIA OFFICE LIBRARY AND RECORDS
Plain tales from the Raj: a catalogue of the BBC recordings
British Library India Office Library and Records, 1981
A catalogue of the recordings (available at the IOLR, Imperial War Museum and School of Oriental and African Studies) of interviews with mainly British people who lived and worked in India from 1900 to 1947.

INESON, Antonia *see* **CLARK, Helen**

INGILBY, Joan *see* **HARTLEY, Marie**

921 **INGLIS, Ruth**
The children's war: evacuation 1939-1945
Collins, 1989
178pp
From interviews and Mass Observation.

922 **INOWLOCKI, Lena**
"Denying the past: right wing extremist youth in West Germany"
Life Stories, no.1, (1985), pp.6-15

923 INSTITUTE OF HISTORICAL RESEARCH
Interviews with historians
University of London Institute of Historical Research, 1989
A series of videotaped interviews with leading historians, each lasting around thirty-five minutes and focussing on guiding influences. Included are: Moses Finley, Christopher Hill, Lawrence Stone, Eric Hobsbawm, Henry Pelling and Margaret Gowing.

924 **INSTITUTIONAL INVESTOR**
The way it was: an oral history of twenty years of finance
New York: Institutional Investor Inc., 1987
376pp
An acccount of two decades of change in US finance through the words of the key figures: the leaders of the financial world like the Rockefellers, Wristons and Rohatyns, as well as the unsung people from a veteran retail salesman to Wall Street policemen. 116 people were interviewed between January and May 1987, each interview lasting two hours or more.

925 **INTERNATIONAL JOURNAL OF ORAL HISTORY**
Vol.1, February 1980-
Published three times per year (February, June and November) with articles, news, reviews, and bibliographies on oral history throughout the world, with an emphasis on theoretical, interdisciplinary and methodological issues.

926 **IRISH IN BRITAIN HISTORY GROUP**
The history of the Irish in Britain: a bibliography
Irish in Britain History Group, 1986
86pp
The only comprehensive bibliography on the subject: it includes some references to oral testimony.

927 **IRVINE, Kathryn**
Getting it taped: a guide to cassette recording
Wellington, New Zealand: Continuing Education Unit, Radio New Zealand, 1985
28pp
How to record oral history: prepared to accompany a radio series (*see also* CARSON, Pam)

928 **IRWIN, Paul**
Liptako speaks: history from oral tradition in Africa
Guildford: Princeton University Press, 1981
221pp; bibliography
Pre-colonial Africa from research conducted in France and the Upper Volta betwen 1970 and 1976.

929 **ISICHEI, Elizabeth**
Igbo worlds: an anthology of oral histories and historical descriptions
Macmillan, 1977
355pp
Collected by the author's students in their home areas and chosen for their typicality. Includes a chapter on African oral history.

930 **ISLAND HISTORY TRUST**
A souvenir history of St.Luke's school
Island History Trust, 1986
8pp broadsheet
Includes memories of the school on London's Isle of Dogs.

931 **ISLINGTON RECALL LOCAL HISTORY GROUP**
Memories are made of this: Westbourne Road area, 1914-1924
Islington Adult Education Institute, 1984
11pp
Memories of housing, streetgames, schooldays and the First World War, including a Zeppelin raid.

ITZIN, Catherine *see* **THOMPSON, Paul**

932 **IVES, Edward D.**
Joe Scott
Urbana: University of Illinois Press, 1978
473pp; bibliography
The life and songs of a ballad artist based on hundreds of interviews with people who knew him and his songs. Looks at how sixty years of oral tradition has shaped the songs.

933 **IVES, Edward D.**
The tape recorded interview: a manual for field workers in folklore and oral history
Knoxville: University of Tennessee, 1980; revised edition, 1984; originally published in 1974 as A manual for field workers
130pp; bibliography
Includes details, in simple language, of how a tape recorder works, interviewing techniques, finding informants, processing, making a transcript and publication. Emphasises the need for thorough preparation.

934 **JACKSON, Brian and MARSDEN, Dennis**
Education and the working class
Ark, 1986 revised edition; previous edition, 1962
296pp; bibliography
A study of the effects of a grammar school education on eighty-eight working-class children and their families in Huddersfield, West Yorkshire.

935 **JACKSON, Brian and MARSDEN, Dennis**
Working class community: some general notions raised by a series of studies in northern England
Routledge & Kegan Paul, 1968; Harmondsworth: Penguin (Pelican), 1972
195pp
A study of the world of working men's clubs, bowling greens, brass bands and textile mills based on research which began in 1958.

936 **JACKSON, Robert**
The prisoners 1914-18
Routledge, 1989
240pp
A broad cross-section of life in prisoner-of-war camps, the Red Cross, internment and escapes during the First World War, drawing on personal narratives from the Imperial War Museum.

937 **JALLA, Danielle**
"Belonging somewhere in the city - social space and its perception: the Barriere of Turin in the early 20th century"
Oral History, vol.13, no.2 (1985), pp.19-34
Housing policy in Turin in Italy.

938 **JAMIESON, Ian**
"Oral history and libraries: some recent developments"
Local Studies Librarian, vol.4, no.2 (Winter 1985), pp.7-9

939 **JAMIESON, Ronda**
Oral history: how to interview
Perth, Western Australia: The Library Board of Western Australia, 1987
One 60-minute audio cassette
From the J.S.Battye Library Oral History Programme.

940 **JANIEWSKI, Dolores**
"'Sisters under their skins?': the effects of race upon the efforts of women tobacco workers to organise in Durham, North Carolina"
Oral History, vol.7, no.2 (1979), pp.31-41
Interviews with black and white women about trade union activities and segregation.

JARDINE, Bob *see* **TURNER, Jane**

941 **JEFFERY, Patricia**
Frogs in the well: Indian women in purdah
Zed Press, 1979
187pp; bibliography
A social anthropological study, using interview extracts, of the seclusion of women by Islamic purdah and how they feel about it.

JEFFREY, David *see* **CROCKER, Andrew**

942 **JELLISON, Charles A.**
Tomatoes were cheaper: tales from the thirties
Syracuse: Syracuse University Press, 1977
240pp
Oral testimony from the American Depression.

943 **JENKINS, David**
The agricultural community in South West Wales at the turn of the twentieth century
Cardiff: University of Wales Press, 1971
291pp; bibliography
A detailed, carefully researched survey, based largely on oral evidence from South Cardiganshire.

944 **JENKINS, Hugh**
Rank and File
Croom Helm, 1980
181pp
Forty verbatim interviews with active members of the Putney Constituency Labour Party about what they think and feel, and how they came to be involved in politics. The author was Member of Parliament for Putney from 1964-79.

945 **JENKINS, Richard**
Hightown rules: growing up in a Belfast housing estate
Leicester: National Youth Bureau, 1982
91pp; bibliography
The 'abnormal' experience of growing up in Belfast since the current troubles began in 1969, from interviews carried out between April 1978 and May 1979.

946 JENKINS, Sara
Past present: recording life stories of older people
Washington, DC: St.Alban's Parish, 1978
150pp
Some practical advice on interviewer training, but mainly edited and illustrated oral history extracts from a project at a day centre for the elderly.

947 JENKINS, Simon and HASTINGS, Max
The battle for the Falklands
Michael Joseph, 1983
372pp
An account of British political decision making and the war's naval and military operations, drawn from interviews with many of the central participants.

948 JENNINGS, Humphrey and MADGE, Charles (eds.)
Mass-Observation day-surveys: May the twelfth, 1937 by over two hundred observers
Faber, 1987; reprint of 1937 edition
440pp
A multi-angled view of a single day and event - George VI's coronation - as recorded by Mass Observation's observers nationwide.

949 JENSEN, Richard
"Oral history, quantification and the new social history"
Oral History Review, vol.9 (1981)
For quantitative analysis.

950 JEWISH WOMEN IN LONDON GROUP
Generations of memories: voices of Jewish women
The Women's Press, 1989
262pp; bibliography
Eight Ashkenazi Jewish women talk about their lives, their feelings and their experiences of anti-semitism, persecution and migration. There are a variety of life stories: from a survivor of Auschwitz to someone brought up in London's East End to a Jewish lesbian growing up in the 1950s.

951 JEWISH WOMEN'S HISTORY GROUP
You'd prefer me not to mention it...: the lives of four Jewish daughters of refugees
Jewish Women's History Group, nd
64pp; bibliography
Life stories spanning the two worlds of the women's movement and traditional Judaism.

952 JIMENEZ, Rebecca S.
"Oral history and the special library"
Catholic Library World, vol.56, no.7 (February 1985), pp.280-2

953 JOB, E.M.
"Retrospective life span analysis: a method for studying extreme old age"
Journal of Gerontology, no.38 (May 1983), pp.369-74
A study of the value of life histories recounted by people over eighty years old.

954 JOHN, Angela V.
"Scratching the surface: women, work and coalmining in England and Wales"
Oral History, vol.10, no.2 (1982), pp.13-26

955 JOHNS, Brenda B. and SMITH, Alonzo
Black oral history in Nebraska: a handbook for researchers and students of oral tradition in black communities
Omaha: University of Nebraska, 1980

956 JOHNSON, Alan
Working the tides: gatemen and masters on the River Mersey
Liverpool: Docklands History Project, 1988
73pp
The world of the Harbour Masters' department of the Mersey Docks and Harbour Board responsible for navigating ships in and out of the Port of Liverpool.

957 JOHNSON, Alan and MOORE, Kevin
The tapestry makers: life and work in Lee's tapestry works, Birkenhead
Liverpool: University of Liverpool/Merseyside Docklands Community History Project, 1987
62pp
The history of men and women who worked at Lee's from its opening in 1908 to closure in 1970, in their own words.

958 JOHNSON, Alexander
"A penny for your thoughts"
History Today, August 1988, pp.7-8
The contribution of local oral history projects in the face of closure due to withdrawal of MSC funding.

959 JOHNSON, Catherine (ed.)
Looking back at Liverpool: an oral history of the Liverpool region 1900-1960
Liverpool, New South Wales: Liverpool City Council, 1986
143pp; bibliography
Australia's Liverpool recalled.

960 **JOHNSON, Charles S.**
Shadow of the plantation
Chicago: Chicago University Press, 1966; first published 1934
215pp
A study of the plantation blacks in Macow County in the Southern States.

961 **JOHNSON, Malcolm**
"That was your life: a biographical approach to later life" in CARVER, Vida (1978)

962 **JOHNSON, Paul**
The Suez War
Macgibbon and Kee, 1957
145pp
Drawn from interviews with participants and political protagonists.

JOHNSON, Rachel *see* **CARSWELL, Jeanne**

963 **JOLLY, Brad**
Videotaping local history
Nashville: American Association for State and Local History, 1982
160pp; bibliography
A basic primer on using video equipment for historical research with some discussion of oral history.

963A **JONES, Audrey**
Farewell Manchester: the story of the 1939 evacuation
Manchester: Didsbury Press, 1989
133pp
Personal recollections by thirty child evacuees, their mothers and hosts, of their traumatic evacuation from Manchester in September 1939.

964 **JONES, Derek (ed.)**
You and your history
Channel Four Television, 1987
A leaflet produced for viewers of 'Years Ahead' which includes a section by Joanna Bornat on making the most of reminiscence.

965 **JONES, Derek and MEDLICOTT, Mary (eds.)**
By word of mouth: the revival of storytelling
Channel Four Television, 1989
45pp; bibliography
Articles and examples of stories passed on by oral tradition from a variety of different British cultures and highlighting the revival of story telling as a stimulus to literacy, as a therapy for older people and as a bridge to understanding in schools. Includes a useful resource section.

966 **JONES, G.I.**
"Time and oral tradition with special reference to Eastern Nigeria"
Journal of African History, vol.6, no.2 (1965)

967 **JONES, G.W.**
"The value of recent biographies, autobiographies and diaries"
Parliamentary Affairs, vol.34 (1981)
Includes an evaluation of oral sources.

JONES, George *see* **DONOUGHUE, Bernard**

968 **JONES, Glenys**
"The use of recall to reinforce the here and now"
New Age, Spring 1984, pp.12-13.

969 **JONES, Glyn M. and SCOURFIELD, Elfyn**
Sully: a village and parish in the Vale of Glamorgan
Cardiff: the authors, 1986
170pp
A local history of Sully, a village in the Vale of Glamorgan which has developed over the last thirty years into a dormitory suburb of Cardiff.

970 **JONES, R. Merfyn**
"Welsh immigrants in the cities of North West England 1890-1930: some oral testimony"
Oral History, vol.9, no.2 (1981), pp.33-41

JONES, R. Merfyn *see also* **HOWELLS, Kim**

971 **JONES, Rosamund**
"Voices of Kentmere: a Lakeland hill farm community"
Oral History, vol.15, no.1 (1987), pp.35-41
Based on interviews with twenty-five Cumbrians.

972 **JONES, Sian**
"Oral history and museum education"
Oral History, vol.12, no.2 (1984), pp.68-71

973 **JONES, Sian and MAJOR, Carl**
"Reaching the public: oral history as a survival strategy for museums"
Oral History, vol.14, no.2.(1986), pp.31-38
The experience of oral history projects in Southampton: Chapel and Northam, and the Caribbean Heritage Project. (*See also* SOUTHAMPTON MUSEUMS)

974 **JOSEPH, Peter**
Good times: an oral history of America in the nineteen sixties
New York: Charterhouse, 1973
472pp
Extracts from interviews with 125 people presented in the Terkel collage style covering the Kennedy years, civil rights and anti-war movements, rock festivals, Johnson, Nixon and the moon landing.

975 **JOSEPH, Pleasant 'Cousin Joe' and OTTENHEIMER, Harriet J.**
Cousin Joe: blues from New Orleans
Chicago: University of Chicago Press, 1987
238pp; bibliography and discography
An oral biography of an established blues singer whose career spanned eighty years.

976 **JOSEPHS, Zoe**
Survivors: Jewish refugees in Birmingham 1933-1945
Warley, West Midlands: Meridian Books, 1988
218pp; bibliography
Initiated by the Birmingham Jewish History Research Group and based on the memories of eighty-seven survivors of Nazism from all over Europe who settled in the West Midlands in the 1930s. They talk of arriving and adapting to the British way of life, internment as aliens and community life.

977 **JOUTARD, Philippe**
"A regional project: ethnotexts"
Oral History, vol.9, no.1 (1981), pp.47-51
An interdisciplinary project in the south-east of France.

978 **JUTTE, Robert**
"Westphalian pedlars: a research project applying oral history in Germany"
Oral History, vol.7, no.1 (1979), pp.54-6

979 **KAHN, Kathy**
Hillbilly women
Garden City, New York: Doubleday, 1973
230pp; bibliography
Based on interviews with nineteen poor women in the Appalachian Mountains who had few opportunities for formal education.

980 **KAHN, Kathy**
Fruits of our labor
New York: Putnam, 1982
370pp
A joint US/USSR project to interview workers in traditional occupations in both countries.

981 **KAHN, Peggy**
"An interview with Frank Watters"
Bulletin of the Society for the Study of Labour History, no.43 (Autumn 1981), pp.54-67
The life of a miner and Communist Party activist in the Scottish and Yorkshire coalfields.

982 **KAHN, Peggy**
"Tommy Mullany"
Bulletin of the Society for the Study of Labour History, no.44 (Spring 1982), pp.49-58
Verbatim transcript of an interview with Mullany, a Yorkshire miner active in the National Union of Miners and a Labour councillor in Doncaster.

983 **KAMINSKY, M. (ed.)**
The uses of reminiscence: new ways of working with older adults
New York: The Haworth Press, 1984
245pp
Originally a special double issue of *Journal of Gerontological Social Work, vol.7, nos.1-2, March 1984.*

984 **KAPLIN, Charles D.**
"Addict-life stories: an exploration of the methodological grounds for the study of social problems"
International Journal of Oral History, no.3 (June 1982), pp.114-28
Oral history as a tool in examining social problems.

KASTENBAUM, R. *see* **COSTA, P.**

985 **KATZ, Esther and RINGELHEIM, Joan**
A catalogue of audio and video collections of Holocaust testimony
New York: Institute for Research in History, 1986
238pp
An exhaustive, annotated listing of thirty-seven American repositories holding 2971 interviews with Jewish survivors.

KAVANAGH, Dennis *see* **BUTLER, David**

986 **KAY, Billy (ed.)**
Odyssey: voices from Scotland's recent past
Edinburgh: Polygon, 1980
112pp; bibliography
Based on a classic BBC Scotland documentary
radio series featuring oral histories of:
Glasgow's Irish; ring-net fishing in Kintyre;
the Lanarkshire Lithuanian community; life
on the remote island of St.Kilda; Dundee's
jute industry; whaling in the Shetland islands;
Tiree emigrants to Canada; land grabbing in
the Highlands; mountaineering as an escape
for Glasgow workers during the inter-war
depression; Scottish courtship and wedding
customs; and working horses in East Coast
farming. (*See also* SMITH, Graham)

987 **KAY, Billy (ed.)**
*Odyssey: voices from Scotland's recent past: the
second collection*
Edinburgh: Polygon, 1982
138pp; bibliography
Oral histories of: the Clydebank Blitz of 1941;
Italians in Scotland; Midlothian mining
villages; women in the Lossiemouth and Nairn
herring industry; Scottish soldiers in Gallipoli
in 1915; pearl fishers; the Glengarnock steel
works in north Ayrshire which closed in
1978; the Neil Clan of Barra; Scotland's
Temperance movement; the 1926 General
Strike in East Fife mining communities;
Glasgow's Jewish community; and the lace
industry in Ayrshire's Irvine Valley.

988 **KAZIN, Alfred**
Writers at work: the 'Paris Review' interviews
*Secker and Warburg, first series, 1958; second
series, 1963; third series, 1968*
368pp

989 **KEARNS, Doris**
Lyndon Johnson and the American dream
Deutsch, 1976
432pp
From the Lyndon B. Johnson Library Oral
History Collection and based on conversations
over four years with Johnson himself about his
childhood and career.

990 **KEDWARD, H.R.**
*Resistance in Vichy France: a study of ideas and
motives in the southern zone, 1940-1942*
Oxford: Oxford University Press, 1978, 1983
311pp; bibliography
An examination of resistance to German
occupation drawing on memoirs, the local
press and oral testimony recorded between
1969 and 1974.

991 **KEEN, Richard**
Coalface
Cardiff: National Museum of Wales, 1982
52pp
Reminiscences from the South Wales coalfield
recorded since the mid-1960s, coupled with
William Jones' remarkable photographs of life
and work underground from the 1900s
onwards.

992 **KEEN, Sam and FOX, Anne Valley**
*Telling your story: a guide to who you are and
who you can be*
Garden City, New York: Doubleday, 1973
153pp

993 **KEESING, Nancy**
*Lily on the dustbin: slang of Australian women
and families*
*Ringwood, Victoria and New York: Penguin,
1982*
188pp

994 **KEILMAN, Chester V.**
"The Texas Oil Industry Project"
Wilson Library Bulletin, vol.40 (March 1966)

995 **KELLY, Jimmy**
"An interview with Ronald Fraser"
Oral History, vol.8, no.1 (1980), pp.52-7

996 **KELLY, Mij and EDENSOR, Tim**
Moving Worlds
Edinburgh: Polygon, 1989
256pp
A collection of twenty stories in which
immigrants, ranging from a Lithuanian in 1913
to a Vietnamese in the 1970s, relate their
experiences of leaving their homeland and
arriving in Edinburgh, Scotland.

997 **KELLNER, Peter and CROWTHER-HUNT,
Lord**
*The civil servants: an enquiry into Britain's
ruling class*
Raven Books, 1980
352pp
Examines the issues surrounding the power
wielded by senior civil servants in selecting
their successors, resisting change and
influencing government. From first-hand
experiences and interviews.

998 **KEMP, Mick**
"I lived in Liverpool Road"
New Age, Winter 1980, pp.18-20.

KENDRICK, Stephen *see* STRAW, Pat

999 KENDRICK, Val
"Oral history in Birmingham"
Talk: the Journal of the National Oracy Project,
no.1 (Spring 1989), pp.4-5
An educational journal which includes much
on storytelling and encouraging young people
to develop their communication skills.

KENNEDY, Elizabeth L. *see* **DAVIS,**
Madeline

1000 KENNEDY, Liam
"Profane images in the Irish popular
consciousness"
Oral History, vol.7, no.2 (1979), pp.42-7
Superstitious and magical beliefs in the oral
tradition of Irish peasant society.

1001 KENSINGTON AND CHELSEA
COMMUNITY HISTORY GROUP
Reminiscence resource pack: Portobello Road
Kensington and Chelsea Community History
Group, 1988
Pack of eight photo-cards
Eight views of Portobello Road between 1904
and 1988 with oral testimony from local
people, designed to stimulate reminiscence in
older people.

1002 KENT, Fred E.
"Recording for posterity"
Oral History, vol.12, no.2 (1984), pp.72-5
Technical advice from the recording engineer
of Edinburgh University's School of Scottish
Studies.

KENYON, Joe *see* **GOULD, Tony**

KERSHAW, Baz *see* **LANGLEY, Gordon**

1003 KEY, Betty McKeever
"Oral history in the library"
Catholic Library World, vol.49 (April 1978),
pp.380-4

1004 KEY, Betty McKeever
Exploring oral history: a how, a why, a who
manual
Baltimore: Maryland Historical Association,
1979

KHALID, R. *see* **SIANN, G.**

1005 KIBBLEWHITE, Liz and RIGBY, Andy
Aberdeen in the general strike
Aberdeen: Aberdeen People's Press, 1977
40pp
Five participant interviews are included: a
boilermaker, messenger boy, postman,
railwayman and a woodworker who was
secretary of Aberdeen Trades Council in 1926.
They talk about clashes with the police and
strike-breaking.

1006 KIBBLEWHITE, Liz and RIGBY, Andy
Fascism in Aberdeen: street politics in the 1930s
Aberdeen: Aberdeen People's Press, 1978
48pp
A study of the activities of the British Union
of Fascists in Aberdeen 1936-9 and their
clashes with anti-fascists, from interviews with
activists.

KIDEL, Mark *see* **MELLOR, Moira**

1007 KIERNAT, J.M.
"The use of life review activity with confused
nursing home residents"
American Journal of Occupational Therapy,
no.33 (1979), pp.306-310

1008 KIGHTLY, Charles
Country voices: life and lore in farm and village
Thames and Hudson, 1984
240pp
Memories of rural England from people living
in seven different areas of the country, all
born around the turn of the century.

1009 KIKI, Albert Maori
Kiki: ten thousand years in a lifetime: a New
Guinea autobiography
Melbourne: Cheshire, 1973
190pp

1010 KIKUMURA, Akemi
Through harsh winters: the life of a Japanese
immigrant woman
Novata, California: Chandler and Sharp, 1981
157pp; bibliography
Based largely on the recorded life story of the
author's mother's experience of coming to
America from Hiroshima in the early 1920s.

1011 KILLIE CAMPBELL AFRICANA LIBRARY
Oral history project relating to the Zulu people:
a catalogue of interviews
Durban: Killie Campbell Africana Library,
University of Natal, 1983
43pp

KIMBALL, Solon T. *see* **ARENSBERG,**
Conrad M.

1012 KING, Helen
"Chloe Fisher on the art of midwifery"
Newsletter of the History Workshop Centre for
Social History, *no.3 (1985), pp.61-7*
An interview with a midwife.

1013 KING, K.S.
"Reminiscing psychotherapy with ageing
people"
Journal of Psychosocial Nursing and Mental
Health Services, *vol.20, no.2 (1982) pp.21-25*

1014 KING, Michael
Te Puea: a biography
Auckland, New Zealand: Hodder and
Stoughton, 1977
331pp; bibliography
A biography of one of the most influential
women in New Zealand politics drawn in part
from taped interviews by the country's
foremost social historian.

1015 KING, Michael
"New Zealand oral history: some cultural and
methodological considerations"
New Zealand Journal of History, *vol.12, no.2*
(1978), pp.104-123
Refers to his experience interviewing native
Maoris.

1016 KINGSCOTT, Judith E.
Oral history in libraries: with special reference
to the Nottinghamshire Oral History Collection
and the Hyson Green Project
Loughborough: Loughborough University of
Technology, 1988
MA thesis
144pp; bibliography
Includes a contemporary study of a complex of
flats in Hyson Green, a deprived inner city
area of Nottingham, and based on recordings
made during an MSC project in 1986-7.

KINNEAR, Jill *see* **EELES, Graham**

1017 KIRBY, David, THOMAS, Delia and
TURNER, Louise (eds.)
Northampton remembers boot and shoe
Northampton: Northampton Borough Council
Community Programme Museum and
Guildhall Project, 1988
79pp
Based on interviews with workers about
aspects of Northampton's staple boot and shoe
industry, including outwork, factory
conditions, trade unionism and employers.

1018 KIRKHAM, Pat, MACE, Rodney and
PORTER, Julian
Furnishing the world: the East London furniture
trade 1830-1980
Journeyman, 1987
136pp; bibliography
Chapters on furniture making, distribution
and marketing, trade unions and talking about
the trade - a compilation of reminiscence.

1019 KIRKLEES SOUND ARCHIVE
Oral history interviews and sound recordings
catalogue
Huddersfield: Kirklees Sound Archive, 1988
72pp
A detailed listing of the Archive's 400 or so
interviews covering the Huddersfield area's
Afro-Caribbean, Asian and Polish
communities; childhood; cinema; folk song
and dance; the engineering, textile and
chemical industries; canals; and the Second
World War. The Archive has also produced a
series of compilation cassettes drawn from the
collection.

1020 KIRKLEES SOUND ARCHIVE
The Polish community in Kirklees
Huddersfield: Kirklees Sound Archive, nd
4pp
A selection of quotes from Polish people
describing their homeland and experiences as
refugees during and after the Second World
War, drawn from the Kirklees Sound
Archive's interviews.

1021 **KIRKLEES SOUND ARCHIVE**
Mill people
Huddersfield: Kirklees Sound Archive, nd
4pp
Extracts from some of the recordings with
textile workers in the Huddersfield area
carried out by the Archive.

KIRKUP, Gill *see* **CARTER, Ruth**

KIRKWOOD-SMITH, Lorna *see* **GREIG,
John**

1022 **KIRRANE, Siobhan**
"Employment Training: the icing on the cake"
Oral History, *vol.17, no.2 (1989), pp.53-5*
The problems of government-funded
temporary work schemes as applied to
Leicester Oral History Archive.

KIRRANE, Siobhan *see also* **CARSWELL,
Jeanne**

1023 **KLAK, Janet**
"Kirkcaldy and its local collections"
LOCSCOT, *vol.1, no.5 (Autumn 1983),
pp.85-6*
Oral history at Kirkcaldy Central Library in
Fife, Scotland.

1024 **KLOCKARS, Carl B.**
The professional fence
Tavistock, 1975
242pp
A case study of a 'fence'(passing stolen
property) based on weekly interviews between
January 1972 and April 1973.

KLOTZ, Heinrich *see* **COOK, John W.**

KLUCKHOHN, C. *see* **GOTTSCHALK, L.**

1025 **KNIGHT, Margot H.**
Directory of oral history in Washington State
Pullman: Washington State University, 1981
76pp

1026 **KOMAROVSKY, Mirra**
Blue collar marriage
*Yale University Press, 1987, second edition;
first edition, 1962*
393pp; bibliography
A sociological study of the family relationships
of fifty-eight stable, working-class families
with twelve years or less schooling.

1027 **KONTTINEN, Sirkka-Liisa**
Byker
Newcastle upon Tyne: Bloodaxe Books, 1985
128pp
A portrait through photographs and oral
history of a working class area of Newcastle on
the verge of extinction through demolition:
the washhouse, the cobbler, the barber, the
pigeon fanciers, the bowls green, the pubs,
shops and houses.

1028 **KORNBLUH, Joyce L. and MIKUSKO,
Brady (eds.)**
Working womenroots: an oral history primer
*Ann Arbor: Institute of Labor and Industrial
Relations, University of Michigan/Wayne State
University, 1979*

1029 **KOSS, Stephen**
"Speaking of the past"
Times Literary Supplement, *5 December 1975,
pp.1435-6*

1030 **KOSS, Stephen**
Nonconformity in modern British politics
Batsford, 1975
272pp
Uses some ten interviews for his study of
religious nonconformity from Victorian times
until the Second World War.

1031 **KOSS, Stephen**
*The rise and fall of the political press in Britain.
Volume 2: the twentieth century*
Hamish Hamilton, 1984
718pp
Several dozen journalists were interviewed
but the author reportedly rarely found 'the
experience as instructive as I would hope'.

KOTKIN, Amy *see* **CUTTING-BAKER, Holly**

1032 **KRAMER, Sydelle and MASUR, Jenny (eds.)**
Jewish grandmothers
Boston, Mass.: Beacon Press, 1976
174pp
An oral history of the immigrant experience of
twelve Ashkenazi Jewish women all born in
Eastern Europe.

1033 **KRANITZ-SANDERS, Lillian**
*Twelve who survived: an oral history of the Jews
of Lodz, Poland, 1930-1954*
New York: Irvington, 1983
Bibliography

1034 KUSNITZ, Peggy Ann
"Oral history: a selective bibliography"
Drexel Library Quarterly, vol.15 (October 1979), pp.50-75
188 items listed to update bibliographies by Fox and Waserman. This issue is a special on 'Managing oral history collections in the library' and contains a number of useful articles.

LA CLARE, Leo *see* **CLARE, Leo La**

1035 LABOV, William
Language in the inner city: studies in the black English vernacular
Oxford: Blackwell, 1977; first published Philadelphia, 1972
412pp
Black youth in US inner cities.

LACEY, Roderic *see* **DENOON, Donald**

1036 LADJEVARDI, Habib
Reference guide to the Iranian Oral History Collection
Cambridge, Mass.: Harvard University Center for Middle Eastern Europe Studies Iranian Oral History Project, 1988
153pp
Details of 126 interviews with individuals, recorded from 1981, who played major roles in political events in Iran from the 1920s to the 1970s: includes prime ministers, cabinet members, the judiciary, media, leaders of tribes and political parties, members of the armed forces and the security agency SAVAK, and foreign diplomats. The vast majority are recorded in Persian, the longest interview is forty-three hours.

LAGENBACH, Randolph *see* **HAREVEN, Tamara K.**

1037 La GUMINA, Salvatore J.
The immigrants speak: Italian Americans tell their story
New York: Center for Migration Studies, 1979
209pp

1038 LAI, Annie, LITTLE, Bob and LITTLE, Pippa
"Chinatown Annie: the East End opium trade 1920-35. The story of a woman opium dealer"
Oral History, vol.14, no.1 (1986), pp.18-30
Winning entry of the London Weekend Television Oral History Competition in 1985.

1039 LAISTERDYKE LOCAL HISTORY GROUP
Remembering Laisterdyke
Leeds: University of Leeds Department of Adult and Continuing Education Pioneer Work, 1988
63pp
A history of an area of Bradford through the memories of people who lived there.

LAMB, J.P. *see* **WALTON, Mary**

1040 LAMBETH COUNCIL
Forty winters on: memories of Britain's post-war Caribbean immigrants
Lambeth Council, 1988
47pp
Memories of early Caribbean migrants, published to commemorate the fortieth anniversary of the arrival of the first ship, SS Empire Windrush, in June 1948.

1041 LAMPHEAR, John
The traditional history of the Jie of Uganda
Oxford: Clarendon, 1976
Oxford Studies in African Affairs
281pp; bibliography
The development of the pastoral Jie political community up to 1915, based on over 200 interviews carried out in Karamoja district in Uganda and Turkhania district in Kenya in 1969-71.

1042 LAN, David
Guns and rain: guerillas and spirit mediums in Zimbabwe
James Currey, 1985
244pp; bibliography
An anthropological study, making use of oral sources.

1043 LANCE, David
"Oral history: some personal reflections on the American experience"
Phonographic Bulletin, no.8 (1974), pp.12-17

1044 LANCE, David
"A museum approach to oral history"
Sound Heritage, vol.3, no.2 (1974)

1045 LANCE, David
"Oral history in Britain"
Oral History Review, vol.2 (1974), pp.64-76
An overview including details of the Imperial War Museum's Department of Sound Records and a list of oral history centres in Britain and Ireland.

1046 LANCE, David
"Oral history in Great Britain: the status of sound recordings and their use"
Phonographic Bulletin, vol.13 (1975), pp.11-21
A comparison between America and Britain: in both cases university social historians have provided the main dynamic for growth.

1047 LANCE, David
"Oral history recordings: a note on legal considerations"
Oral History, vol.4, no.1 (1976), pp.96-7

1048 LANCE, David
"Sound recordings at the Imperial War Museum: setting up a special archive"
Recorded Sound, nos.66-67 (1977), pp.707-9
An outline of the establishment of the Department of Sound Records, which was created in January 1972 and opened to public access in July 1977.

1049 LANCE, David
"Tuning in to the sound of Britain at war"
The Times Higher Educational Supplement, 30 June 1978

1050 LANCE, David
An archive approach to oral history
Imperial War Museum/International Association of Sound Archives, 1978
64pp
Aims to 'provide a body of professional method for the oral history librarian' but it is also an essential text for beginners and established oral historians alike in properly organising, conserving and archiving oral history recordings.

1051 LANCE, David
"Sound archive development and practice: a case study"
Archives and Manuscripts: the Journal of the Australian Society of Archivists, vol.8, no.1 (June 1980), pp.9-16

1052 LANCE, David
"Oral history archives: perceptions and practices"
Oral History, vol.8, no.2 (1980), pp.59-63
The autobiographical narrative approach of US practitioners and the development of an archive-centred methodology.

1053 LANCE, David
"Oral history: criteria for selection for recording in the field" in HARRISON, Helen (ed.)

1054 LANE, Tony
Grey dawn breaking: British merchant seamen in the late twentieth century ·
Manchester: Manchester University Press, 1988
200pp
The first comprehensive study of merchant seamen for eighty years based partially on oral accounts collected by the author, who was himself a merchant seaman for nine years in the 1950s.

1055 LANE, Tony and ROBERTS, Kenneth
Strike at Pilkingtons
Fontana, 1971
266pp
Based partially on oral testimonies from workers at Pilkington Brothers Ltd., glass manufacturers, of St.Helens in Lancashire.

LANGENBACH, Randolph see HAREVEN, Tamara K.

1056 LANGLEY, Gordon and KERSHAW, Baz (eds.)
"Reminiscence theatre"
Theatre Papers, fourth series (1981-2), no.6
A useful overview from the Department of Theatre, Dartington College of Arts, Devon. It covers first steps and early experiments in the Exeter area, basic techniques, set and layout, objects, costumes, character, and scene structure.

1057 LANGLOIS, William J.
"The dissemination of oral history materials"
Phonographic Bulletin, no.22 (1978), pp.34-5

1058 LANGLOIS, William J.
A guide to aural history research
Victoria, British Columbia: Provincial Archives of British Columbia Aural History Programme, 1976
A procedures manual from one of Canada's leading projects. Notable for the introduction of 'aural' for 'oral' in an attempt to broaden the scope of collecting beyond merely spoken word.

1059 LANMAN, Barry A. and MEHAFFY, George L.
Oral history in the secondary school classroom
Provo: Oral History Association, 1988
Pamphlet no.2
Bibliography

1060 LANNING, Greg
"Television History Workshop Project no.1: The Brixton Tapes"
History Workshop, no.12 (Autumn 1981), pp.183-8
An account of an experiment in television history following the Brixton riots in London on 10-12 April 1981, which aimed to enable local people in Brixton to record their own accounts of the events only one week after they had happened. Includes comments on the technical aspects of using video.

1061 LANZMANN, Claude
Shoah: an oral history of the Holocaust. The complete text of the film
Translated from the French
New York: Pantheon, 1985
200pp
With a preface by Simone de Beauvoir.

1062 LAW, Robin
"Early Yoruba historiography"
History in Africa, vol.3 (1976)

1063 LAWRENCE, Jane
It used to be cheating: working together in literacy groups
National Extension College, 1985
119pp
A research project into what students felt about their education based partially on taped interviews.

1064 LAWRENCE, Jane and MACE, Jane
Remembering in groups: ideas from reminiscence and literacy work
Exploring Living Memory/Oral History Society, 1987
38pp
How people working in groups can share their memories about their own living history, with comments on the value of reminiscence.

1065 LAWRENCE, Neil and BUNK, Steve
The stump-jumpers: a new breed of Australians
Marrickville, New South Wales: Hale and Iremonger, 1985
An insight into how a number of famous Australians, in fields as diverse as film-making and big business, have succeeded by using innovation and guile to overcome obstacles.

1066 LAWRENCE, R. and FITZGERALD, J.M.
"Autobiographical memory across the life span"
Journal of Gerontological Social Work, vol.39, no.6 (November 1984), pp.692-8

LAZARUS, W. *see* LESSER, J.

1067 LEE, Gail Margaret
The use of oral history to preserve a record of rural crafts in Great Britain
Loughborough: Loughborough University of Technology, 1988
55pp; bibliography

1068 LEE COMMUNITY EDUCATION CENTRE WOMEN'S HISTORY GROUP
Patchworks
Lee Community Education Centre/University of London Goldsmiths' College, 1987
66pp
Ten older women's recollections, the result of eighteen months of discussion, taping and writing.

1069 LEE COMMUNITY EDUCATION CENTRE WOMEN'S HISTORY GROUP
Home sweet home
Lee Community Education Centre/University of London Goldsmiths' College, 1989
40pp
Homelife in London, Kent and Gateshead in the 1920s and 30s.

1070 LEESON, R.A.
Strike: a live history
Allen and Unwin, 1973
246pp
A distillation of reminiscences of grass-roots participants of industrial disputes between 1887 and 1971.

1071- LEICESTER ORAL HISTORY ARCHIVE
1119 Cassette publications featuring extracts from life story interviews contained in LOHA's wider oral history collection.
Leicester: Leicester Oral History Archive, 1986-9

1071 *Mining memories (C1, 26 mins.)*
Mining at Desford from 1943.

1072 *Cinema (C2, 23 mins.)*

1073 *World War Two evacuee (C3, 20 mins.)*
An evacuee to Leicestershire in 1940.

1074 *Leicester market (C4, 24 mins.)*
Market trading in the 1930s.

1075 *The West End (C5, 31mins.)*
Leicester's West End before the First World War.

1076 *Canals (C6, 50 mins.)*

1077 *Maids and mistresses (C7, 57 mins.)*
Domestic service between the wars.

1078 *New Road (C8, 29 mins.)*
Christmas on the dole.

1079 *Midwife (C9, 30 mins.)*
Memories of a slum midwife and nurse.

1080 *Leicester's slums (C10, 22 mins.)*

1081 *Music hall (C11, 25 mins.)*
Leicester's music hall: its performers and the impact of early cinema.

1082 *Entertainment (C12, 23 mins.)*

1083 *Belgrave (C13, 22 mins.)*
Living in Leicester's Belgrave before the Second World War.

1084 *The Great War (C14, 43 mins.)*
The First World War recalled.

1085 *Holidays (C15, 22 mins.)*

1086 *No fixed abode (C16, 45 mins.)*
A Leicester vagrant talks about alcoholism and homelessness.

1087 *Housing the people (C17, 22 mins.)*
Housing conditions in Leicester before 1939.

1088 *Edwardian Leicester (C18, 28 mins.)*
Daily life in the early years of the century.

1089 *Women's lives (C19, 33 mins.)*
Ordinary women's lifestyles since 1918.

1090 *Public health (C20, 33 mins.)*
Health care in Leicester before the National Health Service.

1091 *Life on the trams (C21, 27 mins.)*
From horse-drawn trams to the arrival of buses.

1092 *Christmas past (C22, 27 mins.)*
Christmas celebrations before 1939.

1093 *Highfields (C23, 26 mins.)*
Children's games and local shops.

1094 *Fascism (C24, 40 mins.)*
The Blackshirts and Oswald Mosley's visit to Leicestershire.

1095 *World War Two (C25, 60 mins.)*
Memories of Leicestershire at war.

1096 *Aylestone (C26, 25 mins.)*
Old Aylestone recalled.

1097 *Unemployment (C27, 28 mins.)*

1098 *Employment (C28, 50 mins.)*
Leicestershire working lives.

1099 *Women in industry (C29, 50 mins.)*
Includes women's work in munitions.

1100 *The three Rs (C30, 50 mins.)*
Memories of school: discipline and the curriculum.

1101 *Home remedies (C31, 45 mins.)*
Cures for everything from cuts to amputations.

1102 *Travel agent (C32, 50 mins.)*
Working in the travel business from 1929.

1103 *Life of a nun (C33, 50 mins.)*
Three nuns talk about their work and the role of convents.

1104 *Swithland, Quorn and Anstey (C34, 54 mins.)*
Leicestershire village life 1900-45.

1105 *The Women's Land Army (C35, 56 mins.)*
Women working on the land in two world wars.

1106 *Farming life (C36, 42 mins.)*
Life and work on Leicestershire farms.

1107 *Theatre (C37, 52 mins.)*
Leicester's Little Theatre and Theatre Royal.

1108 *Leicester shops (C38, 53 mins.)*
Central Leicester shops between the wars.

1109 *Co-operative movement (C39, 51 mins.)*
The development of the co-op movement in
Leicestershire.

1110 *Coffee and cafe (C40, 55 mins.)*
Coffee houses and cafes in Leicester 1900-45.

1111 *Fighting talk (C41, 40 mins.)*
The Leicestershire boxing scene before the
Second World War.

1112 *Boys' homes (C42, 56 mins.)*
Institutional life in various boys' homes in the
1920s, 30s and 40s, notably Desford Boys'
Home.

1113 *Crimes and punishment (C43, 56 mins.)*
Leicestershire crime, police and law
enforcement in the first half of the century.

1114 *All the fun of the fair (C44, 57 mins.)*
Leicester fairs remembered by showmen and
punters.

1115 *Up for the cup! (C45, 59 mins.)*
Leicester City football players remember the
Football Association Cup run of 1949.

1116 *Courting days (C46, 52mins.)*
Growing up and meeting the opposite sex.

1117 *Soar Valley labours (C47, 53 mins.)*
Work in the cement works, shoe factory and
farming.

1118 *Life on the railways (C48, 57 mins.)*
Drivers, signalmen and other railworkers
recall their work.

1119 *Countesthorpe Cottage Home (C49, 54 mins.)*
Ex-Countesthorpe children remember their
time at the home for orphans.

1120 **LEICESTER ORAL HISTORY ARCHIVE**
An introduction to oral history interviewing
Leicester: Leicester Oral History Archive, 1989
13pp booklet and cassette tape
Gives some basic guidance in how to
interview, with some amusing tape
illustrations of how not to do it. Includes an
A-Z of interview technique and a multiple
choice questionnaire suitable for use in
schools.

LEICESTER ORAL HISTORY ARCHIVE *see
also* **CARSWELL, Jeanne; KIRRANE,
Siobhan**

1121 **LEITCH, Roger (ed.)**
The book of Sandy Stewart
Edinburgh: Scottish Academic Press, 1988
129pp; further reading
The life story of one of Scotland's travelling
people based on two years' fieldwork using
tape-recorded reminiscences.

1122 **LEITH LOCAL HISTORY PROJECT**
Leith lives: memories at work. A look at
employment between the wars
Leith: Leith Local History Project, 1985
32pp
Produced under a Manpower Services
Commission scheme and based on interviews
with local people in Leith, Edinburgh's port.

1123 **LEITH LOCAL HISTORY PROJECT**
Leith lives: unemployment - making ends meet.
A look at unemployment between the wars
Leith: Leith Local History Project, 1985
32pp

1124 **LEITH LOCAL HISTORY PROJECT**
Old Kirkgate
Leith: Leith Local History Project, 1985
32pp

1125 **LEITH LOCAL HISTORY PROJECT**
School days
Leith: Leith Local History Project, 1986
32pp

1126 **LEITH LOCAL HISTORY PROJECT**
'It wisnae a'work'
Leith: Leith Local History Project, 1987
32pp

1127 **LEITH LOCAL HISTORY PROJECT**
Your never done
Leith: Leith Local History Project, 1988
32pp

1128 **LEONARD, Diana**
Sex and generation: a study of courtship and
weddings
Tavistock, 1980
315pp; bibliography
A sociological survey of Swansea in the late
1960s based on fifty-four interviews.

1129 **LESSER, J., LAZARUS, W. and FRANKEL,
R.**
"Reminiscence group therapy with psychotic
geriatric patients"
Gerontologist, vol.21, no.3 (1981), pp.291-6

1130 LESSING, Joan (ed.)
Jewish immigrants and the Nazi period in the USA. Volume 3, part 1: Guide to the oral history collections of the Research Foundation for Jewish Immigration, New York
Saur Verlag, 1982
152pp; bibliography

1131 LEVENE, Bruce
Mendocino County remembered: an oral history
Fort Brogy, California: Mendocino County Historical S Society Publications, 1976

1132 LEVINE, Lawrence W.
Black culture and black consciousness: Afro-American folk thought from slavery to freedom
Oxford University Press, 1977
522pp
A variety of sources were used including long narrative oral poems, songs, folktales, proverbs, jokes and verbal games.

1133 LEVINE, Maurice
Cheetham to Cordova: a Manchester man of the thirties
Manchester: Neil Richardson, 1984
56pp; bibliography
Born in 1907 the son of a Lithuanian Jewish immigrant, Levine was one of the first Manchester volunteers to join the International Brigade during the Spanish Civil War.

1134 LEWIS, Brian (ed.)
Privy to Privatisation
Castleford, West Yorkshire: Yorkshire Art Circus, 1988
88pp
Over a hundred people from a coalfield community contribute to a fascinating look at housing and changing family life over three generations.

1135 LEWIS, Brian, DYKE, Mel and CLAYTON, Ian (eds.)
The bus to Barnsley market: journeys into experience
Castleford, West Yorkshire: Yorkshire Art Circus, 1989
96pp
Over a hundred people from Darfield, Snape Hill, Wombwell and Stairfoot near Barnsley talk about education in the broadest sense, including school, WEA, libraries, the Labour Party, church, trade unions, pit work, shops and Barnsley market.

LEWIS, Brian *see also* ROONEY, Ray

1136 LEWIS, Charles N.
"Reminiscence and self-concept in old age"
Journal of Gerontology, vol.26 (1971),
pp.240-3

1137 LEWIS, Charles N.
"The adaptive value of reminiscing in old age"
Journal of Geriatric Psychiatry, vol.6 (1973),
pp.117-21

1138 LEWIS, Myrna I. and BUTLER, Robert N.
"Life review therapy: putting memories to work in individual and group psychotherapy"
Geriatrics, vol.29 (November 1974),
pp.165-174

LEWIS, Myrna I. *see also* BUTLER, Robert N.

1139 LEWIS, Marilyn
An oral history of Walsall
Walsall, West Midlands: Walsall Metropolitan Borough Council Archives Service, 1983
Walsall Chronicle no.5
30pp
Reminiscences of childhood, family life and leisure, and old Walsall.

1140 LEWIS, Oscar
Five families: Mexican case studies in the culture of poverty
New York: Basic Books, 1959
Oral narratives from one rural and four urban families outlining a typical day. Includes the Sanchez family.

1141 LEWIS, Oscar
The children of the Sanchez: autobiography of a Mexican family
Secker and Warburg, 1962; Harmondsworth: Penguin, 1964; first published New York: Random House, 1961
506pp
'Social realism' with the aid of the tape recorder. An example of the American anthropological tradition in which the father and his four adult children in a Mexico City slum tenement family are profiled.

1142 LEWIS, Oscar
La Vida: a Puerto Rican family in the culture of poverty - San Juan and New York
Secker and Warburg, 1967; first published New York: Random House, 1966
599pp
A study of the pseudonymous Rios family: the parents in Puerto Rico, the children in New York.

1143 LEWIS, Oscar
A death in the Sanchez family
Secker and Warburg, 1970; first published New
York: Random House, 1969
119pp
An oral history of the death, wake and burial
of Guadalupe, the maternal aunt of the
Sanchez children Manuel, Roberto and
Consuelo. Originally recorded in Spanish.

1144 LEWIS, Oscar
Pedro Martinez: a Mexican peasant and his
family
Harmondsworth: Penguin, 1980; originally
published New York: Random House, 1964
557pp
The story of a rural Mexican family based on
recordings over twenty years. Born in 1889,
Pedro experienced the 1910 Revolution and
was converted from Catholicism to Seventh
Day Adventism.

**1145 LEWIS, Oscar, LEWIS, Ruth M. and
RIGDON, Susan M.**
Four men: living the revolution: an oral history
of contemporary Cuba
Urbana and London: University of Illinois
Press, 1977
538pp; bibliography
The transcribed stories of four Cuban men
brought up in poverty in Havana and recorded
at Castro's request between 1969 and 1977.

**1146 LEWIS, Oscar, LEWIS, Ruth M. and
RIGDON, Susan M.**
Four women: living the revolution: an oral
history of contemporary Cuba
Urbana and London: University of Illinois
Press, 1977
443pp; bibliography
The status of women in Cuba and their role in
the revolution through the testimony of three
white women and one of mixed race recorded
in 1969-70.

**1147 LEWIS, Oscar, LEWIS, Ruth M. and
RIGDON, Susan M.**
Neighbors: living the revolution: an oral history
of contemporary Cuba
Urbana: University of Illinois Press, 1978
Bibliography
Testimony from five suburban families from
Havana, originally recorded in Spanish in
1969-70.

1148 LEWIS, Peter
A people's war
Thames Methuen, 1986
245pp; bibliography
Written to accompany the Channel Four
television series of the same name about the
Second World War and based on oral
recollections, diaries and letters.

LEWIS, Ruth M. *see* **LEWIS, Oscar**

LI-WEN, Yang *see* **THOMPSON, Paul**

LIBERTY, Margot *see* **STANDS IN TIMBER,
John**

LIBOVICH, Sue *see* **HART, Lorraine**

1149 LICHTMAN, Allan J.
Your family history: how to use oral history,
personal family archives and public documents
to discover your heritage
New York: Vintage Books, 1978
205pp; bibliography

LIDDIARD, Penny *see* **CARVER, Vida**

1150 LIDDINGTON, Jill
"Working class women in the North West"
Oral History, vol.5, no.2 (1977), pp.31-45
Women in the Lancashire cotton industry:
their work patterns and trade union
involvement.

1151 LIDDINGTON, Jill
"Rediscovering suffrage history"
History Workshop, no.4 (Autumn 1977)

1152 LIDDINGTON, Jill
The life and times of a respectable rebel
Virago, 1984
536pp; bibliography
The story of one of the forgotten pioneers of
the women's movement - Selina Cooper,
1864-1946 - told through the oral testimony of
her daughter, unpublished letters,
contemporary documents etc.

1153 LIDDINGTON, Jill
The long road to Greenham: feminism and anti-militarism in Britain since 1820
Virago, 1989
341pp; bibliography
Draws on life story interviews with peace activists and considers the role of the Women's Co-operative Guild's 'white poppy' pacifism of the 1930s and the involvement of women in the Campaign for Nuclear Disarmament (CND), culminating in the establishment of the Greenham Common airbase camp in 1981 against ninety six Cruise nuclear missiles.

1154 LIDDINGTON, Jill and NORRIS, Jill
One hand tied behind us: the rise of the women's suffrage movement
Virago, 1978
304pp; bibliography
Concentrates on radical working class suffragists in Lancashire and Cheshire, many of them textile workers, who fought for a range of women's rights through the Independent Labour Party, the Clarion and Co-op movements and Socialist Sunday Schools. Draws on a number of interviews.

LIDDINGTON, Jill *see also* **EDGE, Y.**

1155 LIDDLE, Peter
The sailor's war, 1914-18
Poole: Blandford, 1988
224pp; bibliography
Derived from his own archive of personal testimonies, now housed at Leeds University, the book reveals the experience of the First World War at sea for junior officers and ratings.

1156 LIDDLE, Peter
The soldier's war, 1914-1918
Poole: Blandford, 1988
224pp; bibliography
Provides a representative account of the daily routine of battle and of being wounded and taken prisoner during the First World War.

1157 LIDZ, Richard
Many kinds of courage: an oral history of world war two
New York: Putnam, 1980
266pp
Survivors from the battles of Britain, Dunkirk and Pearl Harbor, from the Normany landing, and from the prison camps of Germany and Japan tell their stories.

1158 LIEBERMAN, M.A. and FALK, J.M.
"The remembered past as a source of data for research on the life cycle"
Journal of Aging and Human Development, no.14, pp.132-41

1158A LIFE STORIES/RÉCITS DE VIE
No.1, 1985–No. 5, 1989
An international journal of life story-based research published in English and French by the Biography and Society Research Committee of the International Sociological Association.

1159 *Lifetimes: a group autobiography*
Manchester: Institute of Advanced Studies, 1975-1976
A series of seven booklets in which "a group of working people set out to relate their lives in a Manchester overspill town [Partington]". Based on a series of informal transcribed interviews. (*See also* WILKINSON, Greg)

1160 LINDOP, Fred
"An interview with Harry Watson"
Bulletin of the Society for the Study of Labour History, no.39 (Autumn 1979), pp.73-7
Watson was president of the Watermen's, Lightermen's Tugmen and Bargemen's Union 1959-71 and a member of the Communist Party in London's dockland.

1161 LINDOP, Fred
"Unofficial militancy in the Royal Group of Docks 1945-67"
Oral History, vol.11, no.2 (1983), pp.21-33
The Royal Group in London was a focus for post-war militancy with the largest concentration of dockers anywhere in Britain.

1162 LINDQVIST, Sven
"Dig where you stand"
Oral History, vol.7, no.2 (1979), pp.24-30
Describes abandoning the writing of a history of the cement industry in order to encourage workers to record their own life stories.

LING, Geraldine *see* **CATMULL, Mick**

1163 LINKMAN, Audrey
"The Manchester Studies Archive Retrieval Project"
Journal of the Society of Archivists, vol.6, no.7 (April 1981), pp.414-22

1164 LITON, J. and OLSTEIN, S.C.
"Therapeutic aspects of reminiscence"
Social Casework, vol.50 (1969), p.263-8

1165 LITTLE, Bob
"Oral history in East Anglia"
Journal of East Anglian History Workshop,
vol.3, no.2 (1982), pp.5-8

1166 LITTLE, Bob
"Reminiscence books and materials: a review
article"
Oral History, vol.17, no.2 (1989)

LITTLE, Bob and Pippa *see also* **LAI, Annie**

1167 LITTLEJOHN, James
Westrigg: the sociology of a Cheviot parish
Routledge & Kegan Paul, 1963
*International Library of Sociology and Social
Reconstruction*
154pp
The social history of an upland parish in a
rural county in the south of Scotland,
researched between 1949 and 1951.

1168 LIVING ARCHIVE PROJECT
Dig where you stand: a book of ideas
*Milton Keynes: The Living Archive Project/
The Calouste Gulbenkian Foundation, 1989*
24pp; bibliography
A booklet to accompany a documentary arts
initiative in which schools received grants to
use local and oral history in a variety of ways.
Includes oral testimony from a project about
the Buckinghamshire railway town of
Wolverton.

1169 LIVING MEMORY PROJECT
*Growing up in Forest Fields: memories of life in
Nottingham between the wars*
*Nottingham: Nottingham University
Community Action Publishing Project, 1987*
40pp
Reminiscences of a suburb of Nottingham
from its development around the turn of the
century.

1170 *Llafur: The Journal of the Society for the Study
of Welsh Labour History, vol.2, no.2 (Spring
1977)*
A special issue devoted to the industrial unrest
of 1926 featuring many reminiscences from
Welsh participants.

1171 LOCAL HISTORY ARCHIVES UNIT
*I remember: a recall and reminiscence
bibliography and local resource directory*
*Hull: Local History Archives Unit,
Humberside College of Higher Education,
1987*
12pp
The unit has produced a large number of local
history document packs and booklets, and has
a strong local following through its excellent
newsletter.

1172 LOCHEAD, Richard
"Three approaches to oral history: the
journalistic, the academic, and the archival"
*Canadian Oral History Association Journal,
vol. 1 (1975-6), pp.5-12*
Oral history in Canada from 1960-75.

1173 LOCHEAD, Richard
"Oral history: the role of the archivist"
Phonographic Bulletin, no.37, November 1983

1174 LOCK, Alice (ed.)
Looking back at Stalybridge
*Ashton-under-Lyne: Tameside Libraries and
Arts Committee, 1989*
15pp; bibliography
Includes an interview covering schooldays,
local characters and work in the cotton
industry.

1175 LOCK, Graham
*Forces in motion: Anthony Braxton and the
meta-reality of creative music*
Quartet, 1988
412pp
Interviews and tour notes made in England
during 1985 with Braxton, the prominent
African-American composer and jazz multi-
instrumentalist.

1176 LOFTUS, Elizabeth
*Memory: surprising new insights into how we
remember and why we forget*
Addison and Wesley, 1980
207pp

LOFTUS, Elizabeth *see also* **WELLS, Gary L.**

1177 Lo GERFO, Marianne
"Three ways of reminiscence in theory and
practice"
*International Journal on Aging and Human
Development, vol.12, no.1 (1980-1), pp.39-48*

1178 LOH, Morag
*With courage in their cases: the experiences of
thirty-five Italian immigrant workers and their
families in Australia*
*Melbourne: Italian Federation of Emigrant
Workers and Their Families, 1980*

1179 LOH, Morag
Stories and storytellers from Indo-China
Richmond, Victoria: Victorian Indo-Chinese
Refugee Association, 1985, revised edition;
originally published Melbourne 1982
141pp
Sixteen members of Victoria's Indo-Chinese
community relate folk tales.

1180 LOH, Morag and LOWENSTEIN, Wendy
(eds.)
The immigrants
Melbourne: Hyland House, 1977; Penguin,
1978
149pp; bibliography
Based on interviews with immigrants to
Australia in the years 1890-1970.

1181 LOH, Morag and LOWENSTEIN, Wendy
(eds.)
Growing up in Richmond
Melbourne: Richmond Community Education
Centre and Fieldworkers in Oral History, 1979
45pp
Eleven accounts of childhood between 1890
and 1960 aimed at local young people.

LOMBARDI, Jerry *see* **BRECHER, Jeremy**

1182 LONDON HISTORY WORKSHOP CENTRE
SOUND AND VIDEO ARCHIVE
Living memories: recalling and recording the
past
London History Workshop/Thames
Television, 1988
35pp; bibliography
A brief how-to-do-it guide written to
accompany a Thames Television series of the
same name broadcast in September 1988 and
aimed at groups in the London area. Includes
sections on oral history in schools,
reminiscence, and travellers, plus examples of
tape documentation and a contact list of
London projects.

1183 LONDON HISTORY WORKSHOP CENTRE
SOUND AND VIDEO ARCHIVE
SVA Newsletter
Quarterly; no.1 July 1988-
Details of oral and community history
activities in the London area, and of the
archive itself. (*See also* SURRIDGE, O.)

1184 LONGMATE, Norman
How we lived then
Hutchinson, 1971; Arrow, 1973 and 1977
568pp
An exhaustive survey of daily life during the
Second World War based on a vast number of
written recollections from all over Britain.

1185 LOOKBACK GROUP
Middle Park past and present
Lookback Group, 1984
50pp
A group of enthusiastic pensioners from
Middle Park estate in Greenwich, London,
interviewed local schoolchildren and tenants
to compare experiences of change.

1186 *Lore and Language: the Journal of the Centre*
for English Cultural Tradition and Language
Twice annually, vol.1 (1973)-

1187 LOUBERE, Leo A.
The vine remembers: French vignerons recall
their past
Albany: State University of New York Press,
1985
193pp; bibliography

LOVETT, Tom *see* **McNAMEE, Peter**

1188 LOWENSTEIN, Wendy
Weevils in the flour: an oral record of the 1930s
depression in Australia
South Yarra, Melbourne: Hyland House, 1978
464pp; bibliography

1189 LOWENSTEIN, Wendy
The working class and the microphone
Melbourne: National Program Service, 1981
One 48-minute audio cassette

1190 LOWENSTEIN, Wendy and HILLS, Tom
Under the hook: Melbourne waterside workers
remember working lives and class war:
1900-1980
Prahan, Victoria: Melbourne Bookworkers/
The Australian Society for the Study of Labour
History, 1982

LOWENSTEIN, Wendy *see also* **LOH, Morag**

1191 LOWENTHAL, David
The past is a foreign country
Cambridge: Cambridge University Press, 1985
489pp; bibliography
On the social purposes and manipulation of
history.

1192 LUMMIS, Trevor
"The occupational community of East
Anglian fishermen: an historical dimension
through oral evidence"
British Journal of Sociology, vol.28, no.1
(March 1977), pp.51-74
Based on sixty interviews carried out in
1974-6, he criticises the view that oral history
is unreliable because it fails to use sampling
techniques.

1193 LUMMIS, Trevor
"Structure and validity in oral history"
*International Journal of Oral History, vol.2,
no.2 (June 1981), pp.109-20*
Argues that interview technique and the
interviewee's accuracy of memory accounts
for the variable quality of interviews.

1194 LUMMIS, Trevor
"Barrelling sprats"
*Journal of East Anglian History Workshop,
vol.3, no.2 (1982), pp.13-15*

1195 LUMMIS, Trevor
*Occupation and society: the East Anglian
fishermen 1880-1914*
*Cambridge: Cambridge University Press, 1985
212pp; bibliography*
A carefully researched study of fishing
communities, including evidence from
interviews with sixty people from the fishing
families.

1196 LUMMIS, Trevor
*Listening to history: the authenticity of oral
evidence*
*Hutchinson, 1987
175pp; bibliography*
An important book which defines, analyses
and describes oral history and the creation of
reliable oral information.

LUMMIS, Trevor *see also* **THOMPSON, Paul**

1197 LURIE, Nancy O.
*Mountain Wolf Woman, sister of Crashing
Thunder: the autobiography of a Winnebago
Indian*
*Ann Arbor: University of Michigan Press,
1961
142pp*
Recorded in 1958 in both English and
Winnebago, Mountain Wolf Woman describes
how her life changed from being an illiterate
Indian food gatherer to that of a Christian
church member living in a modern house.

1198 LYLE, Guy R.
*The librarian speaking: interviews with
university librarians*
*Athens, Georgia: University of Georgia Press,
1970
206pp*
Sixteen interviews presented with the
minimum of editing.

1199 LYNAM, K.
"Videotaping the Irish experience in Britain"
Irish Studies in Britain, no.1 (Spring 1981)

1200 LYNAM, K.
"The Irish Video Project: the Irish in England
tapes"
*Irish Studies in Britain, no.5 (November 1983-
March 1984)*

1201 LYND, Alice and Staughton
*Rank and file: personal histories by working-
class organisers*
*Boston: Beacon Press, 1973; second edition,
1981
296pp*
Compiled from eighteen transcribed edited
tape recordings with trade union members,
many of them workers in the Chicago area
steel industry. Half were active during the
1930s, the remainder since.

1202 LYND, Robert and Helen
*Middletown: a study in contemporary American
culture*
*Constable, 1929
550pp*
Pioneering oral history.

1203 LYND, Robert and Helen
*Middletown in transition: a study in cultural
conflicts*
*Constable, 1937
604pp*
(*See also* CAPLOW, Theodore)

1204 MABAWONKU, Iyabo
"The collection of oral traditions"
*International Library Review, vol.12, no.1
(January 1980), pp.71-7*
Explains the problems of finance,
environment and dialect common to many
African oral history projects.

1205 MACCOLL, Ewan and SEEGER, Peggy
Shellback reminiscences of Ben Bright, mariner
*History Workshop, nd
48pp; bibliography*
Recorded on three occasions in 1972, Ben
Bright talks and sings about his life and the
sea-going community to which he belonged.

1206 MACCOLL, Ewan and SEEGER, Peggy
*Till doomsday in the afternoon: the folklore of a
family of Scots travellers, the Stewarts of
Blairgowrie*
*Cambridge: Cambridge University Press, 1988
448pp; bibliography*
Based on recordings with four generations
made over twenty years.

1207 MACDONALD, Lyn
They called it Passchendaele: the story of the third battle of Ypres and of the men who fought in it
Joseph, 1978; Macmillan, 1983
253pp; bibliography
An account of one of the key battles of the First World War derived from over 600 stories and eye-witness accounts.

1208 MACDONALD, Lyn
The roses of no man's land
Joseph, 1980; Macmillan, 1984
318pp; bibliography
A unique oral account of the First World War through the eyes of its casualties and medical services, including the women's Voluntary Aid Detachment (VAD).

1209 MACDONALD, Lyn
Somme
Joseph, 1983; Papermac, 1984
366pp; bibliography
Based on interviews with veterans from one of the First World War's most meticulously planned and costly campaigns.

1210 MACDONALD, Lyn
1914
Harmondsworth: Penguin, 1987
446pp; bibliography
Recollections of Kitchener's army in the opening few months of the First World War.

1211 MACDONALD, Lyn
1914-1918: voices and images of the Great War
Joseph, 1988
346pp
A chronological account of the First World War through poems, letters and the personal narrative of those who fought. With research by Shirley Seaton.

1212 MACDONELL, Margaret
The emigrant experience: songs of Highland emigrants in North America
Toronto: University of Toronto Press, 1982
228pp; bibliography
A survey of song traditions reflecting the lives of Gaels in North America compiled from oral sources by a leading Canadian authority on Gaelic culture.

1213 MACDOUGALL, Ian
"The reminiscences of John McArthur, Fife miner"
Oral History, vol.2, no.1 (1974), pp.59-61

1214 MACDOUGALL, Ian (ed.)
Voices from the Spanish Civil War: personal recollections of Scottish volunteers in Republican Spain 1936-39
Edinburgh: Polygon, 1986
369pp; bibliography
Verbatim interviews with twenty Scots International Brigaders from all walks of life, including an accountant, a nurse and a railwayman. They recount memories of battles, injury, being taken prisoner and attitudes towards them on their return to Scotland.

1215 MACDOUGALL, Ian
The Scottish hunger marches: volume one
Edinburgh: Polygon, 1989
192pp
Oral testimonies of those unemployed hunger marchers of the 1930s who converged on Glasgow, Edinburgh and London to demand government action against poverty. Volume two planned for publication in 1990.

1216 MACE, Jane
"Rewriting literature: publishing from adult literacy"
Oral History, vol.7, no.2 (1979), pp.63-7

1217 MACE, Jane
Working with words: literacy beyond school
Writers and Readers Publishing Co-operative for Chameleon, 1979
118pp
A description of the campaign for literacy in the early 1970s incorporating students' and tutors' accounts of their experiences.

MACE, Jane *see also* BAYNHAM, Mike; LAWRENCE, Jane

MACE, Rodney *see* KIRKHAM, Pat

1218 MACFARLANE, James
"Denaby Main: a South Yorkshire mining village"
Bulletin of the Society for the Study of Labour History, no.25 (Autumn 1972), pp.82-100
Comparative perspectives of life in a pit village from verbatim interviews with Robert Shephard, Fred Bramley and Harriet Hallet. *See also* Bulletin, *no.26 (Spring 1973), pp.39-42* for an addendum to this article.

MACK, Joanna *see* HUMPHRIES, Steve

1219 MACKAY, Margaret
"Nineteenth century Tiree emigrant communities in Ontario"
Oral History, vol.9, no.2 (1981), pp.49-60
Migration from an Inner Hebrides island as a result of a potato crop failure.

1220 MACKAY, Margaret
"Oral and documentary sources: a case study"
Phonographic Bulletin, no.30 (July 1981), pp.7-14
The Tiree project of 1973-7 carried out 380 interviews in Gaelic and English, one third on tape.

1221 MACLAREN, A. Allen (ed.)
Social class in Scotland: past and present
Edinburgh: Donald, 1976
195pp
A socio-historical examination of social class and its role in determining attitudes, beliefs and relationships.

MACLEAN, Kay *see* **DAVIS, Cullom**

1222 MACLEOD, Dawn
"Scenes of the near past: born in the stone"
Blackwood's Magazine, November 1980, pp.430-41
Reminiscences of a Cotswold stonemason.

1223 MACMASTER, Neil
Spanish fighters: an oral history of civil war and exile
Basingstoke: Macmillan, 1990
260pp

1224 MACPHAIL, I.M.M.
The Clydebank blitz
Glasgow: Clydebank Town Council, 1974
108pp
Testimony from the air-raids of March 1941.

MADGE, Charles *see* **JENNINGS, Humphrey**

MAJOR, Carl *see* **JONES, Sian**

1225 MAKOWER, Joel
Woodstock: the oral history
Sidgwick and Jackson, 1989
361pp
Extracts from in-depth interviews with the organisers, producers, performers, doctors, policemen, neighbours, audience, and media people at the major music event of the sixties, held one weekend in August 1969.

1226 MANCHESTER, William
The death of a president: November 20-November 25, 1963
Joseph, 1967
784pp
A political documentary of the assassination of John F.Kennedy, based on 266 oral history interviews.

1227 MANN, Nancy D.
"Directory of women's oral history projects"
Frontiers: A Journal of Women's Studies, vol.7, no.1 (1983)
A listing of projects in the United States.

1228 MANSFIELD, Nick
"George Edwards and the Farmworkers' Union and Norfolk and the Great War: oral history in Norfolk Rural Life Museum"
Oral History, vol.14, no.2 (1986), pp.51-58

MANSON, Hugo *see* **FYFE, Judith**

1229 MANTELL, W.
A study in oral history
Knoxville: University of Tennessee Press, 1970

1230- **MANTLE ORAL HISTORY PROJECT**
1240 Cassette publications each around one hour and featuring one or more interviewees from Mantle's oral history archive.
Coalville: Mantle Oral History Project, 1987-9

1230 *Molly (001)*
A story of being adopted, of an institution in Lincoln and starting work in a laundry.

1231 *Harold Hawke (002)*
A childhood in Cornwall, farming, the depression and post-war quarrying in Bardon.

1232 *Winfield (003)*
Memories of Whitwick: childhood games, Whitwick Wakes, shop-work and Whitwick pit.

1233 *H. Blake (004)*
Recollections of a forester on the Beaumanor Estate and mining.

1234 *Eric Hunt (005)*
Bus driving, mining at Desford and Ellistown, and trade unionism.

1235 *One woman's war (006)*
World War Two in Thringstone in the words of a member of the Air Raid Precautions (ARP), including rationing, evacuees and the black market.

1236 *Mining memories (007)*
Miners and their children recall their experiences of home and work in the first forty years of the century.

1237 *Kendrick (009)*
Memories of schooldays, Christmas, Coalville's early shops and the Royal and Ancient Order of Buffaloes (RAOB).

1238 *Sawbridge (011)*
Recollections of a stonemason.

1239 *Phyllis (015)*
Covers a career as a London nurse and a gamekeeper.

1240 *Cox (016)*
Quarrying in Bardon in the early years of the century.

MANTLE ORAL HISTORY PROJECT *see also* **CARSWELL, Jeanne**

MANUNGO, Ken *see* **PEET, Stephen**

1241 **MARKHAM, John (ed.)**
Keep the home fires burning: the Hull area in the first world war
Beverley: Highgate Publications, 1988
94pp
People from Humberside remember the Great War.

1242 **MARLATT, Daphne (ed.)**
Steveston recollected: a Japanese-Canadian history
Victoria, B.C.: Provincial Archives of British Columbia, 1975
104pp; bibliography
A unique oral record, in English, of Vancouver's Japanese-speaking community.

1243 **MARLATT, Daphne (ed.)**
The South End
Boston: Boston Corporation, 1975
Boston 200 Neighbourhood History series
A record of residents in a slum area of Boston.

1244 **MARQUAND, David**
Ramsay MacDonald
Cape: 1977
903pp; bibliography
The author talked to fifty of MacDonald's former friends and colleagues.

1245 **MARSDEN, Dennis**
Workless: an exploration of the social contract between society and the worker
Croom Helm, 1982, revised edition; first edition published by Penguin, 1975, with bibliography
275pp
An analysis of unemployment, its pressures and its effects, through the testimony of the unemployed themselves.

MARSDEN, Dennis *see also* **JACKSON, Brian**

MARSHALL, Jean *see* **EDWARDS, P.J.**

1246 **MARSHALL, John**
"The sense of place, past society and the oral historian"
Oral History, vol.3, no.1 (1975), pp.19-25

1247 **MARSHALL, John**
"The North West Sound Archive"
Oral History, vol.7, no.1 (1979), pp.57-8

1248 **MARSHALL, John**
Voices of the past
Sydney: Sound Information, 1981
Eight audio cassettes
Includes oral histories of social life in New South Wales in the early part of the century.

1249 **MARSHALL, Kathryn**
In the combat zone: an oral history of American women in Vietnam 1966-1975
Boston: Little and Brown, 1987
270pp; bibliography

1250 **MARSON, Dave**
Children's strikes in 1911
History Workshop, 1973
History Workshop Pamphlet no.9
35pp
Draws on a small number of interviews with surviving strikers from the unrest of September 1911 which involved schools in sixty-two towns across Britain.

1251 **MARTIN, Angus**
The ring-net fisherman
Edinburgh: John Donald, 1980
263pp
Traditional fishing methods in the west of Scotland.

1252 **MARTIN, Patricia P.**
Images and conversations: Mexican Americans recall a southwestern past
Tucson: University of Arizona Press, 1983
Edited interviews with thirteen Chicanos living in Tucson, Arizona.

1253 MARX, Trish
Echoes of the second world war
Hemel Hempstead: MacDonald Children's,
1989
96pp
Aimed at children, this illustrated book is
based on the first-hand experiences of people
from different cultures who were children at
the time.

1254 MASANI, Zareer
Indian tales of the Raj
BBC Books, 1987
168pp; select bibliography
Based on a BBC Radio 4 series of the same
name broadcast in 1986. Over fifty Indian men
and women who had worked under the British
were interviewed to redress the balance after
an earlier series, *Plain Tales of the Raj*, had
concentrated on the British experience. (*See
also* ALLEN, Charles; IMPERIAL WAR
MUSEUM; INDIA OFFICE LIBRARY
AND RECORDS; ROYLE, Trevor)

1255 MASON, Alan S. and SAXON, Gerald D.
"The Dallas Mayors Oral History and
Records Project: a program of institutional co-
operation"
American Archivist, vol.45, no.4 (Fall 1982),
pp.472-4
Describes a project to trace the political
history of Dallas in which seven workers
interviewed fifty people over one year.

1256 MASON, Anthony
The General Strike in the North East
Hull: University of Hull Publications, 1970
*University of Hull occasional papers in
economic social history, no. 3*
116pp

1257 MASON, Elizabeth B. and STARR, Louis M.
*The oral history collection of Columbia
University*
New York: Oral History Research Office,
Columbia University, 1979, fourth edition;
third edition, 1973
306pp; bibliography
4000 interviews are indexed by name, subject
and project. (*See also* COLUMBIA
UNIVERSITY)

MASUR, Jenny *see* KRAMER, Sydelle

1258 MATTESON, M.A. and MUNSAT, E.M.
"Group reminiscing therapy with elderly
clients"
Mental Health Nursing, no.4 (1982), pp.177-89
Describes the operation of a group in a
residential home.

1259 MAURER, Harry
Not working: an oral history of the unemployed
New York: Holt, Rinehart and Winston, 1979;
New American Library, 1981
297pp
Interviews with a variety of people in the
United States, from ethnic minority youth to
former corporation employees, arranged in
topic sequence and covering being made
redundant, looking for work etc. A
companion volume to Studs Terkel's *Working*.

1260 MAYFIELD, Chris (ed.)
*Growing up southern: 'Southern Exposure'
looks at childhood, then and now*
New York: Pantheon, 1981
273pp
A compilation of collected articles from
Southern Exposure 1976-81, including
testimony on strikes, family and work.

1261 MAYHEW, Henry
London labour and the London poor
Constable, 1968 (facsimile edition of 1861-62
edition)
4 vols.
A study of poverty: an early example of oral
history.

1262 MAYNARD, John
"Community writing"
Local Historian, no.13 (February 1979),
pp.276-80
A discussion of printed memoirs with a
bibliography.

1263 MAZIKANA, Peter C.
"Archives and oral history: overcoming a lack
of resources"
Information Development, vol.3, no.1 (January
1987), pp.13-16
Addresses the conflict for resources between
oral history and more traditional archival
functions in the USA.

MAZIKANA, Peter C. *see also* MOSS,
William Warner

1264 McBAIN, Janet
Pictures past: recollections of Scottish cinemas and cinema going
Edinburgh: Moorfoot, 1985
80pp; brief bibliography
Oral evidence of 'going to the pictures' in Scotland in the first sixty years of the century, including interviews with cinema owners, projectionists and workers. The author is curator of the Scottish Film Archive.

1265 McCALL, D.F.
Africa in time perspective: a discussion of historical reconstruction from unwritten sources
New York: Oxford University Press, 1969; first published 1964
179pp
For oral history in non-literate societies.

1266 McCALL, Michal M.
"The significance of storytelling"
Life Stories, no.5 (1989), pp.39-48

1267 McCALMAN, Janet
Struggletown: public and private life in Richmond, 1900-1965
Carlton: Melbourne University Press, 1984
325pp
An attempt to construct a social history of Australian twentieth century working-class life through a group biography of one generation.

1268 McCALMAN, Janet
"The uses and abuses of oral history"
Canberra Historical Journal, new series vol.21 (1988)

1269 McCARTHY, H.
"Time perspective and aged persons' attributions of their life experiences"
Gerontologist, vol.17 (1977)

1270 MccGWIRE, Scarlett (ed.)
Transforming moments
Virago, 1989
160pp
Turning points in the teenage years of seventeen women from a variety of backgrounds which altered the course of their lives.

McCLAUCHLAN, J. *see* **HAY, Roy**

1271 McCLELLAN, Angus
The furrow behind me: the autobiography of a Hebridean crofter
Routledge, 1962
202pp
Labour biography using oral sources.

1272 McCLURE, James
Spike island: portrait of a police division
Macmillan, 1980; Pan 1981
532pp
A study of the Merseyside Police's 'A' Division in inner-city Liverpool based on interviews with many of the division's 445 officers over a lengthy period.

1273 McCRACKEN, Jane (ed.)
Oral history: basic techniques
Winnipeg, Canada: Manitoba Museum of Man and Nature, 1974

1274 McCRACKEN, Jane
"The role of oral history in museums"
Canadian Oral History Association Journal, vol.1 (1975-6), pp.34-6

McCRINDLE, Jean *see* **ROWBOTHAM, Sheila**

1275 McDANIEL, George W.
Hearth and home: preserving a people's culture
Philadelphia: Temple University Press
297pp; bibliography
A social and architectural history of the homes of rural blacks in the old American south, which relies on interviews and architectural fieldwork due to the lack of documentary evidence.

1276 McFARLAND, Elaine W., DALTON, Mike and WALSH, Dave
Personal welfare services and ethnic minorities
Glasgow: Glasgow College of Technology, 1987
SEMRU Research Paper no.4
38pp
Featuring interviews with sixty-five Asian and Chinese women about childcare, care of the elderly, advice, information and health.

1277 McLAUGHLIN, Eve
Interviewing elderly relatives
Plymouth: Federation of Family History Societies, 1985, second edition; first edition, 1979
16pp
A useful introduction for genealogists who want to tap living memory.

1278 McKEE, Alexander
Dresden 1945: the devil's tinderbox
Souvenir Press, 1982; Granada, 1983
334pp; bibliography
Based on interviews with the Allied bomber
crews and German survivors, it presents a
powerful case against modern military
planning.

1279 McKENNA, Frank
The railway workers 1840-1970
Faber, 1980
280pp; bibliography

1280 McLEOD, Hugh
"White collar values and the role of religion"
in CROSSICK, Geoffrey *(1977)*

1281 McLEOD, Hugh
"New perspectives on Victorian working class
religion: the oral evidence"
Oral History, vol.14, no.1 (1986), pp.31-49

McMAHAN, Eva *see* CLARK, E.C.

1282 McMAHON, W. and RHUDICK, P.J.
"Reminiscence: adaptational significance in
the aged"
*Archives of General Psychiatry, vol.10 (1964),
pp.292-8*

McMORLAND, Alison *see* BRUCE, Stuart

McMULLIN, Ruth *see* MECKLER, Alan M.

1283 McMURRAY, Campbell
"Oral history and museums: an overview and
critique"
Oral History, vol.14, no.2 (1986), pp.26-30

1284 McNAMEE, Peter and LOVETT, Tom (eds.)
Working-class community in Northern Ireland
Belfast: Ulster People's College, 1987
513pp
Based on interviews with ordinary people
conducted over ten years (to March 1987).
With sections on women and young people,
and a consideration of the two communities -
'Prods' and 'Taigs' - of a divided working
class.

McNEILL, Anthony J.J. *see* HUTCHISON,
Pat

1285 McQUEEN, John
"The work of the School of Scottish Studies"
Oral History, vol.2, no.1 (1974), pp.62-4

1286 McROBERTS, D.
"Catholicity in Glasgow thirty years ago: or
the reminiscences of the last years of the life of
Mrs. Kelly"
Innes Review, vol.14, no.1 (1963)

1287 McSHANE, Harry and SMITH, Joan
No mean fighter
Pluto, 1978
282pp
Based on interviews with McShane, one of the
Scottish labour movement's early activists.

1288 McWILLIAMS, Jerry
*The preservation and restoration of sound
recordings*
Nashville: The American Association for State
and Local History, 1979
138pp; bibliography

MEACHAM, J.A. *see* PERROTA, P.

1289 MECKLER, Alan M. and McMULLIN, Ruth
(eds.)
Oral history collections
New York and London: R.R.Bowker, 1975
344pp
The first volume of a plan to publish an
international directory of oral history projects
and holdings in libraries and archives,
updating the Oral History Association's
Directory of 1971. Lists American centres by
state: UK, Canada and Israel get an eight
page addendum. Each entry comprises a
contact address, a project description and a
note of access restrictions as appropriate.

MEDLICOTT, Mary *see* JONES, Derek

MEEHAN, Betty *see* WHITE, Isobel

1290 MEHAFFY, George L., SITTON, Thad and
DAVIS, O.L.
Oral history in the classroom
Washington D.C.: National Council for the
Social Studies, 1979

MEHAFFY, George L. *see also* LANMAN,
Barry A.; SITTON, Thad

1291 MELLOR, Moira (ed.)
Horsepower
Barnstaple, Devon: Spindlewood, 1985
80pp
Edited tape-recorded recollections by South
Devon people of the role that horses played in
their lives early this century, for both work
and play. Recordings held by Dartington
Rural Archive.

1292 MELLOR, Moira and KIDEL, Mark (eds.)
Yesterday's village
Dartington, Devon: Dartington Rural Archive,
1978; second edition, 1980
56pp
Edited recollections of village life in South
Devon earlier this century, from tape-
recordings and written memoirs.

1293 MELVILLE, Joy
"Down memory lane"
New Society, 12 September 1986, p.23
About Age Exchange Theatre Company.

MELVILLE, Joy *see also* BEAN, Philip

MENDELSOHN, Rona *see* EPSTEIN, E.R.

1294 MENNINGER, Robert
"Some psychological factors involved in oral
history interviewing"
Oral History Review, vol.3 (1975), pp.68-75

1295 MERRIAM, S.
"The concept and function of reminiscence: a
review of the research"
Gerontologist, vol.20, no.5 (1980), pp.604-8

1296 MERRIAM, S. and CROSS, L.
"Adulthood and reminiscence: a descriptive
study"
Educational Gerontology, vol.8 (1982),
pp.275-90

MERRIAM, S. *see also* HUGHSTON, G.

1296A MERSON, Elizabeth
In the country in 1900
Harlow: Longman, 1981
Into the past series vol. 4
24pp

1296B MERSON, Elizabeth, ECHLIN, Shirley and
PURKIS, Sallie
Children in the war, home and school in the
1950s
Harlow: Longman, 1983
Into the past series vols. 10-12
26pp
Originally published as separate volumes by
the three individual authors.

MERSON, Elizabeth *see also* ATTMORE,
Stephen; PURKIS, Sallie

1297 MERTON ORAL HISTORY PROJECT
Throw out your mouldies
Merton Oral History Project/MSC, 1984
40pp
An oral history of change in Merton within
living memory, from open Surrey countryside
to a busy London suburb.

1298 MESSENGER, Betty Thompson
Picking up the linen threads: a study in
industrial folklore
Texas: University of Texas Press, 1978;
Belfast: Blackstaff Press, 1980 (paperback,
1988)
265pp; bibliography
Based on interviews with workers in Ulster's
linen industry in the early decades of this
century, with details of the harsh conditions,
injuries, initiation ceremonies, jokes, songs,
nicknames and stories amongst the mainly
female workforce.

1299 MEYER, Eugenia and DE BONFIL, Alicia
Olivera
"Oral history in Mexico"
Journal of Library History, vol.7 (October
1972), pp.360-5
A description of the Archivo Sonoro, a
Mexican oral history project set up to study
the Mexican Revolution of 1910 which has
expanded to cover rural education, politics
and the Mexican film industry.

MEYER, Michael C. *see* GREENLEAF,
Richard E.

MIDDLETON, Geoffrey *see* PURKIS, Sallie

MIKUSKO, Brady *see* KORNBLUH, Joyce L.

MILLAR, David *see* ABELLA, Irving

1300 MILLAR, James R. (ed.)
Politics, work and daily life in the USSR: a
survey of former Soviet citizens
Cambridge: Cambridge University Press, 1987
Articles analysing 2700 interviews from the
questionnaire-based Soviet Interview Project.

1301 MILLER, Donald and Lorna
"Armenian survivors: a typological analysis of
victim response"
Oral History Review, vol.10 (1982), pp.47-72
An analysis of oral histories of the 1915
massacre.

1302 MILLER, Frederick M.
"Social history and archival practice"
American Archivist, vol.44, no.2 (Spring 1981),
pp.113-24

1303 MILLER, Joseph C. (ed.)
The African past speaks: essays on oral tradition
and history
Folkestone: Dawson, 1980
284pp
For oral history in non-literate societies.
Papers discussing the historical value of oral
traditions.

1304 MILLER, Les and BLOCH, Howard
Black Saturday: the first day of the Blitz: East
London memories of September 7th 1940
Tower Hamlets Arts Project, 1984
35pp
Eighteen personal accounts of East
Londoners' memories of the first day of the
London Blitz in September 1940, collected by
Inner City Theatre.

1305 MILLER, Marc S.(ed.)
Working lives: the 'Southern Exposure' history
of labor in the South
New York: Pantheon Books, 1981
Workers' experiences from coalfields, car
plants, textile mills, tobacco fields and
elsewhere between 1900 and 1980.

1306 MILLER, Merle
Plain speaking: an oral biography of Harry S.
Truman
Gollancz, 1974; Coronet 1976
480pp
A pro-Truman book based on interviews with
the former US president, his friends and
family. Includes a useful preface placing
Truman in American history.

1307 MILLER, Merle
Lyndon: an oral biography
New York: Random House, 1980
645pp; bibliography
Based on interviews with hundreds of the
former US president Lyndon B. Johnson's
colleagues, opponents and friends.

MILLER, Susan *see* **COULTER, Jim**

1308 MILLETT, Freda
Childhood in Oldham 1890-1920
Oldham, Lancashire: Oldham Leisure
Services, 1987
30pp
Interviews with a cross-section of men and
women aged 75-100 covering family life,
leisure, school and starting work.

1309 MILLETT, Freda
Going up town: shopping in Oldham
Oldham, Lancashire: Oldham Leisure
Services, 1988
60pp
Oral histories of shopping in the first quarter
of the century in a northern cotton town, from
both sides of the counter.

1310 MINNS, Raynes
Bombers and mash: the domestic front 1939-45
Virago, 1980
206pp; bibliography
The war according to women based on Mass
Observation sources.

1311 MINTZ, Jerome R.
The anarchists of Casa Viejas
Chicago: University of Chicago Press, 1982
363pp; bibliography
The story of a massacre, following a peasant
uprising, in a small poverty-stricken
Andalusian town in 1933, which had a great
effect on Spain in the years leading up to the
Civil War. Based on interviews conducted in
the 1960s.

1312 MINTZ, Sidney W.
Worker in the cane: a Puerto Rican life history
New Haven: Yale University Press, 1960
Caribbean series no. 2
288pp
About Anastacio Zayas Alvarado, a sugar
cane worker and his wife from interviews
conducted in 1953 and 1956.

1313 MINTZ, Sidney W.
"The anthropological interview and the life
history"
Oral History Review, vol.7 (1979), pp.18-26

1314 MIRZA, Sarah amd STROBEL, Margaret (eds.)
Three Swahili women: life histories from Mombasa, Kenya
Bloomington: Indiana University Press, 1989
157pp; bibliography
Women from different ethnic groups and social backgrounds, all born between 1890 and 1920, talk about the enormous changes in the Swahili Muslim community in Mombasa: the abolition of slavery, the introduction of secular education for girls and the spread of new social attitudes.

1315 MISHLER, Elliot G.
Research interviewing: context and narrative
Cambridge, Mass.: Harvard University Press, 1986
189pp; bibliography
Includes material on the inner consciousness and identity, and mutual interaction within the interview in shaping memory.

1316 MITCHELL, David
"Living documents: oral history and biography"
Biography, vol.3 (Winter 1980)

1317 MOGEY, John Macfarlane
Family and neighbourhood: two studies in Oxford
Oxford University Press, 1956
181pp
A report on the Oxford pilot social survey begun in 1950 to examine the social behaviour of Oxfordians.

1318 MOLINARI, V. and REICHLIN, R.E.
"Life review reminiscence in the elderly: a review of the literature"
International Journal on Aging and Human Development, vol.20, no.2 (1984-5), pp.81-92

MOLTZAN, Jan *see* **SAXON, Gerald D.**

1319 MONTELL, William Lynwood
The saga of Coe Ridge
Knoxville, Tennessee: University of Tennessee Press, 1970
231pp
The story of a Kentucky community originally founded by slaves of the Coe family after the American Civil War up to 1958 when the community broke up. "One of the oustanding examples of the use of oral sources in a local historical study, the story of a transient, undocumented community of black squatters" (*Oral History*).

1320 MONTELL, William Lynwood
Don't go up to Kettle Creek: verbal legacy of the Upper Cumberland
Knoxville: University of Tennessee Press, 1983
247pp; bibliography
Uses material from one hundred interviews. The oral tradition in this area goes back to the late eighteenth century pioneers, and in this volume stories of the Civil War are included.

MONTELL, William Lynwood *see also* **ALLEN, Barbara**

MOORE, Bruce Victor *see* **BINGHAM, Walter Van Dyke**

1321 MOORE, Kevin
The Mersey ship repairers: life and work in a port industry
Liverpool: Docklands History Project, 1988
90pp
In the 1940s Merseyside employed 20,000 people in a host of ship repair trades: boilermakers, shipwrights, fitters, coppersmiths, scalers and painters. Now only a handful remain and this is the story of the workers in their own words, covering their working conditions, hazards and the industry's decline.

MOORE, Kevin *see also* **JOHNSON, Alan**

1322 MOORE, Robert
Pitmen, preachers and politics: the effects of Methodism in a Durham mining community
Cambridge University Press, 1974
292pp; bibliography
An important local study of religious Methodism in the Deerness Valley 1870-1926, based partially on oral sources.

1323 MOORE, Susan
I remember strawberries and sewage: a collection of twenty biographies, reminiscences and photographs of everyday life in the North Warwickshire village of Fillongley
Fillongley, Warwickshire: Susan Moore, 1989
59pp
Based on tape-recorded interviews with the baker, teacher, newsagent, post-lady, housekeepers, builder, farmer, farmer's wife, smallholder and milkman. Includes mention of Woodlands Health Club, an early naturist camp set up in the thirties.

1324   MOOREHEAD, Caroline
Troublesome people: enemies of war 1916-1986
Hamish Hamilton, 1987
344pp; bibliography
The experience of conscientious objectors in
both world wars, and attitudes towards them,
from interviews with survivors.

1325   MORANTZ, Regina Markell, POMERLEAU,
C.S. and FENICHEL, C.H. (eds.)
In her own words: oral histories of women
physicians
Westport/London: Greenwood Press, 1982;
Yale University Press, 1986
284pp; bibliography
A well documented study of nine women at
the Medical College, Pennsylvania.

MORETON, Ginnie *see* **CLARK, Helen**

1326   MORMINO, Gary R. and POZZETTA,
George E.
The immigrant world of Ybor City: Italians and
their Latin neighbours in Tampa City,
1885-1985
Urbana: University of Illinois Press, 1987
369pp; bibliography
A sensitive study based on life stories of a
common yet contrasted heritage.

MORMON CHURCH *see* **CHURCH OF**
JESUS CHRIST OF LATTER-DAY SAINTS

1327   MORNINGSIDE ASSOCIATION/
MORNINGSIDE HERITAGE
ASSOCIATION
Morningside memories
Morningside: Morningside Association/
Morningside Heritage Association, 1986
49pp
Memories of childhood in Morningside from
1900 to the outbreak of the Second World
War.

1328   MORPHY, Howard and Frances
"The 'myths' of Ngalakan history: ideology
and images of the past in Northern Australia"
Man, vol.19 (1984)

MORRIS, P.E. *see* **GRUNEBERG, M.M.**

1329   MORRISH, Alison (ed.)
Caring for Cusworth: servants recall a bygone
era
Doncaster: South Yorkshire Museum and Arts
Service, 1983
30pp
Domestic service at Cusworth Hall in South
Yorkshire, 1912-1952.

1330   MORRISON, James
"Frontier College: workers' education in the
Canadian outback"
Oral History, vol.16, no.1 (1988), pp.40-7

1331   MORRISON, Joan and ZABUSKY, Charlotte
Fox
American mosaic: the immigrant experience in
the words of those who lived it
New York: E.P. Dutton, 1980
457pp
Based on over 100 interviews with a wide
variety of first generation immigrants covering
eighty years from a Russian arrival in 1898. A
vivid, entertaining read, which has been
criticised because of its unquestioning
portrayal of a unified American society and as
an example of oral history validating
conventional mythologies rather than
challenging them.

1332   MORRISSEY, Charles T.
"Oral history as a classroom tool"
Social Education vol.32 (October 1968)
Vermont (USA) history and social studies
teachers' discussion.

1333   MORRISSEY, Charles T.
"Oral history and local history: opportunities
for librarians"
Journal of Library History, vol.4 (October
1969), pp.341-6
Urges librarians to preserve local history
about common people.

1334   MORRISSEY, Charles T.
"Rhetoric and role in philanthropy: oral
history and the grant-making foundations"
Oral History Review, vol.6 (1978), pp.5-19

1335   MORRISSEY, Charles T.
"Oral history reliability is under question"
Library Journal, no.105 (June 1980),
pp.1350-1
Rebuts criticism of the veracity of oral history
and emphasises the value of thorough
preparation.

1336   MORRISSEY, Charles T.
"Why call it oral history? Searching for early
usage of a generic term"
Oral History Review, vol.8 (1980), pp.20-48
Although attributed to Allan Nevins in 1948,
Morrissey finds the term 'oral history' used as
early as 1863.

1337 MORTHLAND, John
"The King remembered, Elvis: an oral history"
Country Music, vol.8 (January/February 1980), pp.45-55
Extracts from interviews with people who knew him.

1338 MORTON, Robin (ed.)
Come day, go day, God send Sunday: the songs and life story told in his own words, of John Maguire, traditional singer and farmer from Co. Fermanagh
Routledge & Kegan Paul, 1973
188pp
An account of the singer's world based on transcribed interviews and including songs.

1339 MOSS, Louis and GOLDSTEIN Harvey (eds.)
The recall method in social surveys
Windsor: University of London Institute of Education, distributed by NFER, 1979
Studies in Education new series no.9
176pp; bibliographies
Important seminar papers discussing the pros and cons of this type of research in various fields. (*See also* GITTINS, Diana)

1340 MOSS, William Warner
Oral history program manual
New York and London: Praeger, 1974
Praeger Special Studies in U.S. Economic, Social and Political Issues
110pp
A useful book which considers large scale oral history projects based on the experience of the J.F. Kennedy Presidential Library Program. There is advice on planning a project, interview techniques, processing interviews and record keeping, transcription, staffing and equipping a major project.

1341 MOSS, William Warner
"The future of oral history"
Oral History Review, vol.3 (1975), pp.5-15

1342 MOSS, William Warner
"Oral history: an appreciation"
The American Archivist, vol.40, no.4 (October 1977), pp.429-39
Looks at the evaluation of oral history and the issue of reliability.

1343 MOSS, William Warner
"Oral history" in BRADSHER, James Gregory (ed.)
Managing archives and archival institutions, Mansell, 1988, pp.148-60

1344 MOSS, William Warner and MAZIKANA, Peter C.
Archives, oral history and oral tradition; a RAMP study
Paris: UNESCO, 1986
97pp; bibliography
Published as part of the Records and Archives Management Programme of UNESCO's General Information Programme. Intended for archivists, curators and information specialists, it lays out archival guidelines based on information gathered from sound professionals in all parts of the world. Available free from UNESCO.

1345 MOTLEY, Mary Penick (ed.)
The invisible soldier: the experience of the Black soldier, World War II
Detroit: Wayne State University Press, 1975
364pp; bibliography
A compilation of fifty-five oral histories from black American soldiers, grouped by fighting unit.

1346 MOZLEY, Ann
"Oral history"
Historical Studies Australia and New Zealand, vol.12, no.48 (April 1967)

1347 MOURBY, Kate
"The wives and children of the Teeside unemployed 1919-39"
Oral History, vol.11, no.2 (1983), pp.56-60
The hardships endured by the families of unemployed men in an area particularly badly hit by the Depression, the key industries being steel, shipbuilding and heavy engineering.

1348 MOYNIHAN, Michael (ed.)
People at war 1939-45
Newton Abbot: David and Charles, 1989; first published 1974
Battle Standards Military Paperback series
216pp
Ten verbatim personal accounts of the Second World War including prisoners-of-war in Germany and Japan, an army cook, Dunkirk, Tunisia, Hiroshima, and the 'Buzz Bomb' campaign of 1944.

1349 MSISKA, A.W.C.
"An attempt to establish an oral history project in the University of Zambia Library, Lusaka Campus"
American Archivist, vol.50 (1987), pp.142-6

MULKAY, Michael J. *see* EDGE, David O.

1350 MULLINS, Samuel and GLASSON, Michael
Hidden Harborough: the making of the townscape of Market Harborough
Market Harborough: Leicestershire Museums, Art Gallery and Record Service, 1984
56pp
Inter-war housing and communities through the reminiscences of residents.

1351 MULLINS, Samuel and GRIFFITHS, Gareth
'Cap and apron': an oral history of domestic service in the Shires, 1880-1950
Leicester: Leicestershire Museums, Art Gallery and Records Service, 1986
Harborough Series, no.2
66pp; bibliography
Based on nearly thirty interviews with former and current domestic servants recorded for the Harborough Museum sound archive in 1985, and supplemented by material from the Leicester Oral History Archive. Covers general servants, butlers, footmen, housemaids, lady's maids, nursery maids, cook-housekeepers and between-maids.

1352 MULTI-CULTURAL EDUCATION CENTRE (LEEDS)
Moving stories: towards a history of the many people of the English cities
Leeds: Leeds City Council, Multi-Cultural Education Centre, Continuing Education Section, 1987
45pp
A pamphlet containing transcripts of talks given on the history of Europeans and West Indians in Bradford and Sikhs in Manchester.

1353 MULTI-CULTURAL EDUCATION CENTRE (LEEDS)
Living history: some biographies from Harehills and Chapeltown, Leeds
Leeds: Leeds City Council Dispersed Tertiary Section Multi-Cultural Education Centre, 1989
102pp
Transcripts of open-ended and unstructured interviews with local people in a Yorkshire city, mainly migrants. Includes material on politics in Jamaica, life for black people in Britain in the 1950s and policing the black community.

1354 MUNCK, Ronnie and ROLSTON, Bill
"Belfast in the 1930s: an oral history project"
Oral History, vol.12, no.1 (1984), pp.15-19

1355 MUNCK, Ronnie and ROLSTON, Bill with MOORE, Gerry
Belfast in the thirties: an oral history
Blackstaff, 1987
209pp; bibliography
Examines working class politics, unemployment and poverty, and argues for the importance of Belfast socialism and its co-existence with sectarianism by focussing on the years between 1932 (and the Outdoor Relief Strike) and 1935 (when there were bloody sectarian riots). Fifty interviews form the base of the book and there is an introduction assessing the historical value of oral testimony.

MUNCK, Ronnie *see also* ROLSTON, Bill

MUNSAT, E.M. *see* MATTESON, M.A.

1356 MUNSON, Henry (ed.)
The house of Si Abd Allah: the oral history of a Moroccan family
Translated from Arabic
New Haven and London: Yale University Press, 1984
280pp; bibliography

1357 MURPHY, John
"The voice of memory: history, autobiography and oral memory"
Historical Studies, vol.22 (1986), pp.157-75

1358 MURRAY, J.F.
The Orkney Sound Archive Project: a report on the setting up and development of a local sound archive operation and an evaluation of its educational potential and the value of the materials produced
Glasgow: SCET, 1982
Occasional working paper Scottish Council for Educational Technology 10
87pp

1359 MUSEUM OF THE JEWISH EAST END
Boris: the studio photographer, 1900-1985
Museum of the Jewish East End, 1986
36pp
Boris Bennett, born in 1900 in Poland, arrived in London in 1922 and quickly established a reputation as the doyen of Jewish portrait photographers, renowned in the 1930s for his wedding photography. He is remembered by clients and colleagues.

1360 MUSTO David F. and BENISON, Saul
"Studies on the accuracy of oral interviews" in
Fourth National Colloquium on Oral History
New York: Oral History Association, 1969

1361 MYERHOFF, Barbara
Number our days: a triumph of continuity and culture among Jewish old people in an urban ghetto
New York: Simon and Schuster, 1978
318pp; bibliography
An anthropological study of elderly Jews (some of them Holocaust survivors) in Venice, California with powerful stories of poverty, neglect, loneliness, ill-health, poor housing and physical danger.

1362 MYERS, C.R.
"An oral history of psychology in Canada"
Canadian Oral History Association Journal, vol.1 (1975-6), pp.30-3
Interviews with Canadian psychologists.

1363 MYERS, John M.
The Westerners: a roundup of pioneer reminiscences
Englewood Cliffs, New Jersey: Prentice-Hall, 1969
258pp
Interviews with pioneers active at the end of the nineteenth and early twentieth centuries.

1364 MYRDAL, Jan
Report from a Chinese village
Translated by Maurice Michael
Heinemann, 1965
374pp
An intimate account of how Communism came to Liu Ling, a small agricultural village in the northern Shensi part of China, through the voices of a cross-section of villagers.

1365 NAMIAS, June
First generation: in the words of twentieth-century American immigrants
Boston: Beacon Press, 1978
234pp; bibliography
The accounts of thirty-one immigrants arriving in the United States between 1900 and 1946.

1366 NATIONAL COUNCIL OF JEWISH WOMEN (PITTSBURGH SECTION)
By myself, I'm a book! An oral history of the immigrant Jewish experience in Pittsburgh
Waltham, Massachusetts: American Jewish Historical Society, 1972
166pp
Produced under the supervision of the University of Pittsburgh's Department of Anthropology.

1367 NATIONAL FILM AND SOUND ARCHIVE (AUSTRALIA)
Oral history interviews list
Canberra: National Film Archive/National Library of Australia, 1981
39pp

1368 NATIONAL LIBRARY OF AUSTRALIA
The Hazel de Berg recordings
Canberra: National Library of Australia, 1989
168pp
A ready-reference guide to a major oral history collection of some 1300 interviews with well-known Australians recorded by Hazel de Berg between 1957 and her death in 1984.

1369 NATIONAL ORAL HISTORY ASSOCIATION OF NEW ZEALAND (NOHANZ)
Oral History in New Zealand
Wellington, New Zealand
52pp
Annual publication of NOHANZ: vol.1, 1988.

NATIONAL SOUND ARCHIVE *see* BRITISH LIBRARY NATIONAL SOUND ARCHIVE

1370 NDIAYE, Raphael
"Oral culture and libraries"
IFLA Journal, vol.14, no.1 (1988), pp.40-6
Argues the case for African libraries to recognise that oral sources pre-date written materials.

1371 NEALE, Margaret
We were the Christmas islanders: reminiscences and recollections of the people of an isolated island - the Australian Territory of Christmas Island, Indian Ocean, 1906-1980
Chapman, Australian Capital Territory: Margaret Neale, 1988
Bibliography

1372 NEE, Victor G. and NEE, Brett de Bary
Longtime Californ': a documentary study of an American Chinatown
New York: Pantheon, 1973
410pp
Oral material was of particular use in this study, due to the lack of written evidence.

NEHRKE, M.F. *see* BOYLIN, W.

1373 NEISSER, Ulric
Memory observed: remembering in natural contexts
San Francisco: Freeman, 1982
433pp; bibliographies
A study in the psychology of memory, relevant to the oral historian in that it challenges the more traditional experimental approach.

1374 NELSON, Hank
P.O.W.: prisoners of war
Sydney: Australian Broadcasting Commission, 1985
Based on oral testimony from Second World War POWs.

1375 NEUENSCHWANDER, John A.
The practice of oral history: a handbook
Glen Rock, New Jersey: Microfilming Corporation of America, 1975
A collection of essays on different aspects of oral history by Joseph Cash, Herbert Herbert, Stephen Ward and Ramon Harris.

1376 NEUENSCHWANDER, John A.
Oral history as a teaching approach
Washington D.C.: National Education Association, 1976
46pp; bibliography
The value to students of process over product: a brief handbook for social science teachers, with examples of a release form and a transcript.

1377 NEUENSCHWANDER, John A.
"Oral history and copyright: an uncertain relationship"
Journal of College and University Law, vol.10, no.2 (1983-4), pp.147-65
American copyright law interpreted by a practising attorney who is also an experienced oral historian.

1378 NEUENSCHWANDER, John A.
Oral history and the law
Denton, Texas: Oral History Association, 1985
Pamphlet series no.1
24pp
Information on the legal status of oral history in the United States.

1379 NEUGARTEN, Bernice L. (ed.)
Middle age and ageing: a reader in social psychology
Chicago and London: University of Chicago Press, 1968
596pp; bibliography
Chapters include: 'Women's attitudes towards the menopause' which involves interviews, and 'The awareness of middle age' based on 100 interviews.

1380 NEVINS, Allan
Gateway to history
Boston: D.C. Heath, 1938
412pp
Described as the 'father of modern oral history' in the United States, Pulitzer prize-winner Nevins is said to have conducted the first oral history interview in 1948. He launched Columbia University's famous oral history collection in the early sixties and became the first secretary of the Oral History Association in 1966. The book's preface urges the launch of an oral history movement in the United States.

1381 NEVINS, Allan
"Oral history: how and why it was born"
Wilson Library Bulletin, no.40 (March 1966), pp.600-1
The beginnings and progress of oral history at Columbia University.

1382 NEVINS, Allan and HILL, Frank Ernest
Ford: the times, the man, the company
Ford: expansion and challenge, 1915-1933
Ford: decline and rebirth, 1933-1962
New York: Charles Scribner's Sons, 1954 (vol.1); 1957 (vol.2); 1963 (vol.3)
Based on the Ford archives' oral history section.

1383 NEW SOUTH WALES STATE LIBRARY
Ethnic oral and local history
Sydney: State Library of New South Wales, 1982
20pp
Papers from a seminar held in February 1982.

1384 NEWBY, Howard
"The dangers of reminiscence"
Local Historian, vol.10 (1973), pp.334-9
Questions the accuracy of oral history based on his experience interviewing agricultural workers who told him what they thought he wanted to hear.

1385 NEWBY, Howard, ROSE, David, SAUNDERS, Peter and BELL, Colin
"Farming for survival: the small farmer in the contemporary rural class structure" in BECHHOFER, Frank and ELLIOTT, Brian (eds.), *The petite bourgeoisie: comparative studies of the uneasy stratum*, *Macmillan, 1981, pp.38-69*

1386 NEWHAM WOMEN'S ORAL HISTORY GROUP
We remember! Oral history project by Newham women
London Borough of Newham Women's Equality Unit, 1987
32pp

1387 NEWMAN, Dale
"Culture, class and Christianity in a cotton mill village"
Oral History, vol.8, no.2 (1980), pp.36-47
A study in North Carolina.

1388 NIBLETT, Chris
"Oral testimony and the social history of technology"
Oral History, vol.8, no.2 (1980), pp.53-7

1389 NICHOLAS, Kate
The social effects of unemployment on Teesside 1919-39
Manchester: Manchester University Press, 1987
254pp; bibliography
An oral history of inter-war unemployment in the north-east of England which looks at the impact of unemployment on living standards, nutrition, health, crime and politics.

1390 NICOLSON, Nigel
Alex: the life of Field Marshall Earl Alexander of Tunis
Weidenfeld and Nicolson, 1973
346pp
In this biography of Lord Alexander of Tunis the author uses oral testimony in a verbatim question and answer format.

NJAMA, Karari *see* BARNETT, Don

1391 NOLAN, Peter
"Attendant dangers"
Nursing Times, vol.85, no.12 (22 March 1989), pp.56-9
Interviews with mental health nurses, many of them repatriated POWs with their own psychiatric problems who had become nurses after the war.

1392 NORFOLK FEDERATION OF WOMEN'S INSTITUTES
Within living memory: a collection of Norfolk reminiscences written and compiled by members of the Norfolk Federation of Women's Institutes
Ipswich: Boydell Press, 1973; first published privately, 1972
159pp

1393 NORRIS, Andrew
Reminiscence with elderly people
Winslow, 1986
80pp
A guide aimed primarily at health and social service workers, this should also be useful for the oral historian as it considers the effects of interviewing on the informants themselves.

1394 NORRIS, Andrew
"Clinic or client? A psychologist's case for reminiscence"
Oral History, vol.17, no.2 (1989), pp.26-30

1395 NORRIS, Andrew and EILAH, Mohammed Abu El
"Reminiscence groups: a therapy for both elderly patients and their staff"
Nursing Times, 78, (11 August 1982), pp.1368-9; reprinted in Oral History, vol.11, no.1 (1983), pp.27-30
Reminiscence as one way in which the psychological needs of the elderly can be catered for as the means of improving their quality of life and bringing nursing staff and patients together. Based on work at Stone House Hospital, Dartford, Kent.

NORRIS, Jill *see* LIDDINGTON, Jill

1396 NORTH KENSINGTON LOCAL HISTORY PROJECT
Women remember
North Kensington Local History Project, nd North Kensington Community History Series no.1
12pp
Extracts from interviews with North Kensington women about housing conditions, health and welfare, immigration, childhood, politics and work as domestics, laundresses, dressmakers and shopworkers.

1397 NORTH KENSINGTON LOCAL HISTORY PROJECT
Multi-racial North Kensington
North Kensington Local History Project, nd
North Kensington Community History Series
no.2
16pp
Oral histories of the various groups who have come to the area since the first Irish migrants arrived at Notting Hill in the early nineteenth century. Notably the Russian and East European Jews in Kensington Park Road, European Volunteer Workers, West Indians and more recently Portuguese and Spanish settlers. Includes memories of Oswald Mosley's parliamentary candidature in North Kensington in 1955.

1398 NORTH KENSINGTON LOCAL HISTORY PROJECT
Our homes, our streets
North Kensington Local History Project, 1987
North Kensington Community History Series
no.3
16pp
Interviews about housing over the century: street life, games, hawkers, kitchens, the Improved Tenants' Association, Bangor Street and the post-war transformation which brought demolition and 'yuppification'.

1399 NORTH TYNESIDE COMMUNITY DEVELOPMENT PROJECT
North Shields: women's work. Final report vol.5
Newcastle: North Tyneside Community
Development Project, 1978
86pp; bibliography
A study of women's work and the conflicts faced by combining work and family.

1400 NORTH WEST SOUND ARCHIVE
Early twentieth century childhood, housing and education
Clitheroe, Lancashire: North West Sound
Archive, nd
14pp
A catalogue of thirty-eight recordings from the NWSA collection of some 50,000. (*See also* HOWARTH, Ken)

1401 NORTH WEST SOUND ARCHIVE
Oral history educational catalogue: abstracts from the North West Sound Archive
Clitheroe: North West Sound Archive, nd
32pp
A listing of 100 extracts covering a variety of topics suitable for use in a school classroom setting, including: canals, First World War, coal mining, bleach workers, railways, children's playsongs, Christmas, cotton workers, basket-making, chemical workers, midwifery, computers, and bookmaking.

1402 NORTH WEST SOUND ARCHIVE
Voice in the crowd: recordings from the collections of North West Sound Archive
Clitheroe: North West Sound Archive, 1987
27pp
A catalogue of the NWSA's holdings of BBC Manchester's early series *Voice in the crowd* in which one person relates their life story. A variety of subjects emerge including: a woman wrestler, a wheelwright, a pirate, a clairvoyant, a witch, a lollipop man, a burglar, a private eye, a vegetarian, an escapologist, a trapeze artist, a 'flapper', boxing booths and the Spanish Civil War.

1403 NORTH WEST SOUND ARCHIVE
Caught in time: the memories of north west England captured in sound
Clitheroe: North West Sound Archive, 1988
Compact disc NWSA 01
An innovative and experimental attempt to present oral history on compact disc with an array of reminiscences, dialect, sounds and music giving a flavour of the region and drawn from NWSA's collection of some 50,000 recordings. Highlights include recollections of a colliery disaster in 1910, running the first computer in 1948, and the sinking of the Lusitania in 1915.

1404 NORTON PARK GROUP
The singing street
Edinburgh: Norton Park Group, third edition,
1989; first published 1951; revised edition
published in 1954 by Albyn Press
16pp
Twenty-three singing street games and dancing rhymes. The booklet accompanies a video of the same name.

1405 NOW AND THEN GROUP
When the lights came on again: recollections of the post-war years (1945-51)
Lee Centre/University of London Goldsmiths' College, 1983
39pp
The result of eighteen months of taping and discussion by a group of people all over fifty years old.

1406 NUNNERLEY, David
President Kennedy and Britain
Bodley Head, 1972
242pp
Absence of official papers encouraged the inclusion of some eighty interviews as a chief source.

NUNNS, Claire *see* **O'CONNELL, Rory**

1407 NWOYE, S.C.
"The land is richer than it looks: thoughts on the preservation of the oral tradition of the Igbos"
Nigerian Libraries, vol.12, no.1 (April 1976), pp.5-17

1408 O'CONNELL, Rory and NUNNS, Claire (eds.)
How we worked: working in Kingston upon Thames, 1900-50
Manpower Services Commission/Royal Borough of Kingston Upon Thames, 1989
20pp
Extracts from Kingston Heritage Project's archive of over 100 interviews covering laundries, shops, family businesses, public services and housework.

1409 O'FARRELL, Patrick
"Oral history: facts and fiction"
Quadrant, November 1979, pp.4-8
A debate in an Australian journal about oral history. (*See also* THORPE, Bill)

1410 O'FARRELL, Patrick
"Reply to Thorpe"
Quadrant, July 1980, pp.58-9

1411 O'FARRELL, Patrick
"The great oral history debate revisited"
Quadrant, July 1987, pp.10-13

O'GRADY, Timothy E. *see* **GRIFFITH, Kenneth**

1412 O'HANLON, Elizabeth
Oral history for religious archives: the Sinsinawa Collection
Dubuque, Iowa: Union Noermann Press, 1978
63pp; bibliography

1413 O'NEILL, Julie
"Village band"
Oral History, vol.15, no.1 (1987), pp.50-3
Brass bands in Woodborough, Nottinghamshire.

1414 O'NEILL, Mark and HUTCHINSON, Gerard (eds.)
The Springburn Experience
Edinburgh: Polygon, 1989
192pp
Locomotive builders from the Springburn district of Glasgow recall their experience of work: trade unions, the war effort, the role of women and the industry's decline.

1415 O'SULLIVAN, Sean
"The work of the Irish Folklore Commission"
Oral History, vol.2, no.2 (1974), pp.9-17

1416 OAKLEY, Ann
"Interviewing women: a contradiction in terms" in ROBERTS, Helen (ed.),
Doing feminist research, Routledge & Kegan Paul, 1981

1416A OATEN HILL AND DISTRICT SOCIETY LOCAL HISTORY GROUP
The Taylors of Canterbury: a family story
Canterbury, Kent: Oaten Hill and District Society, 1989; first edition 1988
Ruth Taylor tells the story of her family in her own words, tape recorded in July 1986.

1417 OBLINGER, Carl
Interviewing the people of Pennsylvania: a conceptual guide to oral history
Harrisburg, Penn.: Pennsylvania Historical and Museum Commission, 1978
84pp
Sociological oral history demonstrating different approaches, with interview guidelines and a sample questionnaire. Draws on the experience of an extensive working people's project.

1418 OGOT, Bethwell
History of the southern Luo. Volume one: migration and settlement, 1500-1900
Nairobi: East African Publishing House, 1967
250pp
A pioneering early study of pre-colonial history based on research done in 1961-2 among the Ugandan Padhola and the West Kenyan Luo.

1419 **OKIHIRO, Gary Y.**
"Oral history and the writing of ethnic history: a reconnaissance into method and theory"
Oral History Review, vol.9 (1981), pp.27-46

1420 **OLCH, Peter D.**
"Oral history: problems and potentials"
The American Journal of Psychiatry, no.124 (February 1968)

1421 **OLCH, Peter D.**
"Oral history and the medical librarian"
Bulletin of the Medical Library Association, no.57 (January 1969), pp.1-4

1422 **OLCH, Peter D.**
"Science and technology" in *Fourth national colloquium on Oral History*, New York: Oral History Association, 1970

1423 **OLCH, Peter D. and POGUE, Forrest C. (eds.)**
Selections from the fifth and sixth national colloquia on oral history held at Asilomar Conference Grounds, Pacific Grove, California, November 13-16, 1970, and Indiana University, Bloomington, Indiana, October 8-10, 1971
New York: Oral History Association, 1972
110pp
Covers oral history and biography, oral history in the ghetto, the Civil Rights Movement, folklore, interviews, cataloguing of records etc.

1424 **OLD OAK HISTORY GROUP**
Matured in oak: Old Oak pensioners remember
Old Oak History Group, 1985
16pp
Recollections of the Old Oak Estate in North West London.

1425 **OLINER, Samuel P. and Pearl M.**
The altruistic personality: rescuers of Jews in Nazi Europe
New York: The Free Press, 1988
419pp; bibliography
The result of the Altruistic Personality Project which interviewed 682 rescuers, non-rescuers and rescued survivors of the Holocaust living in Poland, France, Germany, the Netherlands and Italy under Nazi occupation. Through testimony of dramatic heroism the authors conclude that rescuers were distinguished by common characteristics like a deep empathy and strongly-held moral and ethical values. Included is a section on methodology and the questionnaire used.

1426 **OLIVER, Peter**
"Oral history: one historian's view"
Canadian Oral History Association Journal, vol.1 (1975-6), pp.13-19

1427 **OLIVER, W.H.**
"Oral and other history"
New Zealand Journal of History, vol.12 (1978), pp.99-103
Urges checking oral evidence against written sources.

1428 **OLSON, Germaine L.**
"Oral history from four perspectives"
Journal of Library and Information Science, vol.5, no.2 (October 1979), pp.151-80
An investigation into the growth of oral history in the US and the role of the Oral History Association.

OLSTEIN, S.C. *see* **LITON, J.**

1429 **ONG, Walter J.**
Orality and literature: the technologizing of the word
Methuen, 1982
201pp; bibliography
For oral history in non-literate societies.

1430 **OPIE, Iona and Peter**
I saw Esau: traditional rhymes of youth
Williams & Norgate, 1947
95pp
A collection of rhymes passed on orally from one child to another.

1431 **OPIE, Iona and Peter**
The lore and language of schoolchildren
Oxford: Clarendon, 1959; St Albans: Paladin, 1979
446pp
A classic record of the strange and primitive culture of schoolchildren, based on contributions from 5000 children in Great Britain.

1432 **OPIE, Iona and Peter**
Children's games in street and playground: chasing, catching, seeking, hunting, racing, duelling, exerting, daring, guessing, acting, pretending
Oxford: Oxford University Press 1984; first published 1969
371pp
Derived from contributions from over 10,000 children all over Britain.

1433 OPIE, Iona and Peter
The singing game
Oxford: Oxford University Press 1985, 1988
521pp; bibliography
Children's singing games (with music) based
on surveys and recordings in over 100 schools
all over Britain.

1434 ORAL HISTORY ASSOCIATION
Proceedings of National Colloquium on Oral
History, 1967-1972
New York: Columbia University Oral History
Research Office, various
Five volumes. The proceedings later became
Oral History Review.

1435 ORAL HISTORY ASSOCIATION
Oral history evaluation guidelines
New York: Oral History Association, 1980,
1982
13pp; bibliography
1979 conference report, covering ethical, legal
and interview conduct guidelines.

ORAL HISTORY ASSOCIATION *see also*
OLCH, Peter D.; ORAL HISTORY REVIEW;
POGUE, Forrest C.

1436 ORAL HISTORY ASSOCIATION OF
AUSTRALIA JOURNAL
No.1, 1978-
Articles, reviews, workshop and seminar
reports, newsletters, guides and
bibliographies.

1437 ORAL HISTORY ASSOCIATION OF
AUSTRALIA (SOUTH AUSTRALIAN
BRANCH)
Oral history handbook
Adelaide: Oral History Association of
Australia, 1985
36pp

1438 ORAL HISTORY ASSOCIATION OF
AUSTRALIA (VICTORIAN BRANCH)
'But nothing interesting ever happened to us…':
memories of the twenties and thirties in Victoria
Melbourne: Department of History University
of Melbourne, 1986

1439 ORAL HISTORY: JOURNAL OF THE
ORAL HISTORY SOCIETY
Vol.1, no.1, 1969-
Published by the British Oral History Society
twice yearly in Spring and Autumn. News,
current work, reports on conferences and
meetings, articles, book reviews, technical
advice, results of research and projects in
Britain and abroad. From vol.17 no.2 the
journal was redesigned with new features and
greater use of illustrations. Vol.16, no.1
(Spring 1988) includes a cumulative index.
The contents of *Oral History*'s entire run are
listed in this bibliography.

1440 ORAL HISTORY NEWSLETTER
Vol.1, no.1, April 1978-
Published by the Oral History Association of
Australia.

1441 ORAL HISTORY REVIEW
No.1, 1973-
The publication of the US Oral History
Association containing articles, reviews and
reports of meetings. Beginning as an annual it
became twice yearly from 1987 (vol.15,
nos.1/2). The issues for 1977, 1982, 1983 and
Fall 1988 have extensive oral history
bibliographies. The early annual meetings of
the Association were published as *Proceedings*
between 1966 and 1971. A quarterly
newsletter is also produced for OHA
members. (*See also* ORAL HISTORY
ASSOCIATION)

1442 ORAL HISTORY SOCIETY
Directory of British oral history collections:
vol.1, 1981
Colchester: Oral History Society, 1981
60pp
Compiled by Anne McNulty and Hilary
Troop. Covers 231 collections and includes
name, place and subject indices. Volume two
is still to appear and has been superseded by
the British Library National Sound Archive's
Directory of Recorded Sound Resources.

ORAL HISTORY SOCIETY *see also* ORAL
HISTORY; PURKIS, Sallie

1443 ORCHARD, Imbert
"Tape recordings into radio documentaries"
Sound Heritage, vol.3, no.1 (1974)
Written by a long-time producer from the
Canadian Broadcasting Company.

1444 ORCHARD, Imbert
Martin: the story of a young fur trader
Victoria, British Columbia: Sound and Moving Image Division, Provincial Archives of British Columbia, 1981
Sound Heritage Series no.30
76pp
By one of Canada's pre-eminent practitioners of oral history.

1445 ORSER, Edward
"Racial change in retrospect"
International Journal of Oral History, vol.5, no.1

1446 ORTON, Ian
"Bridging a gap"
Assistant Librarian, vol.75, no.3 (March 1982), pp.34-5
Describes the success of an oral history project in Scotland organised jointly by Dumbarton District Libraries and Strathclyde Council's Education Department in bridging the generation gap. The project reduced loneliness in the old and boredom in the young, forged friendships, and encouraged youngsters to use the library service.

1447 OSBORNE, Richard (ed.)
Conversations with Karajan
Oxford: Oxford University Press, 1989
161pp
From conversations with Herbert von Karajan over the last twelve years of his life covering his life, work, views on the art of conducting and recording techniques. There is very little on his career during the Nazi era.

1448 OSLER, Audrey
Speaking out: black girls in Britain
Virago, 1989
134pp
Sixteen Asian and Afro-Caribbean girls from Birmingham, aged fourteen and fifteen, met once a week for six months to discuss their feelings and experiences. In an anthology of verbatim extracts they talk about racism, sexism, religion, riots, the police, the press, school, family, friends and South Africa.

OTTENHEIMER, Harriet J. *see* JOSEPH, Pleasant

OVERY, Richard *see* PAGNAMENTA, Peter

1449 OWEN, Alwyn and PERKINS, Jack
Speaking for ourselves: echoes from New Zealand's past from the award-winning 'Spectrum' radio series
Auckland, New Zealand: Penguin, 1986
215pp
A selection of interviews conducted over thirteen years by a radio documentary team which specialises in recording 'ordinary' New Zealanders. Includes a chapter on oral history technique.

1450 OWEN-JONES, Sheila
"Women in the tinplate industry: Llanelli, 1930-1950"
Oral History, vol.15, no.1 (1987), pp.42-9

1451 PADEL, Una and STEVENSON, Prue
Insiders: women's experiences of prison
Virago, 1988
202pp
3% of Britain's prison population of around 50,000 are women, most are in their twenties and 65% are eventually acquitted or given non-custodial sentences. Eleven of them speak about the conditions, their own backgrounds and their attitudes to the prison system.

1452 PAGE, Melvin
"Malawians and the Great War: oral history in reconstructing Africa's recent past"
Oral History Review, vol.8 (1980), pp.49-61
Drawing on 180 interviews with participants.

1453 PAGNAMENTA, Peter and OVERY, Richard
All our working lives
BBC, 1984
288pp
A popular history of changing work patterns in Britain since 1914, drawing on the personal memories of workers in the cotton, aircraft, steel, retailing, shipbuilding, chemical, coal, farming, car and electronics industries. Produced to accompany a BBC TV series of the same name, it looks at the issues of competitiveness, unemployment, innovation and trade unionism.

1454 PAHL, Janice and Raymond
Managers and their wives: a study of career and family relationships in the middle class
Harmondsworth: Penguin, 1972
326pp; bibliography
A study of the people who live in private suburban estates around major industrial cities in Britain, based on 172 questionnaires and interviews carried out in the 1960s.

1455 PAKENHAM, Thomas
"The comprehension of Private Copper"
Oral History, vol.9, no.2 (1981), pp.61-6
The background to interviewing for *The Boer War* with some extracts.

1456 PAKENHAM, Thomas
The Boer War
Futura, 1982
659pp; bibliography
An account of one of Britain's most humiliating and costly wars which includes testimony from fifty-two veterans. The tapes are now held by the Imperial War Museum.

1457 PALMER, Joseph W.
"Public libraries as oral history centers: an evaluation"
Collection Building, vol.5, no.3 (Fall 1983), pp.29-38
Based on 105 questionnaires received from 182 US public libraries in eleven states in 1982, and indicating a great variation in library involvement in oral history. Most projects were small and poorly funded.

1458 PALMER, Joseph W.
"Multimedia oral history projects in public libraries: a sampling of successful ventures"
Public Library Quarterly, vol.4, no.3 (Fall 1983), pp.47-62
Examples of library oral history used in publications, slide-tape packs, exhibitions and radio programmes in the States.

1459 PALMER, Joseph W.
Oral history in public libraries
Champaign, Illinois: University of Illinois Graduate School of Library and Information Science, 1984
Occasional Papers no.167
33pp; bibliography
The results of a questionnaire received from 105 US public libraries on oral history projects conducted by library staff and intended for library collections.

1460 PALMER, Roy
"A happy man, a hard life: the story of Arthur Lane (1884-1975)"
Oral History, vol.8, no.2 (1980), pp.30-5
Rural life in Corve Dale, a Shropshire village near Ludlow, before the First World War. Edited from recordings made by Philip Donnellan and Charles Parker.

1461 PALMER, Roy
"The minstrel of Quarry Bank: reminiscences of George Dunn (1887-1975), part one"
Oral History, vol.11, no.1 (1983), pp.62-68
South Staffordshire memories, particularly childhood and schooling.

1462 PALMER, Roy
"The minstrel of Quarry Bank: reminiscences of George Dunn (1887-1975), part two"
Oral History, vol.11, no.2 (1983), pp.61-68
Continues the story with a picture of small-scale Midlands Black Country chain-making.

1463 PAMPLIN, Margaret
"Oral archives"
Journal of the Society of Archivists, vol.6, no.1 (April 1978), pp.33-4

PAPPWORTH, Joanna *see* SELDON, Anthony

1464 PARKER, Tony
Five women
Hutchinson, 1965; Arrow, 1967
189pp
Parker has emerged as Britain's answer to Studs Terkel: his books are meticulously researched, carefully crafted and edited extracts from interviews, presented without comment or interpretation.

1465 PARKER, Tony
People of the streets
Cape, 1968
256pp
Tape-recorded conversations with seven people living in London: an artist, a car washer, a street trader, a musician, a down-and-out, a newspaper seller and a nightwatchman.

1466 PARKER, Tony
The twisting lane: some sex offenders
Hutchinson, 1969; Panther, 1970
242pp
Edited transcriptions of tape-recordings made over eighteen months with eight people who had been convicted of sexual offences.

1467 PARKER, Tony
The frying pan: a prison and its prisoners
Hutchinson, 1970; Panther, 1971
222pp
Based on 200 hours of taped conversations with the inmates and staff of HM Prison Grendon Underwood, Britain's first psychiatric prison, recorded while the author lived in for three months.

1468 **PARKER, Tony**
In no man's land: some unmarried mothers
Hutchinson, 1972; Panther, 1972
159pp
Six portraits of unmarried mothers who talk
frankly about their lives and their attitudes to
a society which treats them as 'outcasts'.

1469 **PARKER, Tony**
*The man inside: an anthology of writing and
conversational comment by men in prison*
Michael Joseph, 1973
159pp

1470 **PARKER, Tony**
Lighthouse
Hutchinson, 1975
288pp
Tape-recorded conversations with lighthouse
keepers from all over Britain drawn from six
months' first-hand research.

1471 **PARKER, Tony**
*The people of Providence: a housing estate and
some of its inhabitants*
*Hutchinson, 1983; Harmondsworth: Penguin,
1985*
373pp
340 hours of interviews with people from a
large London council estate, condensed into
the testimony of fifty-four very different
individuals, resulting in a rivetting book.

1472 **PARKER, Tony**
Soldier, soldier
Heinemann, 1985; Coronet, 1987
244pp
An account of the life of the soldier, and his
wife, in the modern British Army - based on
transcribed interviews with members of the
Royal Anglian Regiment.

1473 **PARKER, Tony**
Red Hill: a mining community
Heinemann, 1986; Coronet, 1988
196pp; bibliography
Interviews with people from one North-East
mining community about the 1984-5 miners'
strike.

1474 **PARKER, Tony**
A place called Bird
Secker and Warburg, 1989
356pp
Interviews with the inhabitants of a Kansas
town who talk about their lives, work and the
impact of the depression of the 1930s.

1475 **PARKER, Tony and ALLERTON, Robert**
The courage of his convictions
Hutchinson, 1962
189pp
The life of an unrepentant and articulate
criminal still waiting for the big 'tickle' that
will enable him to retire, as related to one of
Britain's leading popular oral history writers.

1476 **PARLOPHONE**
The McCartney interview
Parlophone, 1 LP record, CHAT 1, 1980
The Beatles' Paul McCartney interviewed by
Vic Garbarini for *Musician: Players &
Listener* magazine.

1477 **PARSONS, Cheryl**
*Schools in an urban community: a study of
Carbrook, 1870-1965*
Routledge, 1978
Routledge Library in the History of Education
155pp; bibliography
Uses oral evidence to add a new dimension to
the history of elementary education and
community studies.

1478 **PASSERINI, Luisa**
"Work, ideology and consensus under Italian
fascism"
*History Workshop, no.8 (Autumn 1979),
pp.82-108*

1479 **PASSERINI, Luisa**
"Italian working class culture between the
wars: consensus to Fascism and work
ideology"
*International Journal of Oral History, vol.1,
no.1 (February 1980)*

1480 **PASSERINI, Luisa**
*Fascism in popular memory: the cultural
experience of the Turin working class*
*Translated from Italian by Bob Lumley and
Jude Bloomfield*
Cambridge: Cambridge University Press, 1987
Studies in Modern Capitalism
244pp
Based on extensive interviews conducted
between 1976 and 1981 with subjects born
before 1922, this study explores the relation
between state, culture and the working
classes.

1481 PATEL, Bhadra and ALLEN, Jane
A visible presence: black people living and working in Britain today. An annotated anti-racist booklist for young adults, teachers, librarians and community workers
National Book League, 1985
40pp
A useful short bibliography which includes publications based on oral testimony and personal experience. The authors worked for Wandsworth Library Service.

1482 PATERSON, Alan
The law lords
Macmillan, 1982
288pp
Includes in-depth interviews with fifteen law lords.

1483 PATTON, Billy
"'Making ends meet': earning a living in Nottinghamshire, 1900-1950"
Local History, no.1 (July 1984), pp.4-5
Details of the MSC-funded Nottinghamshire Oral History Project which carried out interviews on the lace, hosiery, tobacco and mining industries, and on sport, crime, games, school and remedies.

1484 PEARCE, Cyril
"An interview with Wilfrid Whiteley"
Bulletin of the Society for the Study of Labour History, Spring 1969
Whiteley was one of the Huddersfield Independent Labour Party's proponents and a leading light in the Socialist Sunday School movement.

PEARCE, Elizabeth *see* **RICHARDSON, Yvonne**

PEARL, M. *see* **OLINER, Samuel P.**

1485 PEATE, I.C.
Tradition and folk life: a Welsh view
Faber, 1972
147pp; bibliography
Emphasises the importance of the spoken word.

PECHEL, Peter *see* **STEINHOFF, Johannes**

1486 PECK, A.J. and HERSCHER, U.D. (eds.)
Queen City refuge: an oral history of Cincinnati's Jewish refugees from Nazi Germany
West Orange, New Jersey: Behrman House, 1989
270pp

1487 PECKHAM PUBLISHING PROJECT
So this is England
Peckham Publishing Project, 1984
68pp
A collection about coming to Britain produced by a Black Studies group, with chapters about arrival, housing, work, and education.

1488 PEET, Graham
Peaches, lions and heroes: memories of Bushbury, Oxley and Fordhouses in the words of local people
Wolverhampton: Rhythm Tree Arts, 1989
32pp
Extracts from memories of an area of Wolverhampton in the West Midlands: notably of working at the Goodyear and Stafford Road railway works, but also war and housing.

1489 PEET, Stephen
"'We have a tradition of story telling': oral history in Zimbabwe"
Oral History, vol.16, no.2 (1988), pp.67-72
An interview with Ken Manungo, chief oral historian at the National Archives of Zimbabwe.

1490 PENGELLY, A.H.
"In the beginning was the spoken word"
Proceedings of the Plymouth Athenaeum, vol.5, pp.58-61

1491 PENN, David
"Sound archives: towards computerisation"
Phonographic Bulletin, no.15 (1976), pp.12-16

1492 PENNINGTON, Shelley and WESTOVER, Belinda
A hidden workforce: homeworkers in England, 1850-1985
Macmillan Education, 1989
Women in Society Series
194pp
A study of the predominantly female labour force of homeworkers between 1850 and 1985.

1493 PENTLAND CENTRE/CALTON CENTRE REMINISCENCE GROUPS
Friday night was brasso night
Edinburgh: Workers' Educational Association/ Edinburgh City Museums, 1987
24pp
Reminiscences of childhood, cinema, health, shopping and first jobs.

1494 PEOPLE OF SPITALFIELD
"Where's your horns?"
Spitalfield Books, 1979
Taped accounts of six Jewish children evacuated from Spitalfields, East London, during the Second World War.

1495 PEOPLE OF THURCROFT
Thurcroft: a village and the miners' strike: an oral history
Nottingham: Spokesman, 1986
276pp
The 1984 miners' strike through interviews with fifty members of a South Yorkshire coal village which was originally established in 1909.

1496 PEOPLE'S STORY REMINISCENCE GROUP
Kiss me while my lips are tacky
Edinburgh: Workers' Educational Association South East Scotland District, 1988
30pp
Accounts of family life, leisure, festivals and attitudes to death, drink and temperance, the 'poorshouse', the washhouse, health and courtship. Used as the basis for Edinburgh's innovative museum The People's Story which opened in 1989.

1497 PERDUE, Theda (ed.)
Nations remembered: an oral history of five civilized tribes 1865-1907
Westport, Conn. and London: Greenwood Press, 1980
Contributions in Ethnic Studies Series no.1
264pp; bibliography
A collection of interviews, originally carried out in the 1920s and 1930s by the New Deal Works Progress Administration for the US Government, from the Indians' point of view with much on Indian ways of life.

1498 PERETZ, Elizabeth
"Professionalisation of childcare"
Oral History, vol.17, no.1 (1989), pp.22-8
A study of inter-war health visitors from oral testimonies.

PERKINS, Jack *see* **OWEN, Alwyn**

1499 PERKS, Robert
"Real profit-sharing: William Thomson and Sons of Huddersfield, 1885-1925"
Business History, vol.24, no.2 (1982), pp.156-74
Based partially on interviews with former staff and a relative of George Thomson, a leading Yorkshire exponent of co-operation in textiles.

1500 PERKS, Robert
"'A feeling of not belonging': interviewing European immigrants in Bradford"
Oral History, vol.12, no.2 (1984), pp.64-7
Outlines a project to interview Ukrainians, Yugoslavs, Poles and Italians, and some of the problems involved.

1501 PERKS, Robert
"Everyone has a story to tell: Bradford Heritage Recording Unit and the value of oral history"
The Bradford Antiquary, 3rd series, no.2 (1986), pp.18-27

1502 PERKS, Robert
"Immigration to Bradford: the oral testimony"
Immigrants and Minorities, vol.6, no.3 (November 1987), pp.362-8
An assessment of Bradford Heritage Recording Unit's ethnic community projects.

1503 PERKS, Robert
"'You're different, you're one of us': the making of a British Asian"
Oral History, vol.15, no.2 (1987), pp.67-74
An interview with a Sikh who, through his childhood experiences, outlines changing attitudes and official policy towards migrant groups, and the emergence of overt political racism in Bradford in West Yorkshire.

1504 PERKS, Robert
"Using sound archives: Bradford Heritage Unit's oral history collection"
BASC News, no.2 (1987)
Using oral history in a museum and exhibition context.

1505 PERKS, Robert
"The National Sound Archive"
Oral History, vol.17, no.2 (1989), pp.58-9
The British Library National Sound Archive's
first curator of oral history was appointed in
November 1988: this is a brief account of
progress, holdings and future plans.

PERKS, Robert *see also* **BRADFORD
HERITAGE RECORDING UNIT;
HUMPHRIES, Steve; THOMPSON, Paul**

1506 PERLIS, Vivian
Charles Ives remembered: an oral history
New Haven: Yale University Press, 1974
237pp
An example of a musician's biography written
using fifty-eight transcribed oral history
interviews from the Yale Music Library oral
history collection.

1507 PERROTA, P. and MEACHAM, J.A.
"Can reminiscing intervention alter
depression and self-esteem?"
*International Journal of Aging and Human
Development*, vol.14 (1982), pp.23-30
Assesses the therapeutic value of reminiscing
and questions its short term effectiveness.

1508 PERSCHBACHER, K.
"An application of reminiscence in an activity
setting"
*Gerontologist, vol.24, no.4 (August 1984),
pp.343-53*

1509 PERSONAL NARRATIVES GROUP (ed.)
*Interpreting women's lives: feminist theory and
personal narratives*
Bloomington: Indiana University Press, 1989
277pp
An interdisciplinary collection of articles by
anthropologists, historians, literary scholars
and social scientists looking at the ways life
stories can expand an understanding of
gender. It grew out of a conference of the
same title held in May 1986 at Minnesota
University.

1510 PEUKERT, Detlev
"Ruhr miners under Nazi represssion
1933-1945"
*International Journal of Oral History, vol.1,
no.2 (June 1980), pp.111-127*
Oral recollections of resistance to Nazism.

1511 PEZERAT, Pierrette and POUBLAN, Daniele
"French telephone operators past and
present: the ambiguities of progress"
Oral History, vol.13, no.1 (1985), pp.28-42

1512 PFAFF, Eugene J.
"Oral history: a new challenge for public
libraries"
*Wilson Library Bulletin, no.54 (May 1980),
pp.568-571*

1513 PHILPOT, Terry
"Voices of the past"
Community Care, 9 May 1985

1514 PHIRI, Kings
"Oral historical research in Malawi: a review
of contemporary methodology and projects"
Kalulu [Zomba], no.1 (1976), pp.68-98

1515 PICCADILLY RECORDS
Face to face with John Freeman
*Piccadilly Records, FTF 38501-38505, a series
of five LP records, 1963*
From the famous BBC interview series and
including: Lord Birkett and Frank Cousins
(38501), Dame Edith Sitwell and Cecil Beaton
(38502), Lord Boothby and Lord Reith
(38503), Gilbert Harding and Sir Compton
Mackenzie (38504), and Carl Jung (38505).

1516 PICKARD, Tom
We make ships
Secker and Warburg, 1989
295pp
Verbatim and candid conversations with
shipbuilders drawn from the author's six
months as writer-in-residence in 1986 at a
Sunderland shipyard. The shipyard, Austin
and Pickersgill, closed in 1989, ending 600
years of shipbuilding on the River Wear.

1517 PICKERING, Michael
*Village song and culture: a study based on the
Blunt collection of song from Adderbury, North
Oxfordshire*
Croom Helm, 1982
187pp; bibliography
An interpretation of why a particular song
may have been chosen by a singer and
accepted by his audience.

PICKLES, Helen *see* **ARMSTRONG, Keith**

1518 PIERCE, Preston E.
"Oral history acquisition: some preliminary
considerations"
*Behavioral and Social Sciences Librarian,
vol.5, no.2 (1985-6), pp.67-78*
Touches on bibliographic control of oral
history holdings, problems of video
standardisation and legal issues.

1519 PINCUS, A.
"Reminiscence in ageing and its implications for social work practice"
Social Work, no.15 (1970), pp.47-53

PINTO-DUSCHINSKY, Michael *see* BUTLER, David

1520 PITT, Malcolm
The world on our backs: the Kent miners and the 1972 miners' strike
Lawrence and Wishart, 1979
217pp
A history of mining on the Kent coalfield, ending with the 1972 strike. The author was himself a local miner.

1521 PLUMMER, Ken
Documents of life: an introduction to the problems and literature of a humanistic method
Allen & Unwin, 1983
Contemporary Social Research Series
175pp; bibliography
An excellent introduction to oral history for the social scientist. Includes material on the American anthropological tradition and discusses the development of the life story approach in sociology.

PLUMMER, Ken *see also* FARADAY, Annabel

1522 POGUE, Forrest C.
"The George C. Marshall Oral History Project"
Wilson Library Bulletin, no.40 (March 1966), pp.607-8
300 people associated with the World War Two American general were interviewed.

POGUE, Forrest C. *see also* OLCH, Peter D.

1523 POLLARD, Michael
"Oral tradition and local history"
Local History, vol.9, no.7 (1971), pp.343-7
The value of oral history and folk songs in writing local history in Britain.

1524 POLLARD, Sidney and TURNER, Bob
"Profit sharing and autocracy: the case of J.T.and J. Taylor of Batley, woollen manufacturers, 1892-1966"
Business History, vol.18, no.1 (January 1976)
Makes use of oral evidence alongside other primary sources.

1525 POLLERT, Anna
Girls, wives, factory lives
Macmillan, 1981
251pp; bibliography
Based on interviews with women tobacco workers at Churchmans's in Bristol (part of Imperial Tobacco), who talk about the work process, boredom, their feelings about men and marriage, sexism from supervisors, trade unionism and balancing work with the roles of mother and 'housewife'. The period of research coincided with a one-day strike.

1526 POLYDOR
The Nixon interview with David Frost
Polydor Records PD 4-9401, 1977, 4 LP records
Drawn from nearly twenty-nine hours of interviews. It was the first time Nixon had spoken publicly since his resignation as president on 9 August 1974: he had no control over how the material was edited. It covers his career at home and abroad, and highlights the Watergate Scandal.

POMERLEAU, C.S. *see* MORANTZ, Regina Markell

POMEROY, Barbara *see* DEERING, Mary Jo

POMEROY, Robert W. *see* TRASK, David F.

1527 POPULAR MEMORY GROUP
"Popular memory: theory, politics, method" in CENTRE FOR CONTEMPORARY CULTURAL STUDIES, *Making histories*, Hutchinson, 1982

1528 PORTELLI, Alessandro
"The peculiarities of oral history"
History Workshop, no.12 (Autumn 1981), pp.96-107

1529 PORTELLI, Alessandro
"'The time of my life': functions of time in oral history"
International Journal of Oral History, vol.2, no.3 (November 1981), pp.162-80

1530 PORTELLI, Alessandro
"Oral testimony, the law and the making of history: the 'April 7' murder trial"
History Workshop, no.20 (Autumn 1985), pp.5-35

1531 PORTELLI, Alessandro
"The best trash-can wiper in town: the life and times of Vatero Peppoloni, worker"
Oral History Review, vol.16, no.1 (Spring 1988), pp.69-89
Based on an interview recorded in Turni in central Italy.

1532 PORTELLI, Alessandro
"Uchronic Dreams: working class memory and possible worlds"
Oral History, vol.16, no.2 (1988), pp.46-56
Uchronia is defined as the imagining of what would have happened if a certain historical event had not taken place: an alternative present. Its role in oral history interviewing is assessed in this challenging article.

1533 PORTER, Enid
Cambridgeshire customs and folklore
Routledge & Kegan Paul, 1969
419pp
Curing the sick, magic, calendar customs, games, municipal and university life from interviews.

PORTER, Julian *see* **KIRKHAM, Pat**

1534 POTTS, Bob
The old pubs of Hulme 2: reminiscences
Manchester: Neil Richardson, 1983
32pp
Former residents recall one area of Manchester demolished in the 1960s.

1535 POTTS, Bob
Old pubs of Rochdale Road and neighbourhood
Manchester: Neil Richardson, 1985
36pp
Recollections of pubs in the Collyhurst, Harpurhey and Rochdale Road areas of Manchester.

POTTS, Maggie *see* **FIDO, Rebecca**

POUBLAN, Daniele *see* **PEZERAT, Pierrette**

1536 POWELL, Enoch
"Old men forget"
The Times, 5 November 1981
A critique of oral history.

1537 POWELL, Graeme
"Oral history collections of the National Library of Australia"
Archives and Manuscripts, no.5 (1974), pp.137-42

POWER, Jim *see* **BROMILOW, Anne**

POZZETTA, George E. *see* **MORMINO, Gary R.**

1538 PRESTON, Jo Anne
"Millgirl narratives: representations of class and gender in nineteenth century Lowell"
Life Stories, no.3 (1987), pp.21-30

1539 PRESTONFIELD REMEMBERS GROUP
Changed days
Edinburgh: Workers' Educational Association, 1985
62pp
Family life, wash day, home cures, work, fashion, leisure and trams are amongst the memories from Edinburgh in this first collection.

1540 PRESTONFIELD REMEMBERS GROUP
Just a memory
Edinburgh: Workers' Educational Association, 1988
60pp
Reminiscences of elderly people.

1541 PREVIN, Andre (ed.)
Orchestra
MacDonald and Jane's, 1979
224pp
A look at an how an orchestra ticks from the point of view of the musicians: based on thirty-one interviews by Michael Foss with musicians from great orchestras in Britain and America.

1542 PRICE, Trevor (ed.)
In my life
Wolverhampton: Wolverhampton Heritage Project, 1987
46pp
Edited selections from taped interviews (now held in Wolverhampton Borough Archives) with Wolverhampton people about domestic life, school, work, canals and leisure.

1543 PROBYN, Walter
Angel face: the making of a criminal
Allen & Unwin, 1977
254pp
The life story of a man who had, by 1974, spent thirty of his forty-three years in custodial institutions of some kind: his spectacular escapes from prisons had earned him the nickname 'Angel Face Probyn'. Includes a commentary by Stan Cohen.

1544 PROCTOR, Samuel
"Oral history in the United States"
Phonographic Bulletin, no.13 (1975), pp.6-10
The origins of oral history in the States, the establishment of the Oral History Association in 1967 and progress since then, with some examples.

1545 PUBLIC ARCHIVES OF CANADA
Manual: Sound Archives
Ottawa: Public Archives, Canada, 1975
24pp
Describes the procedures of the Sound Archives, covering acquisitions, interviews, accessioning, cataloguing, preservation etc.(In English and French).

1546 PUGH, Mary Jo
"Oral history in the library: levels of commitment"
Drexel Library Quarterly, vol.15 (October 1979), pp.12-28
Examines varying strategies towards oral history for libraries to adopt, from the collection of books and published manuscripts through serving as a repository of tapes, to setting up an oral history project. She suggests the latter departs from traditional library practice.

1547 PUGH, Patricia M.
"The Oxford Colonial Records Project and the Oxford Development Records Project"
Journal of the Society of Archivists, vol.6 (October 1978)
Originally begun as the OCRP in 1963, an oral history project was added in 1966 and relaunched in 1977 as the ODRP with a grant from the Ministry for Overseas Development.

1548 PULLEN, Brenda
"Keeping the long-stay patients in touch with the 'good old days'"
Health and Social Services Journal, no. 4597, 30 June 1978, pp.738-739

1549 PURKIS, Sallie
"An experiment in family history with first year juniors"
Teaching History, vol.4, no.15 (May 1976)

1550 PURKIS, Sallie
"Oral history"
Journal of East Anglian History Workshop, no.2 (October 1977), pp.6-8

1551 PURKIS, Sallie
"Oral history in the primary school"
History Workshop, no.3 (Spring 1977), pp.113-7

1552 PURKIS, Sallie
At home in 1900
Harlow: Longman, 1981, 1983
Into the Past series no.1
24pp
An introduction to the subject, designed to encourage school children to ask questions and discover oral history for themselves. The series *Into the Past* covers aspects of life in Britain in the first half of this century.

1553 PURKIS, Sallie
In the street in 1900
Harlow: Longman, 1981, 1983
Into the Past series no.2
24pp

1554 PURKIS, Sallie
At school in 1900
Harlow: Longman, 1981, 1983
Into the Past series no.3
24pp

1555 PURKIS, Sallie
Oral history in schools
Colchester: Oral History Society, 1981
20pp; bibliography
An innovative survey aimed at teachers, covering both primary and secondary schools, with examples of work from all over Britain.

1556 PURKIS, Sallie
Arbury is where we live!
Ely, Cambridgeshire: 1981
36pp

1557 PURKIS, Sallie
"Arbury is where we live"
History Today, vol.33 (June 1983), pp.29-32
Details of a school project in Cambridge involving a post-war housing estate.

1558 PURKIS, Sallie
Thanks for the memory
Collins Educational, 1987
How do we know? series
48pp
Assesses the value of oral evidence and offers guidance and examples of how to start an oral history project with particular reference to primary and lower secondary schools.

1558A PURKIS, Sallie, MIDDLETON, Geoffrey and MERSON, Elizabeth
Home, the town and work in the 1930s
Harlow: Longman, 1983
Into the Past series vols. 7-9
26pp
Originally published as separate volumes by the three individual authors.

PURKIS, Sallie *see also* RAVENSDALE, Jack; MERSON, Elizabeth

1559 PUTNEY AND ROEHAMPTON ORGANISATION OF PENSIONERS
We survived! Modern history seen through the eyes of the Putney and Roehampton Organisation of Pensioners History Group
Putney and Roehampton Organisation of Pensioners, 1988
34pp
Extracts from tape-recorded conversations about important twentieth century events as experienced by members of PROP: political education, living conditions, war, the 1945 Labour government, trade unions and the peace movement.

1560 QUEENSPARK BOOKS
Backyard Brighton: photographs and memories of Brighton in the thirties
Brighton: Queenspark Books, 1988
75pp
Photographs of thirty Brighton houses which were knocked down in the 1930s, accompanied by the memories of people who lived in the same area but who challenge the label 'slums' which was used to justify their demolition.

1561 QUEENSPARK BOOKS
Backstreet Brighton: photographs and memories
Brighton: Queenspark Books, 1989
80pp
The sequel to *Backyard Brighton:* thirty demolished streets together with stories from the people who lived in them in the fifties and sixties.

1562 QUEENSPARK RATES GROUP
Brighton on the rocks: monetarism and the local state
Brighton: Queenspark Books, 1983
192pp
Interviews, photographs, statistics and analysis of the effects of monetarism on Brighton people's lives.

1563 RADIN, Paul (ed.)
Crashing Thunder: the autobiography of an American Indian
Nebraska: University of Nebraska Press, 1983; first published 1926
The Native American Autobiography series
215pp
Early oral autobiography.

1564 RAEBURN, Antonia
The militant suffragettes
Joseph, 1973
269pp; bibliography
A history of the suffragette movement from 1905 to 1914: interviews with suffragettes, conducted from 1964, were used as a major source. Includes an introduction by J.B.Priestley.

1565 RAINWATER, Lee
And the poor get children: sex, contraception and family planning in the working class
Chicago: Quadrangle, 1960
Social Research Studies in Contemporary Life
202pp, bibliography
Through intensive interviews with ninety-six working class men and women from Chicago and Cincinnati, this study puts contraceptive behaviour and attitudes in the context of sexual behaviour and social class.

1566 RAINWATER, Lee
Family design: marital sexuality, family size and contraception
Chicago: Aldine, 1965
Social Research Studies in Contemporary Life
349pp; bibliography
From interviews with 409 people in Chicago, Cincinnati and Oklahoma City, this study examines the factors behind family size and the effectiveness of family limitation methods.

1567 RANDALL, John
History of Madeley
Shrewsbury: Salop County Library, 1975: reprint, with new introduction, of 1880 edition
387pp
An early history of the Shropshire coalfield and Coalbrookdale using much oral source material.

1568 RANGER, Terence
"Personal reminiscence and the experience of the people in East Central Africa"
Oral History, vol.6, no.1 (1978), pp.45-78

1569 RANGER, Terence
Peasant consciousness and guerilla war in Zimbabwe: a comparative study
Currey, 1985
400pp; bibliography
The growth of peasant resentment and resistance to alien whites throughout Zimbabwe, and throughout different classes of peasant.

RANGER, Terence *see also* **HOBSBAWN, Eric**

1570 RAVENSDALE, Jack and PURKIS, Sallie
The local history kit
Cambridge: National Extension College, 1982
National Extension correspondence texts: course no.HS31
120pp; bibliography
A practical guide for those wishing to investigate the history of their own area, using oral history as a major source.

1571 RAWICK, George P. (ed.)
The American slave: a composite autobiography
Westport: Greenwood, 1972, 1973
Nineteen volumes
From sundown to sunup: the making of the Black community is an introductory interpretative essay; volumes 2-17 form a series of narratives covering the following states: South Carolina (vols. 2-3), Texas (4-5), Alabama and Indiana (6), Oklahoma and Mississippi (7), Arkansas (8-10), Arkansas and Missouri (11), Georgia (12-13), North Carolina (14-15), Kansas, Kentucky, Maryland, Ohio, Virginia and Tennessee (16) and Florida (17). All are based on interviews carried out under the New Deal Federal Writers' Project of the Works Project Administration in the 1930s. Volumes 18 and 19 are entitled respectively *Unwritten history of slavery* and *God struck me dead* (with bibliography) and consist of interviews conducted by scholars at Fisk University slightly later.

1572 RAWNSLEY, Stuart
"The membership of the British Union of Fascists" in THURLOW, R. and LUNN, K. (eds.), *Essays in British Fascism*, Croom Helm, 1979.

RAWNSLEY, Stuart *see also* **CORKHILL, D.**

1573 REA, Anthony
Manchester's Little Italy
Manchester: Neil Richardson, 1988
44pp
Memories of the Italian district of Ancoats in Manchester recorded by the grandson of Marco Rea, one of the pioneers of the city's ice cream industry.

1574 READ, Daphne (ed.) and RICHARDSON, Gus (compiler)
The Great War and Canadian society: an oral history
Toronto: New Hogtown, 1978
223pp
Recollections of Canadian men and women drawn from over 200 taped interviews recorded in 1974 and covering resettlement of war victims as well as actual war conditions. The introduction contains a useful summary of oral history in North America.

1575 READ, Peter
Down there with me on the Cowra Mission: an oral history of Erambie Aboriginal Reserve, Cowra NSW
Sydney and New York: Pergamon Press, 1984
141pp

1576 READER, W.J.
Imperial Chemical Industries: a history
Oxford University Press, two volumes: 1970 and 1975
Vol.2: The first quarter century, 1926-1952
(569pp; bibliography) is especially relevant. The author found interviews useful for details of inter-personal relationships

1577 READMAN, Alan
"The creation of an oral history archive at the West Sussex Record Office"
West Sussex Archives Society Newsletter, no.12 (January 1979), pp.7-9
Details of the project's aims and methods plus practical advice on techniques, editing and organisation.

1578 REBOUL, P. (ed.)
Those were the days: a collection of tales from and about the Borough of Barnet between the two world wars
Hendon and District Archaelogical Society, 1980
Occasional paper no.5
48pp
Transcribed tape recordings made between 1978 and 1980 with testimony from: a housewife, dentist, policeman, milkman, brewer, bricklayer, commercial traveller, printer, nurse, baker, tunnel miner, carpenter, shopkeeper and postman. Includes a Boer War veteran.

1579 RED LANE OLD RESIDENTS ASSOCIATION
Red Lane reminiscences
Coventry: Red Lane Old Residents Association/Social History Group Community Enterprise Project/Manpower Services Commission, 1983
132pp
A temporary work scheme project in inner city Coventry which included oral history work. The book covers work (textiles, munitions and cars), women at work, home life, school, leisure, religion and the changing community.

1580 REEKIE, Gail
"Women's response to war work in Western Australia 1942-1946"
Studies in Western Australian History, vol.7 (December 1983), pp.46-67
Discusses the reality of women's resistance behind the facade of compliance.

1581 REEKES, Andrew
"Oral history and the Raj: fourth year boys find out about British India through interview"
Teaching History, no.27 (June 1980), pp.4-5
Describes an oral history project at Tonbridge School, Kent, and includes sample questions.

1582 REES, Alwyn David
Life in a Welsh countryside: a social study of Llanfihangel yng Ngwynfa
Cardiff: University of Wales Press, 1950
188pp
A study of the Welsh uplands from questionnaires and interviews carried out between 1939 and 1946.

REICHLIN, R.E. *see* **MOLINARI, V.**

1583 REID, David
"Full of noises"
New Library World, August 1980

1584 REID, Lesley A.
Down memory lane: reminiscences of the Happyhillock 50s group
Dundee: Tayside Regional Council/Lincraig Community Centre, 1988
24pp
An anthology of extracts from a women's group about childhood, household economy, work and leisure between the wars in Dundee.

REID, Stuart *see* **FITZPATRICK, Jim**

1585 REIMER, Derek (ed.)
Voices: a guide to oral history
Victoria, British Columbia: Sound and Moving Image Division, Provincial Archives of British Columbia, 1984
74pp; annotated bibliography
Useful for the novice as it includes details of using tape recorders, the interview and archival practice; with an appendix on 'basic procedures for a small oral history project'.

1586 RENDELL, Brian and CHILDS, Keith
Lessons of a lifetime: memories of Chepstow and the Forest of Dean
Review Graphics, nd
120pp
The result of a scheme at Whitecross School in Lydney in Gloucestershire to bring elderly people into the school to be interviewed, many on video. Includes memories of the tinplating trade, domestic service, the First World War, mining and old Lydney.

1587 RETTER, Janet
Drongan: the story of a mining village
Cumnock: Cumnock and Doon Valley District Council, 1978
85pp
A local history of an Ayrshire village from the 15th century: oral material is used in the later chapters.

1588 REUBAND, Karl-Heinz
"Oral history: notes on an emerging field in historical research"
Historical Social Research [West Germany], no.12 (1979), pp.18-20

RHUDICK, P.J. *see* **McMAHON, W.**

1589 RICHARDS, Denis
Royal Air Force 1939-45
HMSO, three volumes, 1952-3
This official history of the RAF includes material from some 300 interviews.

1590 RICHARDS, Denis
Portal of Hungerford: the life of Marshall of the Royal Air Force Viscount Portal of Hungerford
Heinemann, 1977
436pp
This biography of Lord Portal, who was Chief of Air Staff during the Second World War, is partially based on seventy-five interviews.

1591 RICHARDS, Sam
"Bill Hingston: a biography in sound"
Oral History, vol.10, no.1 (1982), pp.24-46
Traditional music in Dittisham near Dartmouth in Devon.

RICHARDSON, Gus *see* **READ, Daphne**

1592 RICHARDSON, Kenneth
Twentieth century Coventry
City of Coventry/Macmillan, 1972
380pp
Includes over eighty interviews, mainly with notable people, from this Midlands manufacturing city.

1593 RICHARDSON, Neil
The old pubs of Ancoats
Manchester: Neil Richardson, 1987
48pp
An account of 300 pubs which at one time existed in this area of Manchester based partially on personal accounts.

1594 RICHARDSON, Ruth
Death, dissection and the destitute
Routledge and Kegan Paul, 1988; Penguin, 1989
426pp; bibliography
Draws on oral testimony.

RICHARDSON, Ruth *see also* **CHAMBERLAIN, Mary**

1595 RICHARDSON, Sue (ed.)
Manchesters in the Great War
Manchester: Neil Richardson, 1985
88pp; bibliography
Recorded conversations with an 'Old Contemptible', a territorial and a 'Pal', covering action on the Western Front, Gallipoli, Sinai and Italy, 1914-18; with boyhood memories of Cheetham Hill, Oldham Road and Hyde.

RICHARDSON, Sue *see* **ELINOR, Gillian**

1596 RICHARDSON, Yvonne and PEARCE, Elizabeth
"Do you remember?"
Nursing Times, vol.85, no.27 (5 July 1989), pp.54-5
Argues the case for the value of reality orientation with the elderly mentally ill.

1597 RIDDLE, Almeda
A singer and her songs: Almeda Riddle's book of ballads
Baton Rouge: Louisiana State University Press, 1970
191pp
A collection of ballads interspersed with oral testimony of rural life in Arkansas. Edited by Roger Abrahams.

1598 RIDGWAY, Roy
"Remembrance of things past"
BMA News, vol.9, no.8 (1983)

1599 RIDLEY, J.C.
"Recall and reliability of interview data from older women"
Journal of Gerontology, vol.34, no.1 (January 1979), pp.99-105

RIGBY, Andy *see* KIBBLEWHITE, Liz

RIGDON, Susan M. *see* LEWIS, Oscar

1600 RIJKEN, Joke M.S.
"Some remarks on a definition of oral history"
Phonographic Bulletin, no.2 (January 1972), pp.5-7

1601 RINGELHEIM, Joan
"Women and the Holocaust: a reconsideration of research"
Signs, vol.10, no.4 (1985)
An analysis of the importance of testimony drawn from the author's own interviews with women Holocaust survivors.

RINGELHEIM, Joan *see also* KATZ, Esther

1602 RITTER, Lawrence S.
The glory of their times: the story of the early days of baseball: told by the men who played it
New York: Collier, 1971; first published Macmillan, 1966
300pp
Based on tape-recorded interviews with the "greats".

1603 ROACH, Helen (ed.)
Spoken records
Metuchen, New Jersey: Scarecrow Press, third edition, 1970; first edition, 1963
288pp
A discography of spoken recordings which includes oral history.

1604 ROBERTS, Alan
"Paul Thompson, Wendy Lowenstein and one source history"
Oral History Association of Australia Journal, vol.5 (1982-3), pp.25-34

ROBERTS, Alan *see also* DOUGLAS, Louise

1605 ROBERTS, Andrew Dunlop
A history of Bemba: political growth and change in north-eastern Zambia before 1900
Longman, 1973
420pp; bibliography
The pre-colonial history of the Bemba, a Bantu-speaking agricultural people, using oral traditions and interviews recorded in 1964-5.

1606 ROBERTS, Andrew Dunlop
"The use of oral sources for African history"
Oral History, vol.4, no.1 (1976) pp.41-56
Argues for more oral history work with 'ordinary people' in sub-Saharan Africa.

1607 ROBERTS, Elizabeth
"Learning and living: socialisation outside school"
Oral History, vol.3, no.2 (1975), pp.14-28
The educative and maturing influence on children of family and social life between 1890 and 1914, based on oral evidence from eighty-nine people in Barrow and Lancaster.

1608 ROBERTS, Elizabeth
Working class Barrow and Lancaster 1890-1930
Lancaster: University of Lancaster, 1976
Centre for North-West Regional Studies occasional paper no.2
Based on oral testimony and arranged according to subject (food, housing, leisure etc.), followed by brief biographical sketches of the sixty informants.

1609 ROBERTS, Elizabeth
"Working class women in the North West"
Oral History, vol.5, no.2 (1977), pp.7-30
Work, financial management, sexual attitudes and women's role in the home are examined, drawing on the testimony of women from Barrow and Lancaster, the oldest born in 1885.

1610 ROBERTS, Elizabeth
"Oral history and the local historian"
Local Historian, vol.13 (August 1979), pp.408-16
Based on a project which interviewed ninety-five people in Barrow and Lancaster between 1972 and 1976.

1611 ROBERTS, Elizabeth
"Oral history investigation of disease and its management by the Lancashire working class 1890-1939" in PICKSTONE, J.V. (ed.),
Health, diseases and medicine in Lancashire, 1750-1950: four papers on sources, problems and methods, Manchester: University of Manchester Institute of Science and Technology, 1980
Occasional publication Department of History of Science and Technology

1612 ROBERTS, Elizabeth
"Working class standards of living in three Lancashire towns 1890-1914"
International Review of Social History, vol.27, part 1 (1982)

1613 ROBERTS, Elizabeth
"Working wives and their families" in BARKER, T. and DRAKE, M. (eds.), *Population and society in Britain, 1850-1980*, 1982, pp.140-71

1614 ROBERTS, Elizabeth
"The working class extended family: functions and attitudes 1890-1940"
Oral History, vol.12, no.1 (1984), pp.48-55
Argues that the extended family provided a vital network of economic and social support, and is critical of the notion that familial support was motivated by self-interest. Draws on 160 working class interviews from Barrow, Lancaster and Preston, about the period 1890-1940.

1615 ROBERTS, Elizabeth
Voices from the past 1890-1940: an oral history resource for schools
Lancaster: Centre for North West Regional Studies, University of Lancaster, 1984
A teacher's booklet (47pp; bibliography), audio cassette tapes, transcripts and twenty slides covering street life, shops, markets, family life, school, children, work, leisure, housing, food, health and special occasions in the North West.

1616 ROBERTS, Elizabeth
A woman's place: an oral history of working class women 1890-1940
Oxford: Blackwell, 1984
246pp; bibliography
Based on 160 interviews with women from three Lancashire towns, Barrow, Lancaster and Preston, this important book challenges some assumptions about women's status, work and family relationships, and sexual attitudes in the recent past. The culmination of many years' work.

1617 ROBERTS, Elizabeth
"The family" in BENSON, John (ed.) *The working class in England 1875-1914*, Croom Helm, 1985, pp.1-35

1618 ROBERTS, Elizabeth
"Oral history: an introduction"
Local History, February/March 1986

1619 ROBERTS, Elizabeth
"Women's strategies" in LEWIS, Jane (ed.) *Labour and love: women's experience of home and family, 1850-1940*, *Blackwell, 1986, pp.223-47*

1620 ROBERTS, Elizabeth
"The Lancashire way of death" in HOULBROOKE, R. (ed.) *Death, ritual and bereavement*, *Routledge, 1989*

1621 ROBERTS, Helen (ed.)
Doing feminist research
Routledge & Kegan Paul, 1981
207pp; bibliographies
Includes a chapter entitled "Interviewing women: a contradiction in terms" by Ann Oakley.

ROBERTS, Kenneth *see* LANE, Tony

1622 ROBERTS, Robert
The classic slum: Salford life in the first quarter of the century
Manchester: Manchester University Press, 1971; Harmondsworth: Penguin (Pelican), 1973
219pp; Pelican edition includes bibliography
An oral autobiography covering the morality and social structure of a working class area in the North West of England.

1623 ROBERTS, Robert
A ragged schooling: growing up in a classic slum
Manchester: Manchester University Press, 1987; Flamingo 1984; first published 1976
224pp
An oral autobiography.

1624 ROBERTSON, Beth M.
"Keeping the faith: a discussion of the practical and ethical issues involved in donated oral history collections"
Oral History Association of Australia Journal, no.11 (1989), pp.18-29

1625 ROBINSON, Joe
The life and times of Francie Nichol of South Shields
Allen and Unwin, 1975
176pp

1626 ROCHA LIMA, Valentina da
"Getulio: political biography and national myth"
Oral History, vol.16, no.1 (1988), pp.34-9
Political leadership in Brazil.

1627 ROCHDALE LIVING HISTORY
WORKSHOP
*Do you remember?: Some Rochdale people look
back to the turn of the century*
Rochdale: Rochdale Alternative Press, 1975
70pp
A booklet containing three oral
autobiographies and other material covering
mill work, homelife, school and leisure.

1628 ROCHE, Stanley
*Foreigner: the story of Grace Morten as told to
Stanley Roche*
Wellington, New Zealand: Oxford University
Press, 1979
215pp
A biography written from taped interviews
covering childhood in China, and life in
Cambridge, Shanghai and Nazi-occupied
Czechoslovakia before settling in New
Zealand.

RODRIGUEZ, Evangelina *see* DELCROIX,
Catherine

1629 ROGERS, Anna (ed.)
*The war years: New Zealanders remember
1939-1945*
Wellington, New Zealand: Platform
Publishing, 1989
171pp
Taken directly from recordings collected by
the 'Spectrum' radio documentary series, ten
'ordinary' New Zealanders reflect on the
impact of the war on themselves.

1630 ROLLINS, Alfred B.
*Report on the Oral History Project of the John
Fitzgerald Kennedy Library*
Cambridge, Mass.: Harvard University, 1965

1631 ROLSTON, Bill and MUNCK, Ronnie
"Belfast Republicanism in the thirties: the
oral evidence"
Oral History, vol.16, no.2 (1988), pp.34-45

ROLSTON, Bill *see also* MUNCK, Ronnie

1632 ROMANIUK, M.
"Reminiscence and the second half of life"
*Experimental Aging Research, vol.7, no.4
(1981), pp.477-89*

1633 ROMNEY, Joseph
"Legal considerations in oral history"
Oral History Review, vol.1 (1973), pp.66-76
Argues that mutual respect and anticipation
can avoid the worst pitfalls. Issues of contract,
libel, privacy, criminal liability, source
disclosure, ownership and copyright as it
applies in the States are discussed in detail.

1634 ROMNEY, Joseph
"Oral history: law and libraries"
*Drexel Library Quarterly, vol.15 (1979),
pp.39-49*
A discussion of contracts, libel, copyright and
privacy relating to oral history collections in
US libraries.

1635 ROOKE, Andrew
"Oral history librarianship for Zambia"
*Zambia Library Association Journal, vol.12,
no.2 (December 1980), pp.75-83*
Guidelines on techniques and archiving based
on the University of Zambia Department of
History's Joint History Project of 1975.

1636 ROONEY, Ray, LEWIS, Brian and
SCHUHLE, Reini (eds.)
*Home is where the heart is: voices from
Calderdale*
Castleford, West Yorkshire: Yorkshire Art
Circus/Continuum, 1989
96pp
Over 150 people from Halifax, Elland,
Sowerby Bridge, Hebden Bridge,
Todmorden, Brighouse, Mixenden and area,
talk about their houses, homes and
neighbourhoods and how they have changed
during the century. All aspects of housing are
covered from council houses to high-rise flats
and back-to-backs to recent 'yuppification'.

ROOS, Barbara *see* ROOS, J.P.

1637 ROOS, J.P.
"From farm to office: family, self-confidence
and the new middle class"
Life Stories, no.3 (1987), pp.7-20

1638 ROOS, J.P. and ROOS, Barbara
"Upper class life over three generations: the
case of the Swedish Finns"
Oral History, vol.12, no.1 (1984), pp.25-39

1639 ROPER, Michael
"Fathers and lovers: images of the 'older man'
in British managers' career narratives"
Life Stories, no.4 (1988), pp.49-58

1640 ROSALDO, R.
"Doing oral history"
Social Analysis, vol.4 (1980)

ROSE, David *see* **NEWBY, Howard**

1641 ROSEN, B.
"Aural history collections: time for a decision"
Australian Library Journal, no.23 (November 1974), pp.374-9
Argues for the setting up of a central Australian 'aural' history archive.

1642 ROSENBERG, Bruce
The art of the American folk preacher
New York: Oxford University Press, 1970
265pp

1643 ROSENBERG, Deena and Bernard
The music makers
New York: Columbia University Press, 1979
Thirty-two interviews with classical musicians, composers, conductors, critics, managers and scholars from the Project for the Oral History of Music in America at New York City University.

1644 ROSENGARTEN, Theodore
All God's dangers: the life of Nate Shaw
Cape, 1975; originally New York: Knopf, 1974
561pp
An important book in which a black octogenarian tenant farmer from Alabama relates his experiences, including a twelve year gaol sentence for union activity. Extracted from 120 hours of tape.

1645 ROSENSWEIG, Roy
"Automating your oral history program: a guide to database management on a microcomputer"
International Journal of Oral History, vol.5, no.3 (1985)

1646 ROSENTHAL, Robert
"The interview and beyond: some methodological questions for oral historians"
Public Historian, vol.1 (Spring 1978), pp.58-67
Argues that eventual use determines methodology.

1647 ROSS, Alistair
"Children becoming historians: an oral history project in a primary school"
Oral History, vol.12, no.2 (1984), pp.21-31
A project looking at the history of an inner London school and its evacuation to Wiltshire in 1939.

1648 ROSSER, Colin and HARRIS Christopher C.
The family and social change: a study of family and kinship in a South Wales town
Routledge & Kegan Paul, 1965
International Library of Sociology and Social Reconstruction
337pp
A sociological urban community study making use of oral history.

1649 ROTHCHILD, Sylvia (ed.)
Voices from the Holocaust
New York: New American Library, 1981
456pp
A collection of extracts from tapes describing life before, during and after the Jewish Holocaust for Jews now settled in the United States. With a foreword by Elie Wiesel.

1650 ROTHCHILD, Sylvia
A special legacy: an oral history of Soviet Jewish emigres in the United States
New York: Simon and Schuster, 1985
336pp

1651 ROTHNIE, Niall
The bombing of Bath
Bath: Ashgrove Press, 1983
162pp; bibliography
The events and effects of the raids on Bath of 25th and 26th April 1942, which killed 400 people and destroyed 2000 buildings, from the recollections of sixty people including children, ARP wardens, doctors, ambulance drivers, policemen and soldiers.

1652 ROUSSEAU, Ann Marie
Shopping bag ladies: homeless women talk about their lives
New York: Pilgrim Press, 1981
160pp

1653 ROWBOTHAM, Sheila and McCRINDLE, Jean (eds.)
Dutiful daughters: women talk about their lives
Allen Lane, 1977; Harmondsworth: Penguin (Pelican) 1979, 1983
396pp
Fourteen women, aged from thirty to seventy, talk about their childhood, families and work.

1654 ROWBOTHAM, Sheila
"Guardians of India's memory"
New Society, 15 January 1988, pp.28-9

ROWE, D.J. *see* **CLARKE, J.F.**

1655 ROWE, Doc
'We'll call once more unto your house'
Padstow, Cornwall: Padstow Echo, 1982
30pp
An oral history of the traditional annual May Day celebrations in Padstow in Cornwall.

ROWE, Doc *see also* THOMPSON, Paul

1656 ROWLANDS, B.
"Memories of a domestic servant in the first world war"
North East Group for the Study of Labour History Bulletin, no.5, pp.16-28

1657 ROYLE, Trevor
The best years of their lives: the National Service experience 1945-63
Michael Joseph, 1986; Coronet paperback, 1988
350pp
National Service lasted eighteen years and involved over two million men, most of them aged eighteen who spent two years in the services. This is their account of the tedium, skiving, danger and opportunity they experienced.

1658 ROYLE, Trevor
The last days of the Raj
Michael Joseph, 1989
304pp
An account of Britain's withdrawal from India in the 1940s based mainly on spoken recollections with both Indian and British participants. The tapes are now held by the National Sound Archive. (*See also* MASANI, Zareer)

1659 RUBENSTEIN, David
"An interview with Tom Stephenson"
Bulletin of the Society for the Study of Labour History, no.22 (Spring 1971), pp.27-32
Stephenson was secretary and president of the Ramblers' Association.

1660 RUBIN, Don
"Theatre history and oral history"
Canadian Oral History Association Journal, no.2 (1976-7), pp.46-8
A description of a theatre history project in Ontario.

1661 RUBIN, Lillian Breslow
Worlds of pain: life in the working-class family
New York: Basic Books, 1976
268pp; bibliography
Verbatim extracts from intensive interviews of up to ten hours with families from twelve different working class communities around San Francisco Bay. Husbands and wives were interviewed separately and talk about childhood, marriage, stress, sex, work and leisure.

1662 RUMICS, Elizabeth
"Oral history: defining the term"
Wilson Library Bulletin, vol.40 (March 1966), pp.602-5

1663 RUNDELL, Walter
"Main trends in US historiography since the New Deal: research prospects in oral history"
Oral History Review, vol.4 (1976), pp.35-47
A bibliographic article.

1664 RUNYAN, William McKinley
Life stories and psychobiography: explanations in theory and method
Oxford: Oxford University Press, 1982, 1984
288pp; bibliography
A theoretical consideration of the use of biographies in social theory.

1665 RUSSELL, David and WALKER, George
Trafford Park 1896-1939: a selection of photographs and recollections about life in Trafford Park
Manchester: Manchester Polytechnic/ Manchester Studies, 1979
40pp
Extracts from thirty hours of taped memories with members of an industrial community in Manchester devastated by demolition and redevelopment.

1666 RUST, Brian
Discography of historical records on cylinders and 78s
Greenwood Press, 1979
327pp
The best listing available of original spoken word recordings of historic figures, including the earliest Edison recordings of Gladstone (1888) and Florence Nightingale (1890). Copies of many are held by the National Sound Archive.

1667 RYAN, Tony and WALKER, Rodger
Making life story books
British Agencies for Adoption and Fostering,
1985
48pp
Guidelines for life story work with children in
care.

1668 RYANT, Carl
"Comment: oral history and gerontology"
Gerontologist, no.21 (February 1981), pp.104-5

1669 RYANT, Carl
"Oral history and psychohistory"
Journal of Psychohistory, no.8 (Winter 1981),
pp.307-18

1670 RYDEN, M.B.
"Nursing intervention in support of
reminiscence"
Journal of Gerontological Nursing, vol.7, no.8
(1981), pp.461-3

1671 SAFFORD, Jeffrey J.
"The Montana livestock industry through oral
history"
Agricultural History, vol.49 (January 1975),
pp.105-7

1672 SAFIER, Gwendolyn
Contemporary American leaders in nursing: an
oral history
New York: McGraw-Hill, 1977
392pp
Seventeen people involved in the practice,
administration and teaching of nursing
describe their careers, highlighting the
changes since the Second World War.

1673 SAINT, Andrew
Towards a social architecture: the role of school
building in post-war England
New Haven: Yale University Press, 1987
272pp
An unusual example of architectural history
drawing on oral sources, particularly for
understanding the aims, strengths and
weaknesses of the leading architects involved.
The tapes are now lodged with the National
Sound Archive.

SALAFF, Janet W. *see* **SHERIDAN, Mary**

1674 SALISBURY, Harrison E.
The Long March: the untold story
Macmillan, 1985
419pp; note on sources
In the course of researching the book the
author travelled 7400 miles to gather
interviews with many people, including
leading Communists and members of the Red
Army, who marched in the face of Chiang
Kai-Shek.

SALMOND, Anne *see* **STIRLING, Amiria;**
STIRLING, Eruera

1675 SALOME, F.A.
"The methodological significance of the lying
informant"
Anthropological Quarterly, vol.50 (1977)

1676 SALT, Chrys and WILSON, Mervyn
We are one blood: memories of the first sixty
years of the Woodcraft Folk
Co-operative Retail Services Ltd., 1985
52pp
The Woodcraft Folk, set up in 1925, is an
alternative youth organisation for both boys
and girls.

1677 SAMPSON, Anthony
Anatomy of Britain
Hodder and Stoughton, 1962
662pp
One of the first political science books to be
based almost entirely on oral evidence: some
200 interviews.

1678 SAMUEL, Raphael
"Perils of the transcript"
Oral History, vol.1, no.2 (1971), pp.19-22

1679 SAMUEL, Raphael
"Headington Quarry: recording a labouring
community"
Oral History, vol.1, no.4 (1973), pp.107-122

1680 SAMUEL, Raphael
"Local history and oral history"
History Workshop, no.1 (1976), pp.191-208

1681 SAMUEL, Raphael (ed.)
Village life and labour
Routledge & Kegan Paul, 1975
History Workshop series
278pp
An analysis of nineteenth century rural
society: some chapters use oral evidence and
include material on farm workers and quarry
communities.

1682 SAMUEL, Raphael (ed.)
Miners, quarrymen and saltworkers
Routledge & Kegan Paul, 1977
History Workshop series
363pp
Looks at the peculiarities and common features of mineral workers of every class. Includes three detailed local studies: pit life in County Durham, slate quarrying in North Wales and saltworkers in Cheshire.

1683 SAMUEL, Raphael (ed.)
East End underworld: chapters in the life of Arthur Harding
Routledge & Kegan Paul, 1981
History Workshop series
355pp
Based on interviews, recorded in 1973-79, with Arthur Harding (born 1886), probably the last man alive to have been brought up in the 'Jago', the most famous criminal slum of late Victorian London. An example of an interpretative analysis of a single life story with much on criminal activity and prison life.

1684 SAMUEL, Raphael
"Local history and oral history" in BURGESS, Robert G.(ed.) *Field research: a sourcebook and field manual, GAU, 1982*

1685 SAMUEL, Raphael, BLOOMFIELD, Barbara, and BOANAS, Guy (eds.)
The enemy within: pit villages and the miners' strike of 1984-5
Routledge & Kegan Paul, 1986
History Workshop series
260pp
A book of first-hand testimonies - recordings, letters and diaries - about one of Britain's most controversial post-war industrial disputes. Focuses on the local impact on the family economy, kin networks and the mentality of the strike.

1686 SAMUEL, Raphael and THOMPSON, Paul
The myths we live by
Routledge, 1990
History Workshop series
272pp
Papers from the sixth International Oral History Conference on 'Myth and History' held at Oxford in 1987.

1687 SANDERSON, Kay
"Women's lives: social class and the oral historian"
Life Stories, no.4 (1988), pp.27-35

1688 SANTOLI, Al
Everything we had: an oral history of the Vietnam war by thirty-three American soldiers who fought it
New York: Random House, 1981
265pp
A chronological story, from 1965 to the fall of Saigon in 1975, based on interviews with GIs and two female nurses.

1689 SANTOLI, Al (ed.)
To bear my burden: the Vietnam war and its aftermath in the words of Americans and South East Asians
Abacus, 1986
367pp
The author was a teenage infantry sergeant in the Vietnam war and based his book on interviews with forty-eight other veterans with front-line experience.

1690 SARETZKY, Gary D.
"Oral history in American business archives"
American Archivist, vol.44, no.4 (Fall 1981), pp.353-5

1691 SAROFF, Sophie
Stealing the state: an oral history
New York: Community Documentation Workshop, 1983
The story of a Russian Jew who settled in New York, her involvement with the American labour movement and final return to the Soviet Union.

1692 SARSBY, Jacqueline
Missuses and mouldrunners: an oral history of women pottery workers at work and at home
Milton Keynes: Open University Press, 1988
164pp; bibliography
An account of women in the last eighty years of the pottery industry, based on interviews with seventy women.

1693 SATTERFIELD, Archie
The home front: an oral history of the war years in America, 1941-45
New York: Playboy Press, 1981
384pp; bibliography
Focuses on Pearl Harbor, women left behind, rationing and the experiences of Japanese prisoners, black soldiers and those of Italian and German background.

1694 SAUNDERS, Dave
West Indians in Britain
Batsford, 1984
72pp
The personal experiences of three families in London, Birmingham and Bristol; two from Jamaica, one from Barbados. They speak about work, unemployment, family and social life.

SAUNDERS, Peter *see* NEWBY, Howard

SAVAGE, Bryony *see* GREIG, John

1695 SAVILLE, John
"Oral history and the labour historians"
Oral History, vol.1, no.3 (1972), pp.60-2

1696 SAVILLE, John
"Interviews in labour history"
Oral History, vol.1, no.4 (1973), pp.93-106
Looks at three ways in which oral history is especially helpful to labour historians: in illuminating character and personality, for elaborating events and as random samples for future use. He stresses the need for thorough preparation before the interview.

1697 SAWYER, Ralph
Speaking of history: an oral approach to 20th century Australian history
Melbourne: Nelson, 1983
142pp; bibliography
Aimed mainly at secondary school students.

1698 SAXON, Gerald D. and MOLTZAN, Jan
"Reminiscences: from tape to type"
Public Library Quarterly, vol.6, no.3 (Fall 1985), pp.25-31
Describes the Lakewood Oral History Project, a good example of local library/community co-operation which began in 1972.

SAXON, Gerald D. *see also* MASON, Alan S.

1699 SAYDISC
Cotswold characters
Glasgow: Saydisc, nd
One record SDL 222 or cassette CSDL 222, 45 minutes
Seven people born in 1896 discuss life in the Cotswolds around the turn of the century.

1700 SAYDISC
Cotswold craftsmen
Glasgow: Saydisc, nd
One record SDL 247 or cassette CSDL 247, 47 minutes
Older people recall Cotswold sheep, stone walls and roofs, working with oxen, making Gloucester cheese and cider, hurdle making, thatching and wheelwrights.

1701 SAYDISC
Cotswold voices
Glasgow: Saydisc, 1975
One cassette CSDL 267, 46 minutes
Five people, the oldest born in 1885, discuss snuff taking, weather prediction, courtship, bathnights and shopping.

1702 SAYDISC
Down to earth
Glasgow: Saydisc, nd
One record SDL 301 or cassette CSDL 301, 50 minutes
Recorded in 1962, 86 year old Cotswolder Emily Elliot recalls poor rural life around the turn of the century.

1703 SAYDISC
Memories of Osborne
Glasgow: Saydisc, nd
One record SDL 285 or cassette CSDL 285, 50 minutes
Dorothy Blake describes her childhood at Osborne House on the Isle of Wight, and her memories of Queen Victoria, the royal family, a royal Christmas, and tea in the royal nursery.

1704 SAYERS, Peig
An old woman's reflections
Translated from the Irish
Oxford: Oxford University Press, 1978, 1980
133pp
The lives of peasantry and labourers of the West of Ireland, based entirely on oral sources.

1705 SAYWELL, Shelley
Women in war: first hand accounts from World War 2 to El Salvador
Markham, Ontario and New York: Viking Penguin, 1985
324pp; bibliography
Verbatim interviews with twenty five women from all over the world, including a Second World War pilot, members of the resistance movement, a Russian marine, nurses from Vietnam and a war artist in the Falklands War.

SCAFE, Suzanne *see* BRYAN, Beverley

1706 SCARBOROUGH ORAL ARCHIVES
'I remember Scarborough': ten local people reminisce on growing up, living and working in Scarborough in the early part of this century
Scarborough: Scarborough Borough Council, 1987
16pp

1707 SCASE, Richard and GOFFEE, Robert
The real world of the small business owner
Croom Helm, 1987, second edition; previous edition, 1980
170pp
A study of the economic role of small businesses: their managerial, organisational and marketing strategies, and individual attitudes, life styles and relationships.

1708 SCHAFER, Murray
British composers in interview
Faber, 1963
186pp
Interviews with sixteen composers from John Ireland, born in 1879, to Peter Maxwell Davies, born in 1934, which concentrate on the creative process.

1709 SCHAFER, William J. and ALLEN, Richard B.
Brass bands and New Orleans Jazz
Baton Rouge: Louisiana State University Press, 1977
134pp; bibliography and discography
A study of the origins and characteristics of New Orleans jazz using oral biography and interview material from the William Ransom Hogan Jazz Archive at the Howard-Tilton Memorial Library at Tulane University.

1710 SCHIPPERS, Donald J. and TUSLER, Adelaide G.
A bibliography on oral history
Los Angeles: The Oral History Association, 1967
15pp
An annotated list of eighty articles and eighteen institutional publications up to September 1967.

1711 SCHNAPPER, Dominique
"The French Social Security Oral History Project: philosophies, goals and methods"
Oral History Review, vol.5 (1977), pp.39-47
A description of one of France's first oral history projects which began in 1975 and became a model.

1712 SCHNASE, R.C.
"Therapeutic reminiscence in elderly patients"
Journal of Nursing Care, vol.15, no.2 (1982) pp.15-17

SCHUHLE, Reini *see* ROONEY, Ray

1713 SCHULTE, Renee (ed.)
The young Nixon: an oral inquiry
Fullerton: California State University/Fullerton Foundation Oral History Program, 1978
279pp
Part of the Richard Nixon Oral History Project initiated in 1969 by Harry Jeffrey, this is a collection of interviews with people who knew Nixon in his pre-political days in South California.

1714 SCHUURSMA, Rolf
"The sound archive of the Film and Science Foundation and the Dutch Radio Organisation"
Oral History, vol.1, no.2 (1971), pp.23-6

1715 SCHUURSMA, Rolf
"Prospects: oral history archives/audiovisual archives"
Phonographic Bulletin, no.22 (December 1978), pp.22-24

1716 SCHUURSMA, Rolf
"Oral history and sound archives"
Phonographic Bulletin, no.30 (July 1981), pp.20-28
Examines oral history methodology and assesses some of the tensions between sound archivists and oral historians.

1717   SCHUURSMA, Rolf
"Oral history: the role of the archivist"
Phonographic Bulletin, no.37 (November
1983), pp.7-12
Argues that oral history projects should be
closely allied to sound archives.

**1718   SCHWITZER, Joan and THOMPSON,
Katherine**
"Children and young people in wartime"
Oral History, vol.15, no.2 (1987), pp.32-7
North Londoners during the Second World
War.

1719   SCOTSOUN
Tenement tales
Glasgow: Scotsoun, 1976
One cassette
Memories of childhood in Springburn,
Glasgow from Molly Weir.

1720   SCOTSOUN
Four Linmill stories
Glasgow: Scotsoun, 1979
One cassette
Robert McLellan's tales of his boyhood in
Clydesdale.

1721   SCOTSOUN
Lang syne in the East Neuk o' Fife
Glasgow: Scotsoun, 1984
Cassette SSC069 and booklet
Mary Kermack's childhood 1911-17.

SCOTT, Sue *see* **ELINOR, Gillian**

SCOURFIELD, Elfyn *see* **JONES, Glyn M.**

1722   SEABROOK, Jeremy
The unprivileged
*Longman, 1967; Harmondsworth: Penguin,
1973*
137pp
A hundred years of family life and tradition in
a working class street.

1723   SEABROOK, Jeremy
City close-up
*Allen Lane, 1971; Harmondsworth: Penguin,
1973*
283pp
A study of Blackburn in Lancashire based on
interviews with the old and young,
immigrants, students, young married couples,
the hopeless and the derelict.

1724   SEABROOK, Jeremy
A lasting relationship: homosexuals and society
Allen Lane, 1976
232pp
The effects of social change on gays through
forty personal accounts.

1725   SEABROOK, Jeremy
*What went wrong?: working people and the
ideals of the labour movement*
Gollancz, 1978
286pp
"..the beginning of a historical materialist
explanation of contemporary English history."
Includes oral material on the politics of the
unorganised and rank and file.

1726   SEABROOK, Jeremy
Unemployment
Quartet, 1982; Granada (Paladin), 1983
210pp
Unemployed people from the Midlands,
North West and North East speak for
themselves in pubs, job centres, shops and
council estates about the realities of being out
of work in the 1980s.

1727   SEABROOK, Jeremy
Working class childhood: an oral history
Gollancz, 1982
251pp; bibliography
Important historical and political questions
are raised in this oral history of working class
childhood over the last fifty years.

1728   SEABROOK, Jeremy
The leisure society
Oxford: Basil Blackwell, 1988
195pp
Using undocumented oral sources the author
argues that the evolution of a leisure society
imposes its own rigours: that the quest for
leisure affects those that seek it and those that
provide it.

SEDDON, J. *see* **EDGE, Y.**

1729   SEDGWICK, Charles P.
*The life story: a method, with issues, troubles
and a future*
*Christchurch, New Zealand: Department of
Sociology, University of Canterbury, 1980;
second edition, 1984*
Working Paper no.1
77pp; bibliography
Assesses the value of life stories in an
anthropological framework.

1730 SEEGAL, David
"Videotaped autobiographical interviews"
Journal of the American Medical Association,
no.195 (February 1966)

SEEGER, Peggy *see* **MACCOLL, Ewan**

1731 SEERS, C.
"Talking to the elderly and its relevance to
care"
Nursing Times, 1986, occasional papers 82,
pp.51-4

1732 SELDON, Anthony
Churchill's Indian summer
Hodder and Stoughton, 1981
667pp
Uses 225 interviews with retired ministers,
civil servants, journalists and party officials.

1733 SELDON, Anthony
"'Elite' oral history at the London School of
Economics"
Oral History, vol.10, no.1 (1982), pp.12-14

1734 SELDON, Anthony
"Learning by word of mouth"
The Times Higher Education Supplement, 20
August 1982

1735 SELDON, Anthony (ed.)
Contemporary history: practice and method
Oxford: Basil Blackwell, 1988
178pp
Includes a chapter on the problems, benefits
and methodology of interviews, with a
discussion of their reliability and use in written
historical works.

1736 SELDON, Anthony and PAPPWORTH,
Joanna
By word of mouth: 'elite' oral history
Methuen, 1983
258pp
An important book which looks at the theory
and practice of interviewing the leaders rather
than the led. The author interviewed and
corresponded with a great many practising
historians to gauge their experiences of using
oral evidence. There is also an excellent
bibliographical survey of the use of oral
evidence and a description of the British Oral
Archive of Political and Administrative
History, attached to the London School of
Economics.

1737 SELERIE, Gavin (ed.)
The riverside interviews: 1. Allen Ginsberg
Binnacle, 1980 (limited edition)
96pp
Transcribed conversations with the American
poet.

SENIOR, Diana *see* **BARTLETT, Liz**

1738 SENYARD, June (ed.)
I can remember that: recollections of primary
school days, 1904-1959
Carlton, Victoria: Melbourne College of
Advanced Education, 1983
159pp
Interview material collected in 1982 by history
students at Melbourne State College.

SEYD, Pat *see* **HARRISON, R.**

1739 SEYMOUR, John (ed.)
The book of Boswell: autobiography of a gypsy
Gollancz, 1970; Penguin, 1973
191pp
The transcribed account of Sylvester Gordon
Boswell's feelings about being a traveller in
Britain.

1740 SHACKELFORD, Laurel and WEINBERG,
Bill (eds.)
Our Appalachia: an oral history
New York: Hill and Wang, 1977
Interviews with people in eastern Kentucky,
western North Carolina and southwestern
Virginia.

SHAFFER, Deborah *see* **BIRD, Stewart**

1741 SHARNICK, John
Inside the cold war: an oral history
New York: Arbor House, 1987
360pp

SHARPLESS, Rebecca *see* **STRICKLIN,**
David

1742 SHAW, Arnold
Honkers and shouters: the golden years of
rhythm and blues
New York: Collier/Macmillan, 1978
555pp; bibliography and discography
Includes twenty-five interviews with leading
artists, songwriters and record producers who
pioneered R&B between 1945 and 1960, when
R&B became absorbed into mainstream pop.

1743 SHEA, P.
Voices and the sound of drums: an Irish autobiography
Belfast: Blackstaff, 1981
208pp
An oral account of a childhood influenced by the 1916 Rising, the Anglo-Irish War, the Irish Civil War and the author's father's membership of the Royal Irish Constabulary.

1744 SHEPHERDS BUSH LOCAL HISTORY PROJECT
Shepherds Bush memories 1: Bill Massey, trade unionist
Shepherds Bush Local History Project/ Addison Press, 1987
16pp
Based on an interview carried out by Stephen Bird in January 1981 for the project set up under Hammersmith and North Kensington Adult Education Institute.

SHEPLEY, Nigel *see* ARCHER, Stuart

SHEPPARD, Julia *see* FOSTER, Janet

SHERIDAN, Dorothy *see* CALDER, Angus

1745 SHERIDAN, Mary and SALAFF, Janet W. (eds.)
Lives: Chinese working women
Bloomington, Indiana: Indiana University Press/University of Toronto/York University Joint Centre on Modern East Asia, 1984
258pp
Life stories of women from China, Taiwan and Hong Kong from the pre-1949 older Chinese generation through women working in light manufacturing in Taiwan and Hong Kong, to China's rural modernisation.

1746 SHERMAN, E.
"A phenemenological approach to reminiscence and life review"
Clinical Gerontologist, vol.3, no.4 (Summer 1985), pp.3-16

1747 SHETLAND ARCHIVES HISTORY PROJECT
Living memory: a photographic and oral history of Lerwick, Gulberwick and Sound
Shetland: Shetland Amenity Trust, 1986
48pp
Based on 120 hours of interviews recorded between 1985 and 1986 and financed by the Manpower Services Commission Community Programme.

1748 SHETLAND ARCHIVES HISTORY PROJECT
Ahint da daeks
Shetland: Shetland Amenity Trust, 1987
48pp
The outcome of a year-long community history project into the history of the Shetland Islands' parish of Tingwall also covering Whiteness, Weisdale and Scalloway. Essentially the story of crofters and fishermen.

SHILTON, Clare *see* HAINES, Kevin

1749 SHIPLEY COMMUNITY HISTORY GROUP
Shipley fowk talking
Shipley, West Yorkshire: Shipley Community History Group, nd
45pp
Memories of food, housing, work and washday compiled from recordings.

1750 SHOPES, Linda
Using oral history for a family history project
Nashville, Tenn.: American Association for State and Local History, 1980
A technical leaflet.

1751 SHOPES, Linda
"The Baltimore Neighborhood Heritage Project: oral history and community involvement"
Radical History Review, no.25 (1981), pp.26-44
Argues for the integration of oral history projects with existing community groups, and for the value of specific questioning.

1752 SHORES, Louis
"The dimensions of oral history"
Library Journal, vol.92, no.5 (March 1967), pp.979-83

1753 SHORT, David and GREENER, Peter (eds.)
I was born in the High Street wasn't I? Ashwell remembered fifty years ago
Ashwell, Hertfordshire: Friends of Ashwell Village Museum, 1981
32pp
Edited from an evening of recorded reminiscence featuring the memories of the butcher, baker, farmer, midwife, doctor and groundsman from Ashwell, a village near Baldock in rural Hertfordshire.

SHOWALTER, Dennis *see* STEINHOFF, Johannes

1754 SHUMWAY, Gary L.
Oral history in the United States: a directory
New York: Columbia University Press, 1970
120pp
This lists 230 projects, with an additional 93 planned, and 23,115 people interviewed. By 1985 the figure had risen to an estimated 450 projects. The largest in the United States, Columbia University's, had interviewed over 2500 people by 1971.

1755 SHUMWAY, Gary L. and HARTLEY, William G.
An oral history primer
Fullerton, California: California State University Oral History Program, 1973
28pp
A guide to preparation, conducting the interview, formulating questions and making the tapes usable.

SHUMWAY, Gary L. *see also* CURTISS, Richard D.

1756 SIANN, G. and KHALID, R.
"Muslim traditions and attitudes to female education"
Journal of Adolescence, vol.7 (1981), pp.191-200
In-depth interviews with Muslim women in a Scottish town about educational disadvantage.

1757 SIDDALL, Kathy (ed.)
Down Tansh': memories of a scattered community
Castleford, West Yorkshire: Yorkshire Art Circus, 1988
78pp
Anecdotes and pictures about life in a community which was demolished in 1974 to make way for a car park.

1758 SIDER, Gerald
"The ties that bind"
Social History, vol.5 (1980)

1759 SIEDER, Reinhard
"Housing policy, social welfare and family life in 'Red Vienna', 1919-34"
Oral History, vol.13, no.2 (1985), pp.35-48

1760 SIKH FAMILY HISTORY PROJECT
Speaking for ourselves: Sikh oral history
Manchester: Sikh Family History Project, 1986
79pp; bibliography
An oral history of Manchester's Sikh community, one of the oldest of its kind in Britain dating from the 1930s, though it focuses on migration between 1947 and the mid-1950s.

1761 SILVER, Jeremy
"Silence in the museum"
BASC News, no.2 (1987), reprinted from **The Listener,** *16 April 1987*
Looks at issues around the use of oral history and sound in museums.

1762 SILVER, Jeremy
"'Astonished and somewhat terrified': the preservation of aural culture" in LUMLEY, R. (ed.), *The museum time machine, Routledge, 1988, pp.170-195.*

1763 SILVER, Rachel and BRANDENBURGER, Caroline
Establishment wives
W.H.Allen, 1989
240pp
Interviews with forty-three wives of prominent husbands in the law, the arts, the foreign office and civil service, business and industry, medicine and politics, the City, the media, the armed forces, religion and academia. They discuss their marriages, the nature of the Establishment, feminism, playing the dual role of mother and wife, and missed opportunities. Includes interviews with Lady Denning, Patricia Puttnam, Lady Armstrong, Jennifer Sieff, Jane Ashdown, Katherine Trelford, Lady Jakobovits, Anne de Rothschild and Lady Dacre.

SIM, Judith *see* CLARK, Helen

1764 SIMARD, Jean-Jacques
"The horse of hope and the vets"
Oral History, vol.9, no.1 (1981), pp.59-66
A review article about Breton peasantry.

1765 SIMMONS, Leo W.
Sun chief: the autobiography of a Hopi Indian
New Haven: Yale University Press, 1963; first published 1942
460pp
The life story of an American Indian from 350 hours of interviews carried out between 1938 and 1941, as part of a project to study personality through life stories.

SIMPSON, E.J. *see* FERGUSON, I.W.

1766 SIMPSON, Tony
The sugarbag years: an oral history of the 1930s depression in New Zealand
Wellington, New Zealand: Alistair Taylor, 1974; second edition, 1984
168pp
A verbatim oral history of the depression of the 1930s in New Zealand.

1767 SIMS, John
"Oral archives: resources of the National Sound Archive" in GAUR, Albertine (ed.)
South Asian Studies: papers presented at a colloquium 24-25 April 1985, British Library, 1986, pp.124-7
Outlines a collaborative project on the history of broadcasting in India in co-operation with the National Archive of Oral History in Bombay.

SINCLAIR, Ruth *see* FORD, Janet

1768 SINGAPORE ARCHIVES AND ORAL HISTORY DEPARTMENT
Pioneers of Singapore: a catalogue of oral history interviews
Singapore: Singapore Archives and Oral History Department, 1984
171pp

1769 SITTON, Thad, MEHAFFY, George L. and DAVIS, O.L.
Oral history: a guide for teachers (and others)
Austin: University of Texas, 1983
167pp; bibliography
An excellent manual for school oral history covering: selecting a topic, setting up, equipment, technique, transcription, storage, and use in curriculum development and in school magazines.

SITTON, Thad *see also* MEHAFFY, George L.

1770 SKEELS, Jack W.
"Oral history project on the development of unionism in the automobile industry"
Labor History, Spring 1964
Trade unionism in the US car industry.

1771 SKELLEY, Jeffrey
The General Strike, 1926
Lawrence and Wishart, 1976
412pp
A series of regional studies and personal memoirs of the strike.

SLAUGHTER, C. *see* DENNIS, N.

1772 SMITH, Alice K. and WEINER, Charles (eds.)
Robert Oppenheimer: letters and recollections
Cambridge, Mass.: Harvard University Press, 1980
376pp; bibliography
Draws on a number of interviews including those of the Archive for the History of Quantum Physics in the US.

1773 SMITH, Allen (ed.)
Directory of Oral History Collections
Phoenix: Oryx Press, 1988
152pp
A directory of US institutions holding 500 collections, with a subject index. The latest in a series of attempts at a definitive listing. (*See also* COOK, P.; MASON, E.; MECKLER, A.; SHUMWAY, G)

SMITH, Alonzo *see* JOHNS, Brenda B.

1774 SMITH, Anne
Women remember: an oral history
Routledge, 1989
240pp
A varied group of twelve octogenarian women speak openly about the astonishing changes in life styles and values within living memory, about themselves and especially about their feelings as the 'unemancipated generation' born before the First World War.

1775 SMITH, David
"What does history know of nailbiting?"
Llafur, no.1 (1973), pp.34-41
The Welsh labour movement.

1776 SMITH, David (ed.)
A people and a proletariat: essays in the history of Wales 1780-1980
Pluto in association with Llafur, the Society for the Study of Welsh Labour History, 1980
239pp; bibliography
A selection of 'polemical' essays, including discussions about the historical use of language and a defence of oral history as an "absolutely necessary tool" for the modern historian.

1777 SMITH, Graham
"Manpower history: the Arbroath history project. An experience of MSC funded research"
Oral History, vol.12, no.2 (1984), pp.60-63

1778 SMITH, Graham
"Voices on Radio: Billy Kay, the maker of Odyssey"
Oral History, vol.13, no.1 (1985), pp.54-60
Odyssey was a series about Scottish history, based on oral testimony, made by BBC Radio Scotland. (*See also* KAY, Billy)

1779 SMITH, Graham
"From Micky to Maus: recalling the genocide through cartoon"
Oral History, vol.15, no.1 (1987), pp.26-34
An important interview with Art Spiegelman whose strip cartoons of the Nazi horror, *Maus*, were drawn from conversations with his own father about life in Nazi-occupied Poland.

1780 SMITH, J.H.
I remember: reminiscences of Glossop before the first world war
Glossop, Derbyshire: Glossop and District Historical Society, 1975
44pp

SMITH, Joan *see* MCSHANE, Harry

1781 SMITH, Joe
Off the record: an oral history of pop music
Sidgwick and Jackson, 1989
429pp
200 eminent musicians and music business personalities talk about themselves and their careers. The book, by an American record company executive, is arranged to give a chronological account of pop music from jazz and big band to Bono of U2. Gross misconduct, misadventure and bizarre incidents feature strongly, and many legends of popular music are included: Artie Shaw, Woody Herman, Bo Diddley, Alice Cooper, Rod Stewart, Bob Dylan, Van Morrison, Mick Jagger, Roger Daltry, James Brown.

1782 SMITH, Mary F.
Baba of Karo: a woman of the Muslim Hausa
New Haven: Yale University Press, 1981; originally published 1954
299pp
An outstanding early life story of a woman born in 1877.

1783 SMITH, Maurice
Oakbank history trail
Countryside Publications, 1982
48pp
A school project involving members of the local community, investigating the history of the area around Oakbank Secondary School in Keighley, West Yorkshire, using oral history and written sources.

1784 SMITH, Peter J.C.
Flying bombs over the Pennines
Manchester: Neil Richardson, 1988
48pp; bibliography
Accounts by survivors all over the Manchester area of a V-1 attack aimed at the city on December 24th 1944.

1785 SMITH, Tim and WILKINSON, Rob
"Setting up a local recall pack"
Oral History, vol.17, no.2 (1989), pp.43-8
A practical guide for selecting and combining oral history and photographs to produce reminiscence materials.

1786 SMOUT, T.C.
"Scotland: the state of oral history"
Oral History, vol.2, no.1 (1974), pp.11-14
A round-up of individual work and details of activities at the School of Scottish Studies.

1787 SOCIETY FOR RESEARCH ON WOMEN IN NEW ZEALAND
In those days: a study of older women in Wellington
Wellington, New Zealand: Society for Research on Women in New Zealand, 1982
131pp
Based on life story recordings with fifty-one women aged seventy to ninety-two.

SOCIETY FOR RESEARCH ON WOMEN IN NEW ZEALAND see also **ELSE, Ann**

1788 SOCIETY OF AMERICAN ARCHIVISTS (COMMITTEE ON ORAL HISTORY)
"Oral history and archivists: some questions to ask"
American Archivist, vol.36, no.3 (July 1973), pp.361-5

1789 SOCIETY OF ARCHIVISTS SPECIALIST REPOSITORY GROUP
Oral archives in the specialist repository: proceedings of a forum held at the University of Warwick, April 11th 1985
Sheffield: Society of Archivists Specialist Repository Group, 1986
25pp
Contents include papers on the value of oral archives, planning an archive, interviewing techniques, equipment and tape storage.

1790 SOMALI WOMEN'S ASSOCIATION
Our strength comes with us: Somali women's voices
Somali Women's Association, 1987
68pp
Ten women's experiences coming to Britain from Somalia ten to twenty-five years ago: 'We wrote this book for ourselves, to remember our lives and our history'.

1791 SOUND HERITAGE SERIES
Victoria, British Columbia: Aural History Society/Sound and Moving Image Division, Provincial Archives of British Columbia, from 1974
This quarterly published series covers various aspects of life in British Columbia in Canada over the past century, documenting the early settlers' lives and work. Almost all the sources are primary, and the bulk of the written material is usually presented as transcribed interviews. (See also under individual author names)

1792 SOUTH CANNING TOWN AND CUSTOM HOUSE ORAL HISTORY PROJECT
Do you remember?: SOCATATCH Oral History Project
Newham Community News, 1989
8pp
Describes the group's aims to establish a local archive of people's memories of the area.

1793 SOUTHAMPTON CITY COUNCIL LOCAL STUDIES SECTION ORAL HISTORY TEAM
Woolston before the bridge
Southampton: Southampton Local Studies Section, 1989
102pp; bibliography
An excellent exhibition tie-in book about a community on the east side of the River Itchen which was until 1977 (when a permanent bridge was built) connected to Southampton by means of a floating bridge. There are extensive interview extracts covering housing, school, family life, work, leisure, shops, religion and crossing the river: all drawn from some 700 hours of recordings held by the Southampton Museums oral history archive.

1794 SOUTHAMPTON MUSEUMS ORAL HISTORY SECTION
Growing up in Chapel and Northam
Southampton: Southampton Museums Oral History Section, 1986
One sixty-minute cassette tape
Members of a Southampton dockland community recall family life and childhood before the Second World War.

1795 SOUTHAMPTON MUSEUMS ORAL HISTORY SECTION
A working life
Southampton: Southampton Museums Oral History Section, 1986
One sixty-minute cassette tape
Working life in Chapel and Northam, a dock community in Southampton, before the Second World War.

1796 SOUTHAMPTON MUSEUMS ORAL HISTORY SECTION
The Beavis treat
Southampton: Southampton Museums Oral History Section, 1988
8pp
Memories of an annual treat for Southampton children named after a benevolent local alderman.

1797 SOUTHAMPTON MUSEUMS ORAL HISTORY SECTION
Christmas voices
Southampton: Southampton Museums Oral History Section, 1989
One thirty-five minute cassette tape
Southampton people remember Christmas before the Second World War, with carols by a local school.

1798 SOVERVILLE, Ross
"Sound and music services in the National Library"
New Zealand Libraries, vol.45, no.5 (March 1987), pp.104-5

1799 SPADE, Beatrice
"Americans in Vietnam: an oral history project"
History Teacher, vol.8 (February 1975), pp.183-192
A school project to interview Louisiana veterans who served from the 1950s.

SPEARRITT, Peter *see* **DOUGLAS, Louise**

1800 SPINNER: PEOPLE AND PLACES IN SOUTHEASTERN MASSACHUSETTS
An occasional publication of memories and photography: four volumes, 1981-8
Vol.1, 1981: neighbourhood, ethnic history, farming and industry
Vol.2, 1982: folklore, photography, regional culture and oral history
Vol.3, 1984: photography, industrial and ethnic history, cranberries and fishing
Vol.4, 1988: the Federal Writers' Project and the Depression
Influenced by *Foxfire* (*see* WIGGINTON, Eliot) this is the result of work by students at Southeastern Massachusetts University with contributions from people in Fall River and New Bedford. With the assistance of local industrial sponsorship, the project has grown into a major collective history with open membership, a publishing programme, schools projects and exhibitions.

1801 ST.ANN'S REMINISCENCE GROUP
Tales of the old town
Edinburgh: Edinburgh District Council, nd
44pp
Ordinary people's experiences of Edinburgh's south side from the 1920s.

1802 ST.HILL DAVIES, E. and DODWELL, F.
Hidden from history: women in Stevenage 1888-1988
Stevenage, Hertfordshire: Stevenage Museum, 1988
56pp; bibliography
Based on an exhibition of women's experiences held at Stevenage Museum and covering home and family, suffragettes and the vote, the two world wars, work and leisure.

1803 STACEY, Margaret
Tradition and change: a study of Banbury
Oxford University Press, 1970; first published 1960
231pp
A study of migration and the arrival of new industries in an old established Oxfordshire country town, from research carried out in 1948-51.

1804 STACEY, Margaret
Power, persistence and change: a second study of Banbury
Routledge & Kegan Paul, 1975
International Library of Sociology
196pp
An update on change in Banbury based on questionnaires compiled in 1967.

STACKHOUSE, Jan *see* **BRECHER, Jeremy**

1805 STANDS IN TIMBER, John and LIBERTY, Margot with UTLEY, Robert M.
Cheyenne memories
New Haven: Yale University Press, 1967
330pp; bibliography
Oral histories of the North American Cheyenne Indians from one of the last to hear the tribal story. Recorded by Liberty in Montana in 1956.

1806 STANLEY, Jo (ed.)
To make ends meet: women over sixty write about working lives
Pensioners Link, 1989
148pp
Twenty-seven women from varied ethnic backgrounds, all members of The Older Women's Project at Pensioners Link in north London, write of their work experiences in offices, factories, hospitals and shops, from the First World War to today.

1807 **STAPLEY, Laurence**
"An oral history of recorded sound"
Phonographic Bulletin, no.47 (February 1987)
The National Sound Archive's interviewing
programme with people involved in all areas
of the recording industry. (*See also* BRITISH
LIBRARY NATIONAL SOUND
ARCHIVE; ANDERSON, Terri)

1808 **STARR, Louis M.**
"Oral history: problems and perspectives"
Advances in Librarianship, 1971, pp.275-304
An overview of the development of oral
history in the States with some advice to
beginners and an assessment of the reliability
of memory.

1809 **STARR, Louis M.**
"Oral history"
*Encyclopedia of Library and Information
Science, vol.20 (1977), pp.440-63*
Its value compared to other sources, the tape
versus transcript debate and the international
movement.

STARR, Louis M. *see* **MASON, Elizabeth B.**

1810 **STAVE, Bruce M.**
*The making of urban history: historiography
through oral history*
Beverly Hills, Calif.: Sage, 1977
336pp; bibliography
Interviews carried out in 1974-6 and originally
published in *Journal of Urban History*.

1811 **STEDMAN-JONES, Gareth**
"Working class culture and working class
politics in London, 1870-1900"
Journal of Social History, vol.7, no.4 (1974)
Includes material on music.

1812 **STEEL, Donald John and TAYLOR,
Lawrence**
Family history in schools
Philimore, 1973
180pp
Stresses the importance of family history and
aims to encourage historians, teachers and
children to capture memories of old people.

1813 **STEEN, Mike**
Hollywood speaks: an oral history
New York: G.P.Putnam's Sons, 1974
379pp
Twenty-five chapters based on film credit
categories with an interview in each, from
leading lady through producer and
screenwriter to costume design, make-up and
sound recording. Part of the American Film
Institute oral history collection.

1814 **STEINBERG, G.D. and BRENNAN, P.L.**
"Is reminiscence adaptive? Relations among
social activity level, reminiscence and morale"
*International Journal of Aging and Human
Development, vol.18, no.2 (1983-4), pp.99-110*
Based on a study of women.

1815 **STEINHOFF, Johannes, PECHEL, Peter and
SHOWALTER, Dennis**
Voices from the Third Reich: an oral history
Washington, DC: Regnery Gateway, 1989
550pp

1816 **STENBERG, Henry G.**
"Selected bibliography, 1977-1981"
Oral History Review, vol.10 (1982), pp.119-32
For mainly US publications.

1817 **STENT, Ronald**
"The internment of His Majesty's loyal enemy
aliens"
Oral History, vol.9, no.1 (1981), pp.35-40
The story of Jewish refugees interned on the
Isle of Man during the Second World War.

1818 **STEPHENSON, Shirley E.**
"Oral history: today's approach to the past"
*Catholic Library World, no.48 (November
1976), pp.157-61*
Covers oral history in the library and
especially legal problems, transcribing,
funding and equipment.

1819 **STEPHENSON, Shirley E.**
Editing and indexing: guidelines for oral history
*Fullerton, California: California State
University Oral History Program, 1978, 1983*
58pp; bibliography
A practical guide covering transcription style
and standard punctuation, and editing
transcripts.

1820 STEPHENSON, Shirley E.
"Selected bibliography, 1980-1982"
Oral History Review, vol.11 (1983), pp.109-24
For US publications.

STEPHENSON, Shirley E. *see also* CURTISS, Richard D.

1821 STEVENS, Christine
"An Edwardian kitchen garden at St.Fagan's Castle"
Garden History: The Journal of The Garden History Society, vol.13, no.1 (Spring 1985)
An oral account of a now disappeared garden.

STEVENSON, John *see* HALSTEAD, John

STEVENSON, Prue *see* PADEL, Una

1822 STEWART, John
"Oral history and archivists"
American Archivist, vol.36 (1973), pp.361-5

1823 STEWART-PARK, Angela and CASSIDY, Jules
We're here: conversations with lesbian women
Quartet, 1977
152pp
Interviews with British lesbians.

1824 STIELOW, Frederick J.
The management of oral history sound archives
New York: Greenwood, 1986
158pp; bibliography
One of the few texts on the archival considerations of oral history with sections on processing, organisation, microcomputer applications, cataloguing, conservation management and US legal considerations.

1825 STIRLING, Amiria and SALMOND, Anne
Amiria: the life story of a Maori woman, Amiria Manutahi Stirling as told to Anne Salmond
Wellington, New Zealand: A.H. and A.W.Reed, 1976
184pp; bibliography
A life story of a Maori woman born at the turn of the century based on taped interviews.

1826 STIRLING, Eruera and SALMOND, Anne
Eruera: the teaching of a Maori elder, Eruera Stirling as told to Anne Salmond
Wellington, New Zealand: Oxford University Press, 1980
288pp; bibliography
A biography of Stirling, an elder of the Whanau-a-Apanui tribe in Auckland, written from taped interviews and inspired by his determination to pass on traditional knowledge and explain an ancestral way of life to a younger generation.

STOKES, Donald *see* BUTLER, David

1827 STOKES, Edward
United we stand: impressions of Broken Hill 1908-1910
Canterbury, Victoria, Australia: The Five Mile Press, 1983
Bibliography

1828 STONE, Ruth M. and GILLIS, Frank J.
African music and oral data: a catalog of field recordings, 1902-1975
Bloomington: Indiana University Press, 1976
432pp
Concise summaries of material held by individuals and institutions all over the world.

1829 STORM-CLARK, Christopher
"The miners, 1870-1970: a test-case for oral history"
Victorian Studies, vol.15, no.1 (1971), pp.49-74
Includes an excellent discussion of the problem of accuracy in oral history in an actual fieldwork situation.

1830 STORM-CLARK, Christopher
"The miners: the relevance of oral evidence"
Oral History, vol.1, no.4 (1973), pp.72-92
The value of oral testimony in elaborating on miners' family and social lives, as well as providing new information on informal working practices, such as the 'butty system', and working relationships.

1831 STORM-CLARK, Christopher
"Some technical means for higher quality: recording in oral history"
Oral History, vol.6, no.1 (1978), pp.114-119
Recommends using stereo and Dolby noise reduction.

STRAUSS, Anselm L. *see* GLASER, Barney G.

1832 STRAW, Pat and ELLIOTT, Brian
"Hidden rhythms: hidden powers? Women and time in working class culture"
Life Stories, no.2 (1986), pp.34-47

1833 STRAW, Pat and KENDRICK, Stephen
"The subtlety of strategies: towards an understanding of the meaning of family life stories"
Life Stories, no.4 (1988), pp. 36-48

1834 STREE SHAKTI SANGHATANA
'We are making history': women and the Telengana Uprising
Zed Books, 1989
290pp
A collectively produced anthology of life stories of fifteen women, all militants who took part in a mass armed uprising against feudal landlords in the Telengana region of Hyderabad in 1948-51.

1835 STRICKLIN, David and SHARPLESS, Rebecca (eds.)
The past meets present: essays on oral history
Lanham, MD: University Press of America, 1988
151pp
Based on a symposium held in 1985, these essays cover a wide range of topics both methodological and practical, giving a valuable insight into the directions of American oral history.

STROBEL, Margaret *see* MIRZA, Sarah

1836 STUART D.G.
County Borough: the history of Burton upon Trent, 1901-1974
Burton upon Trent: Charter Trustees of Burton upon Trent, 1975
Part one: Edwardian Burton
309pp
Part two: 1914-1974
299pp
A collection of local historical experience compiled from extensive oral research, but lacking in analysis.

1837 SUFFOLK COUNTY COUNCIL INFORMATION AND LIBRARY SERVICE
The past remembered: a catalogue of oral history tapes
Ipswich: Suffolk County Council Information and Library Service, 1988
66pp
(*See also* TAYLOR, Pauline)

1838 SUID, Lawrence H.
Guts and glory: great American war movies
Reading, Mass.: Addison-Wesley, 1978
357pp
Based on over 300 interviews with people in the film industry, the media and the armed forces about selected war films up to the 1970s.

1839 SULLIVAN, Margaret
"Into community classrooms: another use for oral history"
Oral History Review, no.2 (1974), pp.53-8
Secondary school oral history in the USA as a way of encouraging empathy and understanding a multiplicity of views.

1840 SUMMER, Keith
"Sing, say or pay! A survey of East Suffolk country music"
Traditional Music, nos.8/9 (1977/1978), pp.5-53
An account derived from taped interviews with musicians and singers recorded over seven years.

1841 SUMMERFIELD, Penny
Women workers in the second world war: production and patriarchy in conflict
Croom Helm, 1984
214pp
An account of women's working and living conditions, focussing on the implementation of official policy towards women and critical of the war as a period of emancipation. Uses oral testimony drawn from the Mass Observation Archive.

1842 SUMMERFIELD, Penny
"An oral history of schooling in Lancashire, 1900-1950: gender, class and education"
Oral History, vol.15, no.2 (1987), pp.19-31
Based on 120 interviews about schooldays in North Lancashire recorded by an MSC-funded oral history project. Concentrates on discipline and sexuality as influences on gender and class acquisition at school.

SUMMERFIELD, Penny *see also* BRAYBON, Gail

1843 SUMMERS, Anne
"Oral history and the Great War"
Oral History, vol.6, no.2 (1978), pp.49-57
A report on an Oral History Society conference held in 1977.

1844 SURRIDGE, O.
"Oral archives: the London History Workshop"
New Library World, no.86 (1985), p.169

1845 SUTTON BONINGTON LOCAL HISTORY SOCIETY
Remembering Sutton Bonington: the gentry, church, chapel and school days
Sutton Bonington: Sutton Bonington Local History Society, 1986
60pp; bibliography
Oral recollections of life in a rural village on the Nottinghamshire/Leicestershire border.

1846 SUTTON BONINGTON LOCAL HISTORY SOCIETY
Work and leisure: remembering Sutton Bonington 2
Sutton Bonington: Sutton Bonington Local History Society, 1988
80pp; bibliography
Crafts, clubs and local occupations in a Nottinghamshire village.

1847 SUTTON-IN-ASHFIELD LIVING MEMORY GROUP
'It's trew worram tellin' yer!': memories of childhood and growing up in Sutton-in-Ashfield
Sutton-in-Ashfield: Sutton Living Memory Group, 1987
84pp
Members of the group recall their early lives in a small Nottinghamshire town. Very little dialect despite the title.

1848 SUTTON-IN-ASHFIELD LIVING MEMORY GROUP
'Put that light ert!': memories of the second world war in Sutton-in-Ashfield
Sutton-in-Ashfield: Sutton Living Mmeory Group, 1989
68pp
A second collection of short extracts, some from written recollections, some from interviews.

1849 SWAIN, Donald C.
"Problems for practitioners of oral history"
American Archivist, vol.28, no.1 (January 1965), pp.63-9
This issue was an oral history special and includes other useful articles.

SWENSON, Loyd S. *see* BROOKS, Courtney G.

SYKES, R.M. *see* GRUNEBERG, M.M.

1850 SYLVESTER, David
Interviews with Francis Bacon
Thames and Hudson, third edition 1987; first edition 1975
208pp
Extracted from interviews with the artist carried out from 1962.

1851 SYNGE, Jane
"Immigrant communities - British and continental European - in early twentieth century Hamilton, Canada"
Oral History, vol.4, no.2 (1976), pp.38-51

1852 TALSMA, Jaap
"Oral history in the Netherlands"
Higher Education and Research in the Netherlands, vol.24 (1980), pp.41-5

1853 TAWNEY, J.J.
"Oral history programme of the Oxford Colonial Records Project"
Oral History, vol.1, no.3 (1972), pp.49-59

1854 TAYLOR, Arthur R.
Labour and love: an oral history of the brass band movement
Elm Tree, 1983
280pp
Based on interviews with almost 100 people who are or have been involved with brass bands.

1855 TAYLOR, E.
"An interview with Wesley Perrins"
Bulletin of the Society for the Study of Labour History, no.21 (Autumn 1970), pp.16-24
A West Midlands Labour leader, councillor, MP and trade union officer.

1856 TAYLOR, Eric
Women who went to war 1938-1946
Hale, 1988; Grafton paperback, 1989
365pp; bibliography
Based on interviews with many individuals, it tells the story of some of the half million women who fought in the forces during the Second World War: how they acquired new skills, independence and confidence.

TAYLOR, John *see* HUMPHRIES, Steve

TAYLOR, Kay *see* FROST, Debbie

1857 TAYLOR, Lawrence
Oral evidence and the family historian: a short guide
Plymouth: Federation of Family History Societies, 1984
24pp; bibliography

TAYLOR, Lawrence *see* STEEL, Donald John

1858 TAYLOR, Leslie and Griselda
Within living memory: recollections of Old Headington, Oxford
Old Headington, Oxford: The Friends of Old Headington, 1978
72pp

1859 TAYLOR, Pam
"Daughters and mothers - maids and mistresses: domestic service between the wars" in JOHNSON, R. and CHRITCHER, C. (eds.) *Working class culture*, Hutchinson, 1979
Looks at the persistence of living-in domestic service after the First World War, through forty personal accounts, twenty-four of them tape-recorded.

1860 TAYLOR, Pauline
"The past remembered: Suffolk's Oral History Project"
Local Studies Librarian, Autumn 1988, pp.3-6

1861 TAYLOR, Ronald B.
Sweatshops in the sun: child labour on the farm
Boston: Beacon Press, 1973
216pp; bibliography
A study of the exploitation and maltreatment of children of migratory farm workers in the States based on first hand investigative interviews.

1862 TAYLOR, Sandra
"The effect of marriage on job possibilities for women, and the ideology of the home: Nottingham 1890-1930"
Oral History, vol.5, no.2 (1977), pp.46-61

1863 TEAGUE, Michael
Mrs L.: conversations with Alice Roosevelt Longworth
Duckworth, 1981
203pp
Theodore Roosevelt's daughter reveals something of the President's time in the White House.

1864 TEBBUTT, Melanie
Making ends meet: pawnbroking and working-class credit
Leicester: Leicester University Press, 1983
235pp
Extensive use of interviews with pawnbrokers, credit personnel and their customers in Manchester and Salford, illustrating the role of credit on a family's real income level.

1865 TEISER, Ruth
"Transcriber's fancies"
Journal of Library History, vol.5 (April, 1970)

1866-
1870 TELEVISION HISTORY CENTRE
TV History Centre has produced a series of short and accessible pamphlets in association with Channel 4, written to encourage people to record their own history. Some accompanied television documentary programmes and all include resource lists, useful tips and bibliographies. (*See also* LANNING, Greg)

1866 *Making history: 1. The factory (1983, 40pp)*

1867 *Making history: 2. Women (1983, 25pp)*

1868 *Making history: 3. The school (1984, 24pp)*

1869 *Making history: 4. The hospital (1985, 42pp)*

1870 *Making history: 5. Birth control (1988, 48pp)*

1871 TELEVISION HISTORY WORKSHOP
"Morris Motors in the 1960s"
History Workshop, no.16 (Autumn 1983), pp.100-22
A shooting script based on oral history interviews from a five-part television history of Morris Motors at Cowley in Oxford in which 300 local people participated.

1872 TELEVISION HISTORY WORKSHOP CENTRE
Making cars: a history of car making in Cowley by the people who make the cars
Routledge and Kegan Paul, 1985
131pp
Written in conjunction with a Channel Four series and the result of local memories gathered at a pioneering 'history shop' in Cowley, Oxfordshire.

TELFER, Glenn *see* BLAIKIE, Roberta

1873 **TELFORD COMMUNITY ARTS OAKENGATES BOOK GROUP**
Oakengates in the words of Oakengates people: a view of the Oakengates district based on memories and photographs of Oakengates people
Telford, Shropshire: Telford Community Arts, 1987
164pp

1874 **TERKEL, Studs (ed.)**
Division Street, America
Harmondsworth: Penguin, 1970
431pp
America's leading popular oral historian spoke to sixty 'ordinary' people from Chicago over a period of a year about their lives, their city, their society, Vietnam, the Bomb, immigration and the world generally.

1875 **TERKEL, Studs (ed.)**
Hard times: an oral history of the Great Depression
Allen Lane, 1970; originally published New York: Pantheon Books, 1970
462pp
An important book of extracts from interviews with 160 Americans, both famous and unknown, from a variety of backgrounds.

1876 **TERKEL, Studs (ed.)**
Working: people talk about what they do all day and how they feel about what they do
Harmondsworth: Penguin, 1977, 1985; published Wildwood House, revised edition, 1975
479pp
A remarkable and candid book of accounts by over eighty people whose jobs range from stockbrokers to prostitutes, from dustbin men to writers.

1877 **TERKEL, Studs**
American dreams: lost and found
Hodder and Stoughton, 1981; originally published New York: Pantheon Books, 1980
470pp
Comments from 100 people over twenty years of travel by the author, talking about their dreams.

1878 **TERKEL, Studs**
'The Good War': an oral history of world war two
Hamilton, 1985; Harmondsworth: Penguin, 1986
589pp
Interviews with 120 people, both soldiers and civilians, mainly from America but also from many other countries, about their wartime experiences.

1879 **TERKEL, Studs**
Talking to myself: a memoir of my times
Harrap, 1986
337pp
About Terkel's own youth in Chicago and the people he has known.

1880 **TERKEL, Studs**
The great divide: second thoughts on the American dream
Hamish Hamilton, 1989
439pp
Tales of hardship contrasted with wealth: the emergence of a small but wealthy elite and a growing lower class, Wall Street profits, yuppies, religious fundamentalism, Reaganism and liberalism.

1881 **TERRILL, Tom E. and HIRSCH, Jerrold D.**
Such as us: Southern voices of the thirties
Chapel Hill: University of North Carolina Press, 1978
302pp; bibliography
Individual testimonies, mainly from black and white mill hands and farmworkers, about America in the thirties.

1882 **THATCHER, Mary (ed.)**
Cambridge South Asian Archive: third collection of records of the British period in South Asia relating to India, Pakistan, Ceylon, Burma, Nepal and Afghanistan held in the Centre of South Asian Studies, University of Cambridge
Cambridge: Centre of South Asian Studies, 1983
386pp

1883 **THAXTON, Ralph**
"The peasants of Yaocun: memories of exploitation, injustice, and liberation in a Chinese village"
Journal of Peasant Studies, vol.9 (October 1981), pp.3-46
From interviews carried out in 1980 in Henan Province; with some hints on interviewing in rural China.

1883A THOM, Albert
James Chuck: my life in the village
St. Albans, Herts: Albert Thom, 1986
16pp
Childhood, poaching, sewer digging,
unemployment, hay making, hedging and the
two world wars in rural Hertfordshire.

1884 THOM, Deborah
"Women at the Woolwich Arsenal 1915-1919"
Oral History, vol.6, no.2 (1978), pp.58-73
An insight into women's attitudes to working
at Woolwich Arsenal where female labour was
introduced for the first time during the First
World War.

1885 THOMAS, Beth
"Accounting for language shift in a South
Wales mining community"
Cardiff Working Papers in Welsh Linguistics,
no.5 (1987), pp.55-100
A comprehensive analysis of the socio-
historical factors leading to the decreasing use
of the Welsh language in a former mining
community in south-east Wales, from oral
sources.

1886 THOMAS, Delia and TURNER, Louise (eds.)
Northampton remembers the Guildhall
Northampton: Northampton Borough Council
Employment and Training Programme Unit,
1989
88pp
Extracts from interviews covering the
mayoralty, policing, courts and prisons, crime,
political and industrial unrest in Northampton.

THOMAS, Delia *see also* **KIRBY, David**

1887 THOMAS, Hugh
The Suez affair
Weidenfeld and Nicolson, 1967
259pp
The author interviewed many of the leading
protagonists, though many are not identified
due to the Official Secrets Act.

1888 THOMAS-HOPE, Elizabeth
"Hopes and reality in the West Indian
migration to Britain"
Oral History, vol.8, no.1 (1980), pp.35-42
Highlights the significant gap between
expectation and reality.

1889 THOMPSON, Alan
"Times past"
Nursing Times, vol.85, no.6 (8 February 1989),
pp.31-2
Religious reminiscence therapy.

1890 THOMPSON, Derek
"Courtship and marriage in Preston between
the wars"
Oral History, vol.3, no.2 (1975), pp.39-44

1891 THOMPSON, John
On lips of living men
Angus and Robertson, 1962
164pp
Recollections of people who remember
eminent fellow Australians including Nellie
Melba, Max Meldrum, John Curtin, William
Morris Hughes, Sir John Monash and Maurice
O'Shea.

1892 THOMPSON, John
"Oral history in Australia: some problems
discussed at the Australian Folklorists'
Conference, Sydney, November 17-18, 1973"
Archives and Manuscripts, vol.5 (1974),
pp.143-6

THOMPSON, Katherine *see* **SCHWITZER,**
Joan

1893 THOMPSON, Marcia (ed.)
Playing along the canal: from an interview with
Ted Harrison
Canals in Hackney Users Group (CHUG),
1988
50pp
Originally published with an accompanying
cassette. Lively memories of working class
childhood games and pranks in London's East
End.

1894 THOMPSON, Paul
"Memory and history"
SSRC Newsletter, June 1970

1895 THOMPSON, Paul
"BBC archives"
Oral History, vol.1, no.2 (1971), pp.11-18

1896 THOMPSON, Paul
"Problems of method in oral history"
Oral History, vol.1, no.4 (1973), pp.1-55
An important article which looks at the whole
issue of using interviews for social history. It is
followed by an interesting discussion involving
several leading historians transcribed from a
conference held in Leicester in 1972.

1897 THOMPSON, Paul
"Voices from within" in DYOS, Harold
James and WOLFF, Michael, *The Victorian
city: images and realities. Volume one: Past and
present and numbers of people*, Routledge and
Kegan Paul, 1977, pp.59-80; first published in
two volumes, 1973
Based on seventeen interviews with Victorians
drawn from the Essex University archive.

1898 THOMPSON, Paul
"Oral evidence in African history"
Oral History, vol.2, no.1 (1974), pp.65-7

1899 THOMPSON, Paul
The Edwardians: the remaking of British society
Weidenfeld & Nicolson, 1975; Paladin, 1979
382pp; bibliography
Social history based on pioneering oral history
work at Essex University, involving 500
interviews of varied class and geographical
origin. Includes material on politics,
childhood, work and family, with urban and
rural life contrasted.

1900 THOMPSON, Paul
"Oral history in North America"
Oral History, vol.3, no.1 (1975), pp.26-40
An overview of a decade of growth.

1901 THOMPSON, Paul
"The war with adults"
Oral History, vol.3, no.2 (1975), pp.29-38
Rebellion against parental control.

1902 THOMPSON, Paul
"Oral history in Israel"
Oral History, vol.5, no.1 (1977), pp.35-9
Examines the main collections including the
oral history division of the Institute of
Contemporary Jewry at the Hebrew
University of Jerusalem, the Institute of
Jewish Studies' Folklore Research Centre,
and Yad Washem, the Holocaust archive.

1903 THOMPSON, Paul
"The Humanistic tradition and life histories in
Poland"
Oral History, vol.7, no.1 (1979), pp.21-5
The important place of written life histories in
popular culture and the role of Polish
sociologists in developing this trend.

1904 THOMPSON, Paul
"The new oral history in France"
Oral History, vol.8, no.1 (1980), pp.14-20
Late 1970s developments.

1905 THOMPSON, Paul
"Life stories and the analysis of social change"
in BERTAUX, Daniel (ed.) *Biography and
Society*, Sage, 1982

1906 THOMPSON, Paul
"Oral history and the historian"
History Today, June 1983, pp.24-28
An overview which outlines the value of oral
history, basic techniques and some of the
problems.

1907 THOMPSON, Paul
"The family and child-rearing as forces for
economic change: towards fresh research
approaches"
Sociology, vol.18 (1984)

1908 THOMPSON, Paul
"Women in the fishing: the roots of power
between the sexes"
*Comparative Studies in Society and History,
vol.27 (1985)*

1909 THOMPSON, Paul
"Playing at being skilled men: factory culture
and pride in work skills among Coventry car
workers"
*Social History, vol.13, no.1 (January 1988),
pp.45-69*

1910 THOMPSON, Paul
The voice of the past: oral history
*Oxford: Oxford University Press, second
edition, 1988; first edition, 1978*
314pp; detailed bibliography
An essential and definitive handbook, now a
classic text, introducing methods and uses of
oral history, with much practical advice on
interviewing techniques, question approaches,
archiving and community projects. The book
established Thompson as Britain's leading
exponent of oral history. Translated into
Swedish in 1980 and Spanish in 1988.
Available on eight audio cassettes from the
Royal Blind Society of New South Wales in
Australia.

1911 THOMPSON, Paul and BORNAT, Joanna
"Interview with Stephen Peet"
Oral History, vol.10, no.1 (1982), pp.47-55
A documentary film-maker who pioneered
oral history in his BBC series *Yesterday's
Witness*.

1912 THOMPSON, Paul and BURCHARDT, Natasha (eds.)
Our common history: the transformation of Europe
Pluto, 1982
334pp
Twenty-one papers from the First International Oral History Conference held at the University of Essex in 1979. Covers many aspects of contemporary oral history in Europe, including fascism and resistance in the years leading up to and including World War Two, European peasantry and bakers in Paris. Countries included are Italy, Poland, France, Spain, the Netherlands, Norway and Germany.

1913 THOMPSON, Paul, with WAILEY, Tony and LUMMIS, Trevor
Living the fishing
Routledge & Kegan Paul, 1983
History Workshop series
416pp; bibliography
A labour history of fishing based on over 150 life-story interviews with men and women from English and Scottish fishing communities.

1914 THOMPSON, Paul, THOMPSON, Stephen and LI-WEN, Yang
"Oral history in China"
Oral History, vol.15, no.1 (1987), pp.17-25
A good overview.

1915 THOMPSON, Paul with ROWE, Doc
"Ten inches into six feet: low budget equipment for an oral history project"
Oral History, vol.16, no.1 (1988), pp.55-60
An interview with Doc Rowe of London History Workshop Centre Sound and Video Archive.

1916 THOMPSON, Paul with COPELAND, Peter
"Why DAT matters to oral historians"
Oral History, vol.17, no.1 (1989), pp.56-61
An interview with the National Sound Archive's conservation manager about portable digital recording equipment.

1917 THOMPSON, Paul and PERKS, Robert
Telling it how it was. A guide to recording oral history
BBC, 1989
30pp; bibliography and contact list
This brief introduction aimed at beginners accompanied an eight-part BBC Radio Four series of the same name broadcast in May/ June 1989. It covers equipment, interview techniques, archiving and ways of making use of oral history.

1918 THOMPSON, Paul, ITZIN, Catherine and ABENDSTERN, Michele
I don't feel old: the experience of later life
Oxford: Oxford University Press, 1990
256pp; bibliography
Oral accounts of ageing in the past compared with the contemporary experience.

THOMPSON, Paul *see also* SAMUEL, Raphael

THOMPSON, Ruth *see* DOUGLAS, Louise

THOMPSON, Stephen *see* THOMPSON, Paul

1919 THOMPSON, Thea
"A lost world of childhood"
New Society, 5 October 1972

1920 THOMPSON, Thea
Edwardian childhoods
Routledge & Kegan Paul, 1981, 1982
232pp
Memories of nine Edwardian children from a variety of backgrounds in their own words.

1921 THOMPSON, Willie and HOBBS, Sandy
"British Communists on the war, 1939-1941"
Oral History, vol.16, no.2 (1988), pp.23-33
Based on interviews with fourteen members of the Communist Party of Great Britain living in central Scotland.

THOMSON, David *see* EVANS, George Ewart

1922 THORNTON, Joan (ed.)
It were no laughing matter
Castleford, West Yorkshire: Yorkshire Art Circus, 1987
127pp
Memories about life in the Calder Valley between 1930 and 1945, featuring millworkers and miners, weddings and war work.

1923 THORNTON, Joan (ed.)
No time for dying: voices of retirement
Castleford, West Yorkshire: Yorkshire Art
Circus, 1989
88pp
From a project in conjunction with Doncaster
Library Service: extracts from seventy
interviews with pensioners expressing their
feelings about retirement and talking about
their varied leisure activities.

1924 THORNTON, Susan and BROTCHIE, Janet
"Reminiscence: a critical view of the empirical
literature"
British Journal of Clinical Psychology, vol.26
(1987), pp.93-111
Concludes that there is little evidence of an
age-specific process of reminiscence, that its
functions are unclear and that its value as
therapy is in doubt.

1925 THORPE, Bill
"Further verbals in the oral history debate"
Quadrant, 1980, pp.54-8
See also O'FARRELL, Patrick for the rest of
this Australian debate.

1926 TIBBOTT, Minwell S.
Welsh fare
Cardiff: National Museum of Wales, 1976
84pp
A selection of traditional Welsh recipes from
the turn of the century derived from the
memories of older people.

1927 TIBBOTT, Minwell S.
Laundering in the Welsh home
Cardiff: National Museum of Wales, 1981
22pp
The methods of washing and drying clothes,
and the role of the washerwoman, from oral
sources.

1928 TIBBOTT, Minwell S.
Cooking on the open hearth
Cardiff: National Museum of Wales, 1982
31pp
Open hearth cooking was dominant in Wales
up to the turn of the century.

1929 TIBBOTT, Minwell S.
"Furnishing, fashion and fetish: a Welsh
study"
Local Historian, vol.18, no.4 (November 1988)
A study of the custom of covering table legs in
industrial South Wales.

1930 TITON, Jeff Todd
"Life story"
Journal of American Folklore, no.93 (July/
September 1980), pp.276-92
Distinguishes between life stories and life
histories.

1931 TOLAND, John
Adolf Hitler
Garden City: Doubleday, 1976
1035p; bibliography
The life and career of Hitler drawing on over
250 interviews recorded in 1970-2 with his
adjutants, secretaries, chauffeur, pilot,
doctors, generals, architects and leading
politicians.

1932 TOLLIDAY, Steve
"Militancy and organisation: women workers
and trade unions in the motor trades in the
1930s"
Oral History, vol.11, no.2 (1983), pp.42-55

1933 TOLSTOY, Nikolai
Victims of Yalta
Corgi, 1979; originally published Hodder and
Stoughton, 1977
640pp
A hundred people were interviewed about the
forcible repatriation of prisoners-of-war to the
Soviet Union at the end of the Second World
War.

TOMLIN, David *see* **FARRELL, Terrance and**
James

1934 TONKIN, Elizabeth
"Implications of oracy: an anthropological
view"
Oral History, vol.3, no.1 (1975), pp.41-9
Includes a useful bibliography of oral history,
social anthropology and African history.

1935 TONKIN, Elizabeth
"Steps to the redefinition of oral history:
examples from Africa"
Social History, vol.7 (October 1982), pp.329-35

1936 TORANSKA, Teresa
Oni: Stalin's Polish puppets
Translated from the Polish
Collins Harvill, 1987
384pp
Five revealing interviews with post-war Polish
communist leaders, made in the early 1980s.

1937 **TOSH, John**
The pursuit of history: aims, methods and new directions in the study of modern history
Longman, 1984
205pp; bibliography
The final chapter is devoted to 'History by word of mouth' in which the author assesses the value of oral history in the light of his own work in African history.

1938 **TOTTENHAM HISTORY WORKSHOP**
How things were: growing up in Tottenham 1890-1920
Tottenham History Workshop, 1982
114pp
Memories of Tottenham in north London before the end of the First World War covering childhood illnesses, relations with the police, street games, and getting the first job.

1939 **TOWER HAMLETS ARTS PROJECT**
Auschwitz and East London
Tower Hamlets Arts Project, 1983
24pp
A collection of personal statements, some from Holocaust survivors, linking the events of Auschwitz and the East End. Produced to coincide with the opening of an exhibition in Stepney.

1940 **TOWER HAMLETS ENVIRONMENT TRUST**
The Jewish East End: an education pack
Tower Hamlets Environment Trust, 1988
57pp
Eight sections give the flavour of Jewish life in London's East End, 1880-1930. Includes oral history, photographs, documents, teachers' notes, question sheets and resource lists.

1941 **TOWNSEND, Colin and Eileen**
War wives
Grafton, 1989
320pp
Testimony from the 'unsung heroines' of the Second World War: the housewives of Britain and Germany left to cope after their menfolk joined the forces.

1942 **TOWNSEND, Peter**
The family life of old people: an enquiry in East London
Harmondsworth: Penguin, 1977 (abridged edition); first published 1963
331pp; bibliography
Based on 203 interviews carried out in Bethnal Green in 1954-5.

1943 **TRASK, David F. and POMEROY, Robert W. (eds.)**
The craft of public history: an annotated select bibliography
Westport, Connecticut and London: Greenwood, 1983
481pp
Chapter ten (pp.351-417) concentrates on oral history: its theory, techniques, evaluation and usage in various fields including schools, the arts, ethnic minorities, gerontology, science, labour and local history, military history, political and social history and women's studies. It comprises an exhaustive selection of books, manuals and articles about oral history in the United States. Prepared under the auspices of the National Council on Public History.

1944 **TRELEVEN, Dale E.**
"Oral history, audio technology and the TAPE system"
International Journal of Oral History, vol.2, no.1 (1977)
This describes an alternative to transcription in which the Timed Access to Pertinent Excerpts system produces a time-coded abstract.

TRELEVEN, Dale E. *see also* **GALLACHER, Cathryn A.**

1945 **TREVOR-ROPER, Hugh R.**
The Last Days of Hitler
Macmillan, 1947
280pp
An early example of 'instant history' based on two main oral sources: evidence at the Nuremburg Trials and some forty-two interviews carried out by the author as an intelligence officer.

1946 **TRINDER, Barrie**
"Oral history in adult education: some experiences in Shropshire"
Oral History, vol.1, no.3 (1972), pp.63-70

TRUDGEON, Roger *see* **WHITE, Helen**

1947 **TUFT, N.**
"Dramatic exchange"
New Age, no.23 (Autumn 1983), p.7
Discusses a theatre company which uses reminiscence.

1948 TURNER, Jane and JARDINE, Bob
Pioneer tales
Milton Keynes: People's Press of Milton Keynes, 1985
96pp
Interviews and photographs of thirty of the first settlers to Britain's newest and most publicised 'new town', giving an insight into the first ten years. The People's Press has also published a number of autobiographies of local people.

TURNER, Louise *see* **THOMAS, Delia; KIRBY, David**

1949 TURNER, Michele
Stuck!: unemployed people talk to Michele Turner
Ringwood, Victoria and New York: Penguin, 1983
263pp

1950 TURNER, Naomi
Which seeds shall grow? Men and women in religious life
Blackburn, Victoria: Collins Dove, 1988
Based on interviews with 100 Roman Catholic nuns and fifty priests.

1951 TURNER, Robert
"The contribution of oral evidence to labour history"
Oral History, vol.4, no.1 (1976), pp.23-40
Includes a useful bibliography.

1952 TURNER, Robert
"Towards an oral history of labour"
Bulletin of the Society for the Study of Labour History, no.27 (Autumn 1973), pp.63-71

TURNER, Robert *see also* **POLLARD, Sidney**

1953 TURNER-BISSETT, R.A. (ed.)
Beccles reflections
Beccles, Suffolk: Sir John Lehman School, 1985
39pp

TUSLER, Adelaide G. *see* **SCHIPPERS, Donald J.**

1954 TWADDLE, Michael
"On Ganda historiography"
History in Africa, vol.1 (1974)

1955 TYACK, Geoffrey
"Service on the Cliveden estate between the wars"
Oral History, vol.5, no.1 (1977), pp.63-87
Domestic service at a large country house in the Chilterns twenty-five miles from London.

1956 ULSTER FOLK AND TRANSPORT MUSEUM
No two ways about it: some early memories of Belfast by Paddy McParland
Holywood, Co. Down: Ulster Folk and Transport Museum, 1989
A cassette of extracts from interviews with McParland in which he recalls his family's coal delivery business and the redevelopment of Belfast which has had such impact on community life.

1957 ULSTER SOCIETY FOR ORAL HISTORY
Newsletter, no.1 (February 1984)-
Twice-yearly covering developments in Northern Ireland.

1958 UNIVERSITY OF LEEDS DEPARTMENT OF ADULT AND CONTINUING EDUCATION
Saltaire: our memories, our history
Leeds: University of Leeds, 1984
Pioneer work publications
28pp
Recollections of life in Saltaire, a model textile village in West Yorkshire, in the twentieth century produced by members of a community history group.

1959 URDANG, Stephanie
And still they dance: women, war and the struggle for change in Mozambique
Earthscan, 1989
256pp; bibliography
Based on tape-recorded interviews with women since independence in 1975.

URRY, James *see* **BARWICK, Diane**

UTLEY, Robert M. *see* **STANDS IN TIMBER, John**

1960 VAN DYNE, Larry
"Oral history: sharecroppers and presidents, jazz and Texas oil"
Chronicle of Higher Education, December 24, 1973

1961 VAN RIEL, Rachel (ed.)
All in a day's work
Castleford, West Yorkshire: Yorkshire Art Circus, 1985
54pp
A butcher, a brickie, an engineer and workers in liquorice, glassworks and munitions speak of their workdays.

1962 VAN RIEL, Rachel (ed.)
Bathtime
Castleford, West Yorkshire: Yorkshire Art Circus, 1985, 1988
32pp
Memories of medicinal baths, rugby baths, tin baths in front of the fire and slipper baths.

VAN RIEL, Rachel *see also* ADAM, Rachel

1963 VAN VORIS, W.H.
Violence in Ulster: an oral documentary
Amherst: University of Massachusetts Press, 1975
326pp; bibliography
Based on the recorded memories of 'hundreds' of people in Northern Ireland.

1964 VANSINA, Jan
Oral tradition as history
James Currey, 1985; first edition, Oral tradition: a study in historical methodology, *Routledge & Kegan Paul, 1965*
258pp; bibliography
A good general introduction: an account of the process by which oral history is produced and an analysis of the role of the oral tradition, based principally on the author's fieldwork in Central Africa.

1965 VANSINA, Jan
"The power of systematic doubt in historical inquiry"
History in Africa, vol.1 (1974), pp.109-127

1966 VEGH, Claudine
I didn't say goodbye
Translated from the French
Caliban, 1984; originally published 1979
179pp
Written by a psychiatrist, herself the daughter of a Holocaust victim, and based on interviews with French Jews whose parents were deported to extermination camps. Translated by Ros Schwartz.

1967 VIGNE, Thea
"Parents and children 1890-1918: distance and dependence"
Oral History, vol.3, no.2 (1975), pp.6-13

1968 VIGNE, Thea and HOWKINS, Alun
"The small shopkeeper in industrial and market towns" *see in* CROSSICK, Geoffrey

1969 VINCENT, David
Bread, knowledge and freedom: a study of nineteenth-century working-class autobiography
Europa, 1981; Methuen, 1982
221pp; bibliography

1970 VINCENT, David
"The decline of oral tradition in popular culture" in STORCH, Robert D.(ed.), *Popular culture and custom in nineteenth century England, Croom Helm, 1982*

1971 VISUAL EDUCATION CORPORATION
Grass roots: an oral history of the American people
Momence, Illinois: Visual Education Corporation, 1976
Six cassettes varying from 60 minutes to 90 minutes (5421/01-06), with a listener's guide
Interviews with people born mainly in the nineteenth century from six parts of the United States: Northeast, South, Midwest, Southwest, Farwest and Northwest. Subjects covered include: New England farmers, Maine coal miners and lumber camps, Pennsylvania sailors, former Southern slaves and cotton workers, Blues music, Southern courtship and marriage, Kansas, Oklahoma and Arkansas homesteading and farming, Indians, Texas oilfields, cowboys, Colorado mining, Utah Mormons, Barbary Coast sailors, Northwest railroading and logging.

1972 WAGNER, Anton
"The uses of oral history in Canadian theatre history research"
Canadian Oral History Association Journal, vol.4, no.1 (1979), pp.10-13
A critique of the way oral history has been used in this field.

WAILEY, Tony *see* THOMPSON, Paul

1973 WAKE, Joan
How to compile a history and present day record of village life
Northampton: Northampton and Soke of Peterborough Federation of Women's Institutes, 1935, third revised edition
95pp

1974 WALE, Michael
Vox pop: profiles of the pop process
Harrap, 1972
320pp
A series of interviews with performers,
promotors, managers and agents in the pop
business.

WALKER, Curt *see* ELINOR, Gillian

WALKER, George *see* RUSSELL, David

WALKER, Martin *see* COULTER, Jim

WALKER, Rodger *see* RYAN, Tony

1975 WALLER, Prue
"Spinning Room: the making of a
documentary film"
Oral History, vol.17, no.2 (1989), pp.60-1
Details of a museum video based on
interviews with former Chatham Royal
Dockyard workers.

1976 WALLER, Robert J.
The Dukeries transformed: the social and
political development of a twentieth century
coalfield
Oxford: Clarendon, 1983
Oxford Historical Monographs
319pp; bibliography
A history of a mining community following the
opening of seven new pits in post-1918
Nottinghamshire.

1977 WALSALL AGE CONCERN
A stroll around Bloxwich
Walsall: Walsall Leisure Services Library and
Information Division Local History Centre,
1989
31pp
Reminiscences of old Bloxwich recorded by an
MSC scheme.

1978 WALSALL LIBRARY AND MUSEUM
SERVICES
Walsall at war
Walsall: Walsall Library and Museum
Services, 1986
Walsall Chronicle no.8
Includes a fourteen page section by Joyce
Hammond entitled "Eye witness" of
reminiscences of the home front in Walsall in
the Second World War. Walsall Local History
Centre has published a number of cassettes of
recordings used in this and other booklets,
covering Second World War experiences,
family and street life in the Walsall area of the
West Midlands.

WALSH, Dave *see* McFARLAND, Elaine W.

1979 WALTERS, Raymond
"The last word: call it oral history"
New York Times Book Review, 2 January 1972
A brief survey of the development of oral
history in the USA.

1980 WALTHAM FOREST ORAL HISTORY
WORKSHOP
'Touch Yer Collar; Never Swaller': memories of
childhood illnesses before the Health Service
Waltham Forest Oral History Workshop, 1984
32pp
The first of a series from an outstanding North
London project.

1981 WALTHAM FOREST ORAL HISTORY
WORKSHOP
Pig's head and pease pudding: memories of the
butchery trade and the uses of meat before the
second world war
Waltham Forest Oral History Workshop, 1985
38pp
Includes a short section on vegetarianism.

1982 WALTHAM FOREST ORAL HISTORY
WORKSHOP
Cottage loaves and plain bricks: memories of
bread and bread making in Waltham Forest
1913-50
Waltham Forest Oral History Workshop, 1986
54pp

1983 WALTHAM FOREST ORAL HISTORY
WORKSHOP
Bullseyes: a history of sweet making in Waltham
Forest
Waltham Forest Oral History Workshop, 1988
58pp

1984   WALTON, John K.
The Blackpool landlady: a social history
Manchester: Manchester University Press, 1978
229pp
Based on the author's doctoral thesis:
readable, amusing, and using oral evidence
skilfully.

1985   WALTON, Mary and LAMB, J.P.
Raiders over Sheffield: the story of the air raids
of 12th and 15th December 1940
Sheffield: Sheffield City Libraries, 1980
169pp
The story of Second World War air raids
based on interviews with ninety people and
written reminiscences from another fifty-five.

1986   WANDOR, Michelene
Once a feminist: stories of a generation.
Interviews by Michelene Wandor
Virago, 1990
243pp
Published to mark the twentieth anniversary
of the first Women's Liberation Conference at
Ruskin College, Oxford including verbatim
interviews with Sheila Rowbotham, Juliet
Mitchell, Anna Davin, Sally Alexander,
Catherine Hall and Audrey Wise.

1987   WARD, Ben (ed.)
Our heritage: voices from the past collected by
the East Cleveland Heritage Project oral history
team
Loftus, East Cleveland: East Cleveland
Heritage Project/MSC, 1987
48pp
The third in a series of oral history booklets
based on interviews collected in East
Cleveland and North Yorkshire from 1983.
This one covers family life, transport, pills and
potions, and prices. (*See also* WILSON,
Gloria)

1988   WARD, Colin and HARDY, Dennis
"The Plotlanders"
Oral History, vol.13, no.2 (1985), pp.57-70
Recollections of pioneer city dwellers in the
South East of England who seized the chance
before 1940 to get a plot of land in the country
or by the seaside for a bungalow or chalet.

WARD, Colin *see also* **CROUCH, David;**
HARDY, Dennis

1989   WARD, Elizabeth
Father-daughter rape
The Women's Press, 1984
247pp; bibliography
Moving personal accounts by nine women
victims of incest, originally recorded in
Australia and set in a theoretical and political
context.

WARD, Stephen *see* **HARRIS, Ramon I.**

1990   WASERMAN, Manfred J.
"Manuscripts and oral history: common
interests and problems in the history of
medicine"
Bulletin of the Medical Library Association,
vol.58 (April 1970), pp.173-6

1991   WASERMAN, Manfred J. (ed.)
Bibliography on oral history
New York: Oral History Association, 1975;
original edition, 1971 (40pp)
53pp
An annotated listing of US published articles
and books.

1992   WATERS, Frank
Book of the Hopi
Harmondsworth: Penguin, 1977, 1978;
originally published 1963
345pp
Source material recorded by Oswald White
Bear Fredericks.

1993   WATERS, Mavis
"Craft consciousness in a government
enterprise: Medway dockyardmen,
1860-1906"
Oral History, vol.5, no.1 (1977), pp.51-62

1994   WATKINS, Owen C.
The Puritan experience: studies in spiritual
autobiography
Routledge & Kegan Paul, 1972
270pp; bibliography
For early religious biography.

1995   WATSON, Catherine (ed.)
Boots and all: an oral history of farming in
Victoria
Collingwood, Victoria: Friends of the Earth,
1984
108pp
Agriculture in Australia.

1996   **WAUGH, Maureen (ed.)**
Memories of Holborn
Holborn Local History Group/London
Borough of Camden Libraries and Arts
Department, 1986
36pp
Reminiscences by twenty people about family,
childhood, school, housing, work,
entertainment, festivals and the Second World
War, drawn from an adult education class
which met at the Central Institute over three
years.

1997   **WEA CARDENDEN WOMEN'S
DISCUSSION GROUPS**
Wartime memories of Cardenden women
Fife: WEA, 1986
42pp

1998- **WEA PORTSMOUTH LOCAL HISTORY
2016   GROUP**

1998   *Memories of childhood in Portsmouth*
Southsea: WEA, 1980
36pp

1999   *Memories of Lake Road*
Southsea: WEA, 1980
46pp

2000   *Saturday and Sunday: a childhood memory*
Southsea: WEA, 1980
8pp

2001   *Sixty two years a Fratton pharmacist*
Southsea: WEA, 1980
16pp

2002   *Memories of downtown Portsmouth*
Southsea: WEA, 1980
100pp

2003   *Memories of Church Street School*
Southsea: WEA, 1980
8pp

2004   *A Pompey boy in the 30s and 40s*
Southsea: WEA, 1981
29pp

2005   *Point boy and the powerstation*
Southsea: WEA, 1982
17pp

2006   *Gateway to Queen Street*
Southsea: WEA, 1982
46pp

2007   *Memories of Kingston Road*
Southsea: WEA, 1983 and 1988
90pp; bibliography

2008   *Portsmouth at war*
Southsea: WEA, 1983
Two volumes: 93pp and 76pp
Second World War memories.

2009   *Memories of a window dresser*
Southsea: WEA, 1985
24pp

2010   *Memories of Albert Road*
Southsea: WEA, 1985
96pp; bibliography

2011   *Memories of St.Agatha's school*
Southsea: WEA, 1985
11pp

2012   *Memories of Charlotte Street*
Southsea: WEA, 1987
56pp

2013   *Memories of Fawcett Road*
Southsea: WEA, 1988
72pp

2014   *Going to work in Portsmouth between the wars*
Southsea: WEA, 1988
Books three and four: 28pp and 29pp

2015   *Portsea*
Southsea: WEA, 1989
41pp; bibliography

2016   *Memories of Stamshaw*
Southsea: WEA, 1989
44pp; bibliography

2017   **WEA WEST OXFORDSHIRE ORAL
HISTORY GROUP**
In service
Oxford: WEA West Oxfordshire Oral History
Group, nd
Broadsheet no. 4
65pp; bibliography
Transcripts of interviews - questions included -
with nine people who were in service from
1900-1940.

2018   **WEART, Spencer R. and DE VORKIN, David
H.**
"The voice of astronomical history"
Sky and Telescope, February 1982

2019 WEBB, Beatrice
My apprenticeship
Cambridge: Cambridge University Press for London School of Economic and Political Science, 1979 (facsimile reprint of first edition 1926)
429pp; bibliography
Includes a section on interviewing, pp.361-3. Sidney and Beatrice Webb were pioneers in using oral history methods, most notably in their trade union histories.

2020 WEBER, Arlene
"Mining the nuggets of the past or, oral history observed"
Journal of Library History, vol.6 (July 1971), pp.275-81
Amusing reminiscences from the fifth national colloquium on oral history.

WEBSTER, N. *see* **BARNES, J.A.**

2021 WEIGHTMAN, Gavin and HUMPHRIES, Steve
Christmas Past
Sidgwick and Jackson, 1987
176pp
An original look at Britain's single most important festival, which through personal recollections charts its rise during the twentieth century. Written in conjunction with a London Weekend Television programme of the same name.

WEIGHTMAN, Gavin *see also* **HUMPHRIES, Steve**

WEINBERG, Bill *see* **SHACKELFORD, Laurel**

2022 WEINBERGER, Barbara
"Towards an oral history of the police"
Journal of the Police History Society, no.2 (1987), pp.36-8

WEINER, Charles *see* **SMITH, Alice K.**

2023 WELFORD, A.T.
Ageing and human skill: a report centred on work by the Nuffield Unit for Research into the problems of ageing
Oxford University Press, 1958
300pp

2024 WELLER, Ken
'Don't be a soldier!': the radical anti-war movement in North London 1914-1918
Journeyman Press/London History Workshop Centre, 1985
96pp
Using interviews with over twenty participants, the author argues that the anti-war movement grew out of the syndicalist and industrial movements, the radical wing of the women's movement and organisations critical of the Labour movement.

2025 WELLS, Gary L. and LOFTUS, Elizabeth (eds.)
Eyewitness testimony: psychological perspectives
Cambridge: Cambridge University Press, 1984
374pp; bibliography
Written with reference to evidence and the legal system, with sections on acquisition, retention and retrieval of information.

2026 WELSH FOLK MUSEUM
On the best side: memories of life in Rhyd-y-car
Cardiff: Welsh Folk Museum/National Museum of Wales, nd
One cassette
Two women recall their childhood from the turn of the century to the 1930s when they lived in a row of workmen's cottages near Merthyr Tydfil in South Wales which were re-erected at the Museum as examples of early industrial housing.

2027 WERBNER, Pnina
"Rich man, poor man - or a community of suffering: heroic motifs in Manchester Pakistani life stories"
Oral History, vol.8, no.1 (1980), pp.43-8

2028 WESSEX STREET GROUP
The happiest time
Oxford House, nd
32pp
A women's group, meeting at the old school in Wessex Street in London's Tower Hamlets, recall their memories of childhood. Taped and transcribed by M. Ashworth.

WEST, Kath *see* **HAYNES, Debbie**

WEST, Richard *see* **HOWARD, Anthony**

2029 WEST HOWE HISTORY GROUP
'West Howe proper': a part of Dorset remembered by local people
Wimborne, Dorset: Word and Action, 1982
120pp
Tape-recorded group reminiscences of farming, brickmaking, potteries and gypsies in an area of Bournemouth.

2030 WEST NEWCASTLE LOCAL STUDIES MULTI-CULTURAL PROJECT
Newcastle new era
Newcastle-upon-Tyne: West Newcastle Local Studies, 1988
35pp
The story of the arrival of migrant groups in Newcastle's West End including: Chinese, Irish, Bengalis, Indian Hindus and Sikhs, Nigerians, Pakistanis, Sudanese, West Indians and Welsh. Oral history extracts and family photos.

WEST OXFORDSHIRE ORAL HISTORY GROUP *see* **WEA**

2031 WESTALL, Robert
Children of the Blitz: memories of wartime childhood
Viking, 1985; Harmondsworth: Penguin, 1987
237pp
An original collection of children's reminiscences of wartime life.

2032 WESTON, Murray
"The British Video History Trust: recording people and places"
BASC News, no.3 (1988)
Outlines a scheme to video oral testimonies to broadcast standards.

WESTOVER, Belinda *see* **DAVIDOFF, Leonore; PENNINGTON, Shelley**

2033 WESTWOOD, Sallie
All day every day: factory and family in the making of women's lives
Pluto, 1984
259pp
Based on interviews carried out over a year at a hosiery factory in the Midlands with women of mixed ethnic backgrounds.

2034 WHINCOP, April
"Using oral history in museum displays"
Oral History, vol.14, no.2 (1986), pp.46-50
The experience of Lancaster Maritime Museum in presenting the fishing industry.

2035 WHISTLER, Nancy
Oral history workshop guide
Denver: Denver Public Library/Colorado Center for Oral History, 1979
55pp; bibliography

2036 WHITAKER, W.R.
"Why not try videotaping oral history"
Oral History Review, vol.9 (1981), pp.115-24
Covers equipment and editing; with a short bibliography.

2037 WHITE, Helen M.
"Thoughts on oral history"
American Archivist, vol.20 (January 1957)

2038 WHITE, Helen and TRUDGEON, Roger
"Birmingham's gun quarter: a skilled trade in decline"
Oral History, vol.11, no.2 (1983), pp.69-83

2039 WHITE, Isobel, BARWICK, Diane and MEEHAN, Betty
Fighters and singers: the lives of some Australian aboriginal women
Sydney and Boston: Allen and Unwin, 1985
226pp; bibliography

2040 WHITE, J.D.
"Scottish Lithuanians and the Russian revolution"
Journal of Baltic Studies, vol.6, no.1 (1975)

2041 WHITE, Jerry
Rothschild buildings: life in an East End tenement block 1887-1920
Routledge & Kegan Paul, 1980
History Workshop series
320pp
The author talked to twenty-two people who grew up in the buildings, which were a 'model dwelling' in London's East End, from the 1890s onwards. Includes material on working class Jewish history, architecture, space and community, with accounts by women of their personal lives.

2042 WHITE, Jerry
"Police and people in London in the 1930s"
Oral History, vol.11, no.2 (1983), pp.34-41

2043 WHITE, Jerry
The worst street in North London: Campbell Bunk, Islington, between the wars
Routledge & Kegan Paul, 1986
History Workshop series
312pp; bibliography
Working class life presented in the informants' own words; findings "of the utmost importance to planners, social workers...policemen and academics".

2044 WHITE, Margaret
And grandmother's bed went too: poor but happy in Somers Town
The St.Pancras Housing Association of Camden, 1988
130pp
Nearly thirty people were recorded recalling housing conditions, family life, school, street games, neighbours, outings, hop-picking, pawn shops and unemployment between the wars. It includes the St. Pancras Housing Association's rehousing project in Somers Town.

2045 WHITEHEAD, Margaret
Now you are my brother: missionaries in British Columbia
Victoria, British Columbia: Sound and Moving Image Division, Provincial Archives of British Columbia, 1981
Sound Heritage series no. 34
92pp
Based almost entirely on transcribed interviews with missionaries and members of their families, born between 1870 and 1919. Includes brief biographies of the informants.

2046 WHITTINGHAME, R.C.I.
Looking back on a village 1875-1975: Holywell-cum-Needingworth
Needingworth, Cambridgeshire: Holywell C.E. School, 1975
A primary school project.

WHITTLE, Tony *see* **ARMSTRONG, Keith**

2047 WHYMAN, John
"Oral history and its possibilities"
Cantium, Spring 1972, pp.2-6
A brief introduction and history of oral history in Britain.

2048 WICKS, Ben
No time to wave goodbye
Bloomsbury, 1988
288pp
A compilation of moving personal testimony, both written and oral, from several hundred of the three and a half million child evacuees in Britain during the Second World War.

2049 WICKS, Ben
The day they took the children
Bloomsbury, 1989
128pp
A further illustrated collection of Second World War evacuee stories.

2050 WIDDOWSON, John D.A.
"Oral history and tradition in an urban setting"
Lore and Language, vol.2, no.9 (1978), pp.43-56

2051- WIGGINTON, Eliot (ed.)
2059 The *Foxfire* series brings together material from *Foxfire*, a magazine of oral history experiences first produced in 1966 by high school students at Rabun Gap-Nacochee School in the Southern Appalachians region of Georgia. In 1989 sales approached eight million copies in the series, with royalties going to The Foxfire Fund Inc. A Broadway play version, *Foxfire*, was broadcast in 1987. It has become a model for schools oral history all over the world. Wigginton was described by a *Time* magazine cover story in 1979 as one of fifty emerging leaders.

2051 *The Foxfire book*
Garden City, New York: Doubleday, 1972
384pp
Hog dressing, log cabin building, mountain crafts, food, snake lore, hunting tales, faith healing and moonshining.

2052 *Foxfire 2*
Garden City, New York: Anchor Press/Doubleday, 1973
410pp
Ghost stories, spinning and weaving, midwifery, burial customs and wagon making.

2053 *Foxfire 3*
Garden City, New York: Anchor Press/Doubleday, 1975
511pp
Animal care, musical instruments, hide tanning and butter churning. Includes a cumulative index for volumes 1-3.

2054 *Foxfire 4*
Garden City, New York: Anchor Press/
Doubleday, 1977
496pp; bibliography
Water systems, fiddle-making, horse trading, sassafras tea, berry buckets, gardening, logging and wood carving.

2055 *Foxfire 5*
Garden City, New York: Anchor Press/
Doubleday, 1979
511pp; bibliography
Ironmaking, blacksmithing, flintlock rifles and bear hunting.

2056 *Foxfire 6*
Garden City, New York: Anchor Press/
Doubleday, 1980
507pp
Shoemaking, gourd banjos, toys and games. Includes a cumulative index for volumes 4-6.

2057 *Foxfire 7*
Garden City, New York: Anchor Press/
Doubleday, 1982
510pp

2058 *Foxfire 8*
Garden City, New York: Anchor Press/
Doubleday, 1984
510pp

2059 *Foxfire 9*
Garden City, New York: Anchor Press/
Doubleday, 1986
493pp
The general stores, a praying rock, an Indian potter, quilting, home cures and log cabin building.

2060 **WIGHAM, Eric**
Strikes and the government 1893-1981
Macmillan, 1982
248pp
Includes testimony from ministers, employers, union leaders and conciliators.

WILDIG, Susan *see* **WRIGHT, Jenny**

2061 **WILKIE, James**
"Alternative views in history: historical statistics and oral history" *see* GREENLEAF, Richard E. and MEYER, Michael C. (eds.), *1973*
On the political history interview.

2062 **WILKINS, Rachel**
Turrets, towels and taps
Birmingham: Birmingham Museums and Art Gallery, 1984
24pp
The history of Birmingham's Public Washing-Baths based on a 1983 project to record those who used and worked in them. There is an accompanying cassette tape of personal accounts.

2063 **WILKINSON, Greg**
"Understanding Lifetimes"
Oral History, vol.4, no.2 (1976), pp.89-94
Lifetimes is a series of booklets in seven parts which is a collective autobiography of Partington, a Manchester overspill development. (*See also* LIFETIMES)

WILKINSON, Rob *see* **SMITH, Tim**

2064 **WILLEY, Bob**
From all sides: memories of world war II
Gloucester: Alan Sutton, 1989
240pp
Verbatim accounts of the day when war broke out from British, German, Czech, Russian, Polish and French people with experiences on the home front as well as the front line. Includes interviews with Sue Ryder, President Herzog of Israel, and Georges Simenon. Collected by Willey and his sixth form school pupils.

2065 **WILLIAM, Eurwyn**
Rhyd-y-car
Cardiff: National Museum of Wales, 1987
28pp
Commemorates the re-erection of a small terrace of iron workers' houses from Merthyr Tydfil at the Welsh Folk Museum: with taped extracts from their erstwhile inhabitants. (*See also* WELSH FOLK MUSEUM)

2066 **WILLIAMS, Bill**
"The Jewish immigrant in Manchester: the contribution of oral history"
Oral History, vol.7, no.1 (1979), pp.43-53
An important article by one of Britain's leading historians of Jewish life.

2067 **WILLIAMS, Bill and LINKMAN, Audrey**
"Recovering the people's past: the archive rescue programme of Manchester Studies"
History Workshop, no.8 (Autumn 1979)

2068 **WILLIAMS, Claire**
Open cut: the working class in an Australian mining town
Sydney and Boston: Allen and Unwin, 1981
222pp; bibliography

2069 **WILLIAMS, Kitty**
"Pennine Oral History"
Old West Riding, vol.4, no.2 (Winter 1984)
Based on recordings carried out by a project at Hebden Bridge in West Yorkshire. Copy tapes are available at Halifax Central Library.

2070 **WILLIAMS, Ned**
Black country folk at work
Wolverhampton: Uralia Press, 1989
96pp
A mixture of written autobiographies and oral interviews about Black Country people's experiences of work. Includes: coal mining, iron making, starting work, nail and chain making, cooperage, the firebrick trade, making glass, working with lead, leather working, dressmaking, lock making, making motorcycles and switchgear, pork pie making, spot welding, office and administrative work, transport, cinema, newsagents, post delivery, window dressing and cobbling.

2071 **WILLIAMS, Patricia (ed.)**
Children at war
BBC Books, 1989
48pp
Twelve childhood memories of the Second World War from around the world, linked to a BBC Schools TV and radio series.

2072 **WILLIAMS, Philip**
Hugh Gaitskell: a political biography
Cape, 1979
1007pp
300 people were interviewed to make up for deficiencies in written evidence. Described as "an academic justification for the use of interviews" (*see* JONES, G.W., 1981).

2073 **WILLIAMS, Philip**
"Interviewing politicians: the life of Hugh Gaitskell"
Political Quarterly, vol.51, no.3 (1980)

2074 **WILLIAMS, Thomas Harry**
Huey Long
New York: Vintage, 1981; first published Knopf, 1969
884pp; bibliography
A political biography in which 295 individuals were interviewed for this Pulitzer Prize-winning study.

2075 **WILLIAMS, Val**
Women photographers: the other observers 1900 to the present
Virago, 1986
192pp; bibliography
A history of twentieth century women photographers, based in part on interviews.

2076 **WILLIAMS, William Morgan**
The sociology of an English village: Gosforth
Routledge & Kegan Paul, 1956
International Library of Sociology and Social Reconstruction
246pp

2077 **WILLIAMS, William Morgan**
A West Country village. Ashworthy: family, kinship and land
Routledge & Kegan Paul, 1963
Dartington Hall Studies in Rural Sociology
228pp; bibliography
The effects of rural depopulation on family and kinship in pseudonymous 'Ashworthy', based a research carried out in 1957-8.

2078 **WILLIAMSON, Harold**
Toolmaking and politics: the life of Ted Smallbone: an oral history
Birmingham: Linden Books, 1987
The story of an International Brigader, shop steward and CND activist (in his retirement), based on carefully edited interviews.

2079 **WILLIS, Roy**
A state in the making: myth, history and social transformation in pre-colonial Ufipa
Bloomington: Indiana University Press, 1981
African Systems of Thought series
322pp; bibliography
The development of part of the East-Central African plateau from fieldwork conducted in 1962, 1964 and 1966.

WILLMOTT, Peter *see* **YOUNG, Michael**

2080 WILLOWBROOK URBAN STUDIES
CENTRE
*The good old days? School memories of a
Southwark oral history group*
Willowbrook Urban Studies Centre Good Old
Days Group, 1989
23pp
Teachers, lessons, discipline, treats, sport,
clothing, food and health are recalled by a
group in south London.

2081 WILSON, Amrit
Finding a voice: Asian women in Britain
Virago, 1978
192pp
A vivid picture through personal experiences
of Asian women's struggles: the difficulties of
emigration and adapting to a new country,
racism and exploitation at work.

2082 WILSON, Gloria (ed.)
*Voices: memories of home life by the East
Cleveland Heritage Project oral history team*
Loftus, East Cleveland: East Cleveland
Heritage Project, 1985
38pp
The first in a series of booklets of personal
recollections from the North East of England,
including chapters on rug making, allotments
and self-sufficiency, kitchen ranges, home
cooking, children's games, washing and
cleaning, pigs and early radios.

2083 WILSON, Gloria (ed.)
*More voices: some more spoken memories
collected by the East Cleveland Heritage Project
oral history team*
Loftus, East Cleveland: East Cleveland
Heritage Project/MSC, 1986
48pp
This second volume in the series includes
interviews about traditions, tin baths, earth
closets, trips and holidays, ironstone mining in
East Cleveland, leisure at home and
childhood. (*See also* WARD, Ben)

2084 WILSON, H.H.
*Pressure group: the campaign for commercial
television*
Secker and Warburg, 1961
232pp
One of the first post-war contemporary
histories to use systematic oral testimony.

WILSON, Mervyn *see* SALT, Chrys

2085 WILSON, Rhonda
*Good talk: the extraordinary lives of ten ordinary
Australian women*
Ringwood, Victoria: Penguin, 1984

2086 WILTON, Janis
*Balancing the books: oral history for the
community*
Sydney, Australia: Ethnic Affairs Commission
of New South Wales, 1983
52pp; bibliography
A handbook prepared by the Oral Histories
Project of the Ethnic Affairs Commission.

2087 WILTON, Janis
Ethnic oral and local history: the state of the art
Richmond, Victoria: Clearing House on
Migration Issues, 1987
15pp; bibliography

2088 WINDHILL LOCAL HISTORY PROJECT
Memories of Windhill
Shipley, West Yorkshire: Windhill Local
History Project, 1985
24pp
Conversations with local people on life in
Windhill, Shipley and surrounding areas.

2089 WINSTANLEY, Michael J.
''The rural publican and his business in East
Kent before 1914''
Oral History, vol.4, no.2 (1976), pp.63-78

2090 WINSTANLEY, Michael J.
''Some practical hints on oral history
interviewing''
Oral History, vol.5, no.1 (1977), pp.122-30
Focusses on the equipment itself and the
elimination of unwanted background noise.

2091 WINSTANLEY, Michael J.
Life in Kent at the turn of the century
Folkestone: Dawson, 1978
236pp
Based on 180 interviews collected between
1974 and 1977, it covers fishing, horse-dealing,
fishing, hop-picking and agriculture. One of
the first publications emerging from the
University of Kent oral history project.

2092 WINSTANLEY, Michael J.
''Voices from the past'' in MINGAY, G.E.
(ed.) *The Victorian countryside*, Routledge and
Kegan Paul, 1981

2093 WINSTANLEY, Michael J.
The shopkeeper's world 1830-1914
Manchester: Manchester University Press, 1983
230pp; bibliography
Interviews are quoted at length in this
innovative study of late Victorian and
Edwardian changes in retailing: grocers,
butchers, greengrocers, saddlers,
pawnbrokers and village shopkeepers are
included, many of them from Kent.

2094 WINTER, Edward Henry
Beyond the mountains of the moon: the lives of
four Africans
Routledge & Kegan Paul, 1959
276pp
The life stories of two men and two women of
the Amba tribe who live in the mountains to
the west of Uganda, recorded in 1950-2.

2095 WIERLING, Dorothee
"Women domestic servants in Germany at the
turn of the century"
Oral History, vol.10, no.2 (1982), pp.47-57

2096 WITLEY POINT TENANTS ASSOCIATION
Rising above it
Witley Point Tenants Association, 1989
22pp
Recollections from residents of a post-war
housing estate in Roehampton: changing
living conditions, the war, first impressions,
vandalism and social problems on the Alton
Estate and more recent issues.

WITTLINGER, R.P. *see* **BAHRICK, H.P.**

2097 WOBERTON, Terry
"An oral history of lesbianism"
Frontiers, no.4 (Fall 1979), pp.52-4
An issue devoted to lesbian history.

2098 WOLCOTT, Reed
Rose Hill
New York: Harper and Row, 1976
381pp
A superb portrait of a remote farming town of
1700 people in North Carolina, based on
ninety interviews recorded in 1972-4 with
teachers, housewives, politicians, preachers,
tobacco buyers, bootleggers, bankers, farmers
and felons, old and young, black and white.

2099 WOOD, Conrad
"Ten years of the Department of Sound
Records of the Imperial War Museum"
Oral History, vol.11, no.1 (1983), pp.9-12
A survey of progress and a summary of
holdings.

2100 WOODBERRY DOWN MEMORIES GROUP
Woodberry Down memories: the history of an
LCC housing estate
ILEA Education Resource Unit for Older
People, 1989
80pp
Memories of tenants and members of an
ILEA adult education class from a north
Hackney housing estate which was a London
County Council show estate when its first
residents arrived in 1948.

2101 WOODHEAD, John
"The Bentley Colliery disaster"
Bulletin of the Society for the Study of Labour
History, no.31 (Autumn 1975), pp.66-92
This pit disaster, caused by a firedamp
explosion, in 1931 killed forty-five men and
boys. Survivors and by-standers relate their
experiences, and the author was impressed by
the accuracy of their oral recall when checked
against documentary sources.

WOODS, Robert T. *see* **HOLDEN, Una P.**

2102 WOODS, Ruby
"From the pit"
Oral History, vol.7, no.2 (1979), pp.59-62
The autobiography of a Durham miner's
daughter which includes vivid descriptions of
experiencing mental illness.

WORKERS' EDUCATIONAL
ASSOCIATION *see* **WEA**

2103 WORPOLE, Ken
"The history lark"
New Socialist, May/June 1984, and Oral
History, vol.12, no.2 (1984), pp.19-20

2104 WRIGHT, Jenny and WILDIG, Susan
Birchills: an oral history
Walsall: Walsall Metropolitan Borough
Council Archive Service, 1984
65pp
A comparison of differing life styles by
contributors from the Birchills area of Walsall
in the West Midlands.

2105 WRIGHT, Maisie
"Oral history from Cuckfield"
West Sussex History, no.35 (September 1986),
pp.31-3; and no.36 (January 1987), pp.22-5
Extracts from transcripts of three recordings
held at West Sussex Record Office.

2106 WRIGHT, Mel
"Using the past to help the present"
Community Care, no.533 (11.10.1984), pp.20-3

2107 WRIGHT, Mel
"Priming the past"
Oral History, vol.14, no.1 (1986), pp.60-5
Personal experiences using reminiscence in social work with older people in London.

2108 WRIGHT, Mel
"Making history"
Community Care, 5 February 1987, pp.23-5
Elderly people and young people on community service orders benefitted from a reminiscence project in London's Lewisham.

2109 WRIGHT, Mel
A sense of history: reminiscence work with elderly people
London Borough of Lewisham Social Services Department Training and Staff Development, 1988
28pp; bibliography
An excellent introductory booklet which integrates oral history and reminiscence, with useful chapters on starting a reminiscence group and lists of local and national resources. Included are extracts from the work of oral history groups in the Lewisham area including a Vietnamese group, the Calabash Jamaica Project History Group and the Bellingham History Group.

2110 WRIGHT, Mel
"Seaside postcards, the Beano and the Sex Pistols: the use of oral history" in GLENDENNING, Frank and PHILLIPSON, Chris (eds.), *Voluntary action and community work with older people*, Keele: Beth Johnson Foundation/Centre for Social Gerontology at University of Keele, 1988, pp.66-70

2111 WRIGHT, Mel
"'Shine on Harvest Moon': behind a tea dance that goes beyond the foxtrot"
Generations: Bulletin of the British Society of Gerontology, no.10 (Summer 1989), pp.8-9

WRIGHT, Mel *see also* GINGELL, Maria

2112 WRIGHT, Simon
Memories of the Salford Blitz, Christmas 1940
Manchester: Neil Richardson, nd
32pp
Recollections of 22-23 December 1940 when 276 bombs and some 10,000 incendiaries left over 1000 casualties.

2113 WRIGLEY, J.R.
"A Sunday in September"
The Historic Record, no.13 (September, 1989), pp.8-30
Transcripts of 'audio documents': both famous and rare recordings relating to the outbreak of the Second World War, including speeches and reminiscences.

2114 WRIGLEY, Kathryn
Directory of Illinois oral history resources
Springfield: Oral History Office, Sangamon State University, 1981
54pp

WYNCOLL, Keith *see* EDWARDS, Alison

2115 WYNCOLL, P.
"General strike in Nottingham"
Marxism Today, vol.16 (1972), pp.172-80
Based partially on interviews.

2116 YARNELL, Terry
Collecting traditional music, a handbook for the guidance of the non-professional
Privately published: 11, Shelley Ave., London E12, 1976
47pp
A pocket guide containing some useful information on fault finding when using a tape recorder.

YE, Sang *see* ZHANG, Xinxin

2117 YEATMAN, Jack
"Solent Archives for Education: a radio experiment"
Oral History, vol.6, no.2 (1978), pp.87-92
In 1973 BBC Radio Solent waived copyright on its sound archive tapes to enable their use in educational resource materials.

YOCOM, Margaret *see* CUTTING-BAKER, Holly

2118 YORK ORAL HISTORY PROJECT
York memories: nine first hand accounts of life in York 1900-1939
York: York Oral History Project, 1984
48pp
Memories of the York area: rural childhood, tenant farming, domestic service at Heslington Hall, Blue Coats School, the means test in the 1930s, the 'monkey run', cattle markets, theatres and cinemas.

2119 YORK ORAL HISTORY PROJECT
"Upstairs and down at Heslington Hall"
New Age, Autumn 1984, pp.10-12
Memories of domestic service in York.

2120 YORK ORAL HISTORY PROJECT
York memories at work: personal accounts of working life in York before 1952
York: York Oral History Project, 1985
52pp
Drawn from YOHP's archive, this second collection covers monumental masonry, Rowntree's chocolate works, munitions, railway workers and French polishing.

2121 YORK ORAL HISTORY PROJECT
York memories at home: personal accounts of domestic life in York, 1900-1960
York: York Oral History Project/York Castle Museum, 1987
74pp
Washing and ironing, cleaning, cooking and baking, shopping and household economy, families, bathing, health and sickness, Christmas, games and entertainments.

2122 YORK ORAL HISTORY PROJECT
York memories of stage and screen: personal accounts of York's theatres and cinemas 1900-1960
York: York Oral History Project, 1988
74pp

2123 YOUNG, Michael and WILLMOTT, Peter
Family and kinship in East London
Routledge & Kegan Paul, 1986; first published 1957
Reports of the Institute of Community Studies
234pp; bibliography

2124 YOUNG, Peter
Power of speech: a history of Standard Telephones and Cables 1883-1983
Allen & Unwin, 1983
221pp
A company history, appropriately using some oral testimony.

ZABUSKY, Charlotte Fox *see* **MORRISON, Joan**

2125 ZACHERT, Martha Jane
"The implications of oral history for librarians"
College and Research Libraries, vol.29 (March 1968), pp.101-3
Examines the creation, handling, access and finding aids relating to oral history in libraries.

2126 ZACHERT, Martha Jane
"Sources: oral history interviews"
Journal of Library History, vol.5 (January 1970), pp.80-7
Techniques for getting the maximum information from an interviewee.

2127 ZAHN, Wilfred
"Preservation and storage of tape recordings"
Phonographic Bulletin, no.15 (1976), pp.5-6

2128 ZBOROWSKI, Mark and HERTZOG, Elizabeth
Life is with people: the culture of the shtetl
New York: Schocken, 1964
452pp
An account of life in the East European Jewish 'shtetls' before their destruction by Nazism, based on interviews with survivors.

2129 ZHANG, Xinxin and YE, Sang
Chinese lives
Edited and translated from Chinese by W.J.F. Jenner and Delia Davin
Macmillan London, 1987; Penguin edition, 1989
367pp
An innovative oral history of contemporary China, based on interviews with a wide range of informants, capturing both the typical and the individual.

ZIMMERMAN, Robert *see* **COLLINS, James**

2130 ZIMMERMAN, William
Instant oral biographies: how to interview people & tape the stories of their lives
New York: Guarionex, 1979; third edition, 1982
100pp
An enthusiastic guide to recording family history. (Cover title: *How to tape instant oral biographies*)

2131 ZORBAUGH, Harvey Warren
The gold coast and the slum: a sociological study of Chicago's Near North Side
Chicago: University of Chicago Press, 1976; facsimile reprint of the 1929 first edition
287pp
Early oral history and community studies.

2132   **ZUCKEMAN, Harriet**
Scientific elite: Nobel laureates in the United States
New York and London: Free Press, 1977
335pp
The careers of Nobel prize-winners in science using oral testimony. Includes an appendix which considers the methodology and value of oral evidence, entitled 'Interviewing an ultra-elite'.

INDEX

Crafts 322, 355, 383, 513, 536, 539, 540, 1067, 1700, 1846, 2051, 2053-6, 2059
Cricket 425
Crime and criminals 140, 259, 378, 427, 882, 883, 1024, 1113, 1389, 1402, 1466, 1475, 1483, 1543, 1683, 1886; *see also* police
Crystal Palace (London) 506
Cuba 1145-7
Cuckfield 2105
Cumberland 207
Cumbria 68, 333, 535, 851, 971
Cutlery trade 175
Cycling 34, 351
Cypriot community *see* ethnic communities
Czechoslovakia 430, 1628, 2064

Dallas (USA) 1255
Dance and dancing 412, 1019
Death 330, 338, 1496, 1594, 1620, 2052
Demolition worker 322
Denmark 430
Dentists 11, 637, 1578
Depression (Inter-war)
    in Australia 172, 237, 238, 303, 1188
    in Canada 227
    in New Zealand 1766
    in United Kingdom 67, 298, 716, 986
    in USA 62, 317, 942, 1474, 1800, 1875
Derbyshire 442, 481, 1780
Devon 496, 1291, 1292, 1591
Dialect and language 516, 517, 540, 993, 1035, 1403, 1885
Diaries 611, 967
Diet *see* cooking; food
Disability 10, 570, 1596, 2102
District Audit Service 435
Divers and diving 427
Docks and dockworkers 39, 81, 108, 231, 532, 858, 956, 1160, 1161, 1190, 1321, 1793-5, 1975, 1993
Doctors 11, 33, 83, 105, 152, 388, 734, 1325, 1753; *see also* health; hospital; medicine; nursing
Domestic service and servants 40, 131, 321, 547, 627, 691, 739, 785, 1077, 1329, 1351, 1396, 1586, 1656, 1859, 1955, 2017, 2095, 2118, 2119
Doncaster 982, 1923
Dorset 2029
Drongan 1587
Drugs 143, 719, 878, 984, 1038
Dulles, John Foster 409, 857
Dundee 490, 491, 493-5, 796, 986, 1584
Durham 76, 331, 479, 1322, 1682, 2102
Dustmen 427, 1876

East Anglia 327, 431, 568, 1165, 1192, 1194, 1195; *see also* Norfolk; Suffolk
East Cleveland *see* Cleveland

Edinburgh 161, 162, 633, 731, 732, 996, 1215, 1404, 1493, 1496, 1539, 1540, 1801; *see also* Leith
Education *see* oral history in schools; school; teachers
Egypt 74
Eire *see* Ireland
El Salvador 6, 1705
Electronics industry 1453
Elites 243, 456, 1733, 1736, 1880, 2132
Elland 1636
Embroidery 322
Emigration 527, 1212, 1219, 1220; *see also* migration; immigration
Engineering 315, 1019, 1347, 1961
Entrepreneurs 141
Equipment *see* oral history techniques
Escapologists 1402
Eskimos 365, 368, 501
Essex 681
Estonia 430
Estonian community *see* ethnic communities
Ethics *see* oral history and copyright
Ethnic communities in Canada
    Hungarian 447
    Japanese 230, 1242
Ethnic communities in United Kingdom
    Afro-Caribbean/West Indian 25, 31, 36, 159, 195, 197, 200, 201, 247, 274, 391, 464, 530, 658, 705, 710, 833, 973, 1019, 1040, 1352, 1353, 1397, 1448, 1481, 1487, 1694, 1888, 2030, 2109
    Asian 18, 31, 195, 197, 200, 201, 274, 828, 867, 996, 1019, 1276, 1352, 1448, 1503, 1756, 1760, 2027, 2030, 2081
    Chinese 31, 195, 1038, 1276, 2030
    Cypriot 31
    Estonian 195, 197
    German 195, 197
    Iranian 529
    Irish 40, 195, 197, 200, 274, 527, 926, 986, 1199, 1200, 1397, 2030
    Italian 31, 195, 197-200, 867, 987, 1352, 1500, 1573
    Jewish *see* Jewish community
    Latvian 195, 197
    Lithuanian 195, 197, 986, 996, 2040
    Nigerian 2030
    Polish 31, 195, 197, 198, 528, 867, 1019, 1020, 1500
    Portuguese 1397
    Russian 1397
    Somali 1790
    Spanish 1397
    Sudanese 2030
    Ukrainian 195, 197, 198, 200, 867, 1352, 1500
    Vietnamese 195, 274, 677, 996, 2109
    Yugoslav 195, 197, 200, 1500
    See also immigration; Jewish community; racism
Ethnic communities in USA
    Generally 806, 1331, 1800

London *(continued)*